VIRGINIA STATE LIBRARY

List of the Colonial Soldiers
of Virginia

Special Report of the Department of Archives and
History for 1913

H. J. ECKENRODE, Archivist

CLEARFIELD

Originally Published as
a "Special Report of the Department
of Archives and History for 1913"
in the *Thirteenth Annual Report of
the Library Board of the Virginia
State Library, 1915-1916*
Richmond, 1917

Reprinted
Genealogical Publishing Co., Inc.
Baltimore, 1961
Baltimore, 1965
Baltimore, 1974
Baltimore, 1976

Reprinted for
Clearfield Company, Inc by
Genealogical Publishing Co , Inc.
Baltimore, Maryland
1995, 1997, 2000

Library of Congress Catalogue Card Number 62-51491
International Standard Book Number: 0-8063-0099-X

Made in the United States of America

List of the Colonial Soldiers of Virginia

Preface.

When colonial warfare is mentioned, the mind goes back to the first English planting on American soil, to helmeted and breast-plated soldiers with pikes and muskets, who were the necessary accompaniment of the settler in the wilderness. Virginia was essentially a military colony and remained so for many years; every man was something of a soldier as well as farmer and jack-of-all-trades. Guns, pistols, and armor were part of the regular house furnishing. Danger was always to be apprehended from the Indians, who, in 1622, after many threatenings, rose against the small, sickly colony and decimated it. This massacre inaugurated a war which lasted for several years, ending in the extermination of many tribes in eastern Virginia. Twenty-two years later, in 1644, the massacre was repeated on a smaller scale, followed by inevitable retaliation.

Extension westward, beyond the first limit of settlement, the peninsulas between the James, York, and Rappahannock, brought the colonists into contact with other tribes, and small forts were erected in various places and garrisoned with rangers, who for a long period guarded this head-of-tidewater frontier against the savages. Fighting was frequent.

The Indian troubles culminated in 1676 with Bacon's Rebellion. Nathaniel Bacon raised a force of some hundreds of men to punish the Indians for long-continued depredations, and finally crushed the Indian power east of the Blue Ridge. Soon after this campaign he was obliged to turn his arms against Governor Sir William Berkley, who resented his raising troops without proper governmental authority, and in the ensuing curious little war a large part of the able-bodied population served on one side or the other. All of these fighting-men ought to be mentioned in a list of the colonial soldiers of Virginia, but the muster-rolls, if they ever existed, which is unlikely, have long since been lost.

At this time, the closing quarter of the seventeenth century, warlike spirit had not died out in Virginia, but it notably dwindled in succeeding generations, until the colony at length became that ultra-peaceable, cavalier-Quaker community which A. G. Bradley, the historian of the great French war, so warmly condemns. The reasons for the change are obvious. Cut off from the wars of Europe, far distant from the French in Canada, untroubled by Indians, eastern Virginia lived a singularly tranquil, undisturbed, monotonous life. Military ambitions require a strong military tradition and some active spur to the imagination, and the Virginians as a rule were easy-going people, bent on getting as much pleasure out of their environment as possible. Only a small proportion of the later settlers were of the military caste; as in all colonies, the greater number of immigrants were industrious citizens hopeful of bettering their condition. In a new country, undisturbed by war for the long period of three-quarters of a century, 1675-1750, a distinctly peaceful and unadventurous planter civilization developed. In the same way, all the other English colonies were unwarlike,

4

unenterprising communities given over to the purely material pursuits of commerce and agriculture. Among the French in Canada it is true that a singularly bold class of adventurers arose, but here again economic conditions determined the development. The fur-trade was the chief resort of the poor and struggling French colony, and fur-trading is an occupation necessarily leading men into wilderness life with its perils and wanderings, especially as furs begin to grow scarce in the neighborhood of the settled territory. Canadian war-methods, evolved from border life, were wholly at variance with European military practices of that day, which engagingly grouped troops in the densest formations in order to afford the enemy every convenience in killing them. American warfare had become Indianized, and it has always retained traces of Indian ideas. Nowhere in North America did the military traditions and military spirit of eighteenth century Europe influence the people.

From time to time Virginia, like other colonies, was drawn to a slight extent into the current of European war, but her secure position, protected by layers of colonies from the French in the north and by other layers of colonies from the Spanish in the south and by the Blue Ridge from the Indians, made war for her an adventure of the few restless spirits of her population. More nearly military colonies were Massachusetts, New Hampshire, South Carolina, and Georgia, made so not by any inheritance of military blood but by the unhappy necessities of contiguity.

In the early years of the eighteenth century the southern frontier of Virginia became involved in Indian troubles as a result of the Tuscarora War in North Carolina. Alexander Spotswood, the governor, managed to avert war by making treaties with the discontented tribes along the Virginia-Carolina border. But in 1715 the governor of South Carolina appealed to Virginia for aid in the Indian war then devastating that province, and Spotswood asked the assembly for a military grant on the ground that Virginia herself lay in danger of invasion along her southwestern boundary. Spotswood, with the consent of the council, had sent arms and men, chiefly friendly Indians, to South Carolina. When the assembly met, however, it raised an issue with the governor, and the session ended without the grant of relief for the sister colony. Militarism certainly did not dominate Virginia at this period.

For a generation the quiet life of eastern Virginia flowed along quite undisturbed by any visions of war,—a condition that could not last. Willy-nilly the colonies were being drawn into the great imperial struggle between England and Latin Europe. In the Cartagena expedition of 1740, when provincials for the first time served England in war, the Old Dominion furnished four hundred men, most notable of whom, next to ex-Governor Spotswood himself, was Lawrence Washington, half-brother of George. ([1]) Massachusetts sent five hundred men on this expedition, the largest colonial contingent. ([2]) The whole venture was wretchedly mismanaged, and the greater part of the provincials died of disease.

Six years later Virginia again contributed troops, this time for an expedition to conquer Canada. Neither the attack on Cartagena nor that on

([1]) Campbell's History of Virginia, 417.
([2]) Doyle's English Colonies in America, 5, 409.

Canada directly concerned her, and it is probable that the losses of the former expedition had gone little way towards firing her with martial ardor. At all events the Virginia contingent in 1746 numbered, one hundred men, as against several thousand for Massachusetts, seventeen hundred for New York, and one thousand for Connecticut, colonies which had everything to gain in case of success. Pennsylvania, North and South Carolina, and Georgia did not respond. The invasion proved abortive, and the peace of Aix-la-Chapelle in 1748 ended the war.

In Virginia the only effect of the War of the Austrian Succession was to inspire some Indian raids beyond the Blue Ridge; the profound peace of the east was not touched. But the hour was coming for war to strike nearer home, since after 1748 the French began to plan a line of settlements along the Ohio, connecting Canada with Louisiana—that is, the vast Louisiana of those days. In 1753 they built forts within the territory claimed by Virginia, which is now a part of Pennsylvania owing to the complaisance of inefficiency of the Virginia representatives in the boundary settlement made during the Revolution. By this aggression the far away Canadian struggle was brought almost to the headwaters of the Potomac. In the following war, begun on her own soil, Virginia entered on that long military career destined in the end to bring her a peculiar glory.

At the opening of the French and Indian War the colony retained her immemorial militia system, but in the tidewater it had degenerated into something of a farce. It was, by all accounts, a strangely English survival, for the commanding officer in each county was his honor the county-lieutenant and the other officers were for the most part of the gentry. The whole able-bodied male population made up the rank and file, and the militia musters were great occasions, when the scattered population came together, shouldered arms for as brief a period as conscience allowed and then feasted and made merry. Thackeray in "The Virginians" has described one of these scenes, and it is a good caricature of some of the musters in eastern Virginia. But west of the tidewater, where the people were expert riflemen and hunters, the militia took on another character. It was commanded there by the most vigorous and experienced men, and it was well qualified for frontier warfare, and for the defensive operations of regular war, as Dunmore found to his cost at the Great Bridge in 1775. In 1750 the whole militia of the colony numbered about 30,000 men, the greater part very ignorant of the most rudimentary military knowledge.

When the French built forts at Presqu' Isle on Lake Erie and Fort le Boeuf, further south, and began expelling English Indian-traders, Dinwiddie, the governor of Virginia, sent George Washington, then a surveyor and ambitious militia officer, to warn the French off English soil. Washington carried out his mission successfully, though the interlopers, of course, had no thought of abandoning their hold on the Ohio Valley on Dinwiddie's complaint. The governor then began to make plans to raise a force to meet them. After much wrangling he succeeded in obtaining a grant of money from the assembly and raised a force of 300 men, which was commanded by John Fry under a colonial commission as colonel, with Washington as second in command, bearing the rank of major. This force was not exactly militia and not regular but combined the characteristics of both branches; it was the beginning of the Virginia regiment, which became a regular military organization of the highest efficiency in border fighting. Two independent companies from New York and South Carolina, paid by the English government, were joined with the Virginians.

Dinwiddie's first move was to send Ensign Ward with forty men to build a post at the junction of the Alleghany and Monongahela rivers, a site selected by Washington. A considerable French detachment, coming up, ejected Ward and turned the block-house into the world-renowned Fort Du-Quesne. The Virginia regiment thereupon advanced to Will's Creek, at which point Fry encamped, while Washington with 150 men crossed the Alleghanies to a trading station called "The Great Meadows," where it was learned that the French were also advancing. Washington, taking 40 of his men ahead on a scouting expedition, chanced to run into them. A skirmish followed, and Jumonville, the officer commanding the handful of French, was killed with several others. This was the first blood shed in the war, and the English took the initiative, so that the French, with no prevision of twenty years after, branded Washington as an assassin, and actually succeeded in cheating him into admitting it.

Washington after this brush fell back to the Great Meadows, where Fry had meanwhile died. He now commanded 350 men, counting the South Carolina company, and he proceeded to throw up a slight entrenchment euphemistically styled "Fort Necessity." A little later the French arrived in overwhelming force and surrounded the fortification, pouring a hot fire into it from the shelter of the woods; the Virginians replied with spirit. When night ended the skirmish, Washington had lost twelve men killed and forty-three wounded of the Virginia force, and his total casualties probably neared a hundred. His position was desperate, and he was ready to treat for terms of surrender, which were surprisingly light. Among the articles, however, was a clause referring to the first skirmish as "l'assassinat de Jumonville," and Washington signed his name to the paper under the impression that the translation read: "The killing of Jumonville." Two Virginia officers, Robert Stobo, a Scotchman, and Jacob Van Braam, a Dutchman, were given to the French as hostages for the discharge of the conditions of capitulation, and thus the first act ended.

Stobo, prisoner at Quebec, had a very romantic and harrowing experience indeed. Among Braddock's papers, captured on the Monongehala, was a plan of the Quebec fortification which Stobo had furnished; for this he was condemned to death, but escaped to act as a guide to Wolfe in 1759. Stobo is said to have served Smollett as a model for Lismahago, and in later days certainly inspired Gilbert Parker's "The Seats of the Mighty," wherein he appears as Captain Robert Moray, a very highly idealized rendition of the eccentric soldier of fortune.

After this disaster the Virginia assembly voted $20,000 for military purposes, and Dinwiddie recruited his force, which served as an auxiliary to Braddock's command in the following year 1755, when the British government decided to strike at Fort DuQuesne and the French menace. Braddock divided his little army into two skeleton brigades, the first commanded by Sir Peter Halkett and composed of the 44th regiment of the line—700 men—and 230 New York, Maryland, and Virginia rangers; the second, under Col. Dunbar, was made up of the 48th regiment—650 men—170 Carolinians, and about the same number of Virginians. There was a total of something over two thousand men. The Virginia companies included about 450 men; besides these the two English regiments had been considerably recruited in the colony, so that of Braddock's entire force of 2,000 or thereabouts, probably 600 were Virginians, a creditable showing. Braddock despised the provincial troops, whom he attempted to drill into imitation regulars, and Bradley has abused them roundly, though they won commendatiòn for their valor on the fatal July 9, 1755, the day of Braddock's defeat. Bradley dismisses them casually: "Most of the hundred or so Virginia riflemen, about whose action in this fight a good deal of fable has gathered, were here. They did their duty, and fought gallantly behind trees according to back-woods custom. But the contemporary plan of the battle shows the attack on the rear guard to have been far weaker than where the mass of the demoralized red coats drew the bulk of the fire." ([3]) Washington did not serve in this campaign as an officer of Virginia troops but as volunteer aid, having resigned his commission in disgust because the British regulations made the youngest ensigns of regulars rank the highest colonial officers, the pleasing manner in which the imperial government exhibited its contempt for provincial military prowess. The Virginia companies in Braddock's expedition were commanded by Captains Waggoner, Cock, Hogg, Stephen, Polson, Peyronie, Mercer, and Stewart; and there was a troop of Virginia light horse. The other provincials included the remains of two independent companies from New York and a hundred pioneers and guides called hatchet-men. ([4]) Several of the Virginia companies were in the battle; Peyronie, a Frenchman in the Virginia service, and all of his officers were killed; only one officer escaped in Polson's company. Nearly all of the Virginia troops present were killed or wounded. Captains Peyronie and Polson were among the killed and Stephen, Waggoner and Stewart among the wounded.

In August, 1755, the assembly voted $40,000 for the war, and the governor and council decided to increase the Virginia regiment to sixteen companies of 1,500 men. At the same time Washington was placed in command with ranking of colonel; his chief subordinates were Lieutenant-Colonel Adam Stephen and Major Andrew Lewis, ([5]) both excellent soldiers. "Peyton Randolph raised a volunteer company of one hundred gentlemen, who, however, proved quite unfit for the frontier service." The Virginia regiment in 1756 numbered about 1,400 men. It was composed partly of militia drafted from the eastern counties, but much more largely of the class of restless, unemployed men who hang on every advancing frontier. Bradley has seen fit to speak disparagingly of this force and of the public spirit in Virginia, but somewhat unjustly: "Washington, with a thousand raw soldiers, low-class Southern white men, to whom authority was specially odious, was struggling in defense of a frontier nearly four hundred miles in length. Virginia, it should be said, was notoriously touchy on the subject of her boundaries. Her white population at this time was larger than that of the Transvaal Boers to day, who have placed some forty or fifty thousand men in the field. It was three times that of Natal, who has sent out to war

---

([3]) A. G. Bradley's Struggle with France for North America, 101.
([4]) Campbell, 472.
([5]) *Ibid.*, 486.

many thousands of her best sons upon no greater provocation. Her frontier counties were swimming in blood and ringing with passionate appeals for succor. It was an occasion, one would have supposed, when the sons of her numerous aristocracy and still more numerous yeomanry would have responded in thousands to the call of their own harried people at least, if not to that of the mother country. They were an outdoor people, bread to the use of horse and gun, and cherished a sort of pride that, without the martial ingredient, seems to lack significance. The existence of slavery made even their time very much their own. The fear of a slave insurrection might influence numbers available for distant adventure; but one looks in vain among the squires and yeomanry of the Southern colonies for the faintest spark, at this burning period, of the spirit that one would particularly expect in such a class. The natural fire of youth and love of glory and adventure, to say nothing of patriotic sentiment, that was so conspicuously present with after generations of the same breed, seems in this one to have been almost an unknown quantity. Considerably less than half the officers who commanded the few hundred ill-paid mercenaries that so tortured Washington belonged to the gentry class, and represented their total contribution to the defense of the province, and the long and fierce struggle with France.

"A mere handful of Washington's own class are grouped round his youthful and commanding figure in this war. Whatever may have been the virtues of the Southern planter of this generation—and they were not inconsiderable—the love of soldiering and a generous public spirit were assuredy not among them." (⁶)

And Doyle has said: "Virginia has incurred severe—it may reasonably be contended exaggerated—condemnation for the part which her citizens played. She has been reproached for her tardy co-operation, for her inadequate grants alike of men and money. The blame has probably been the more freely bestowed because the antecedents in Virginia and the conditions of life there justified other expectations. The training and temper of the Virginia planters might have been thought to insure a certain aptitude for military duties. . . . Yet undoubtedly in the struggle against France the help of Virginia was given grudgingly and inadequately. That was largely due to causes for which individual Virginians of that day could not be fairly held responsible. These were two. Firstly, there was the dread of a servile insurrection. . . . The danger, too, was greatly increased by the lack of communication among a widely dispersed population. The same cause, too, helped in other ways to paralyze the military life of Virginia just as it paralyzed her economical and religious life. It was no easy matter to organize a system of defense in a country where there was no regular administrative unity." (⁷)

In contradistinction to Virginia and other colonies, Bradley thus pictures Massachusetts: "Three colonies, Pennsylvania, Maryland, and Virginia, with some half-million whites, to say nothing of rude and populous North Carolina, could only wring from this large population a wretched, half-hearted militia of 2,000 men, recruited largely from the burnt-out victims of the frontier. Where, one may well ask, were the squires of Virginia and Maryland, who swarmed along the eastern counties of both provinces, and

(⁶) The Struggle with France for North America, 133.
(⁷) English Colonies in America, 5, 428.

whose comfortable homesteads reached to within a hundred miles of the scene of this bloody war, of their fellow-countrymen's long agony, and of the impudent invasion of their country? To mention a dozen or two young men of this class who rallied to Washington, would only be to aggravate the case, if such were possible, in the face of these statistics. Men of substance and education, accustomed to horse and gun, 'outdoor' men in fact or nothing, were quietly staying at home by thousands, unstirred by feeling of patriotism or vengeance and apparently untouched by the clash of arms and the ordinary martial instincts of youth. . . . Washington, whose local patriotism no one will dispute and whose example shone like a beacon light amid the gloom, cursed them often and soundly in his letters for doing nothing. It was fortunate for these colonies that Pitt came forward to save them . . . the tobacco squires of the Seven Years' War were lamentedly wanting in those generous and martial impulses which supply almost the only motive for pride of race, and quite the only one where high culture and learning are absent, as was here the case. . . . Turn to Massachusetts at that day, who alone sent to the front ten or fifteen thousand close-fisted, industrious farmers, men whose labor was their daily bread, and whose absence from the homestead was, for the most part, a serious matter."

These statements are fiery and somewhat overlook the facts. In another place Bradley says of New England: "They were much the most warlike group of the British colonies, not from choice, but from necessity," and, so saying, explains the whole case. New England was menaced by Canada, that is, by a hostile, civilized state on her border; New England trade was disturbed by French cruisers, and for more than a generation this condition had continued. New England military expeditions were usually conducted against a civilized enemy occupying fortified places, like Louisbourg. For this reason New England was fully aware of the French peril, something the Southern colonies never awakened to. Virginia at no time was in danger of conquest; her frontier beyond the Blue Ridge was harassed by Indians and severely harassed, but the Blue Ridge divided the colony at the middle of the eighteenth century in a most striking way. East of the mountains, especially east of the tidewater line, Virginia was another England. The mode of life was thoroughly civilized and commonplace; the people knew nothing whatever of the arts of the wilderness. Beyond the mountains lay the savage American frontier, a world apart, where men lived as frontiersmen lived until yesterday in an isolation and primitiveness requiring special knowledge. Eastern Virginians were little more fitted to cope with Indians and backwoods warfare than Braddock's troops, and Indians were the only enemy to be fought on the Virginia frontier; the French as an organized force were only to be found at Fort DuQuesne, a long and most arduous journey distant. Eastern Virginians had lost the art of Indian warfare several generations before, and it was useless to expect them to be of any service in the peculiar guerilla fignting of the frontier without considerable training. Such war was without glory and attended by the most extreme discomfort. It is not at all peculiar that the imagination of the tidewater youth was not enraptured.

As a matter of fact, we see the Indian and Indian fighting through a veil of romance totally wanting to the people of the colonial period. The provincials drew all their romantic ideas from the old world; they dreamed of the gaiety and fashion of London and of the tented fields of Europe. The Indian for them was a sordid reality, one which the seaboard American had gotten rid of and which he wished to permanently remain rid of; he could little understand the taste of frontiersmen willing to live on the edge of the Indian country and squat on Indian lands when practicable, and he had little solicitude for their safety. The scalping of obscure immigrants on the border, often half-Indianized as they were, aroused him as little as the outrages committed on American citizens in Mexico to-day arouse the average American. It was something out of his ken. Doubtless he should not have been indifferent, but so he was.

Because of the idealization of Indian life by Cooper and his school the French and Indian War appears to us as one of the most fascinating periods in history. It did not appear thus to the generation that lived through it, one having no appreciation of wild adventure but preferring the tame in literature and in life; it was a generation that wrote dull verses in the dreary style of Pope and thought that the quintessence of existence lay in the art of making flourishing bows and paying complicated compliments to women on all possible occasions.

But after the Revolution Americans, partly out of hatred for England, partly because of the new ideas arising from the struggle, began to look on the mother country with a notable diminution of that ardent, naïve admiration and desire of imitation characteristic of the colonial era, seeking, instead, to find a romantic element in American life. There, fortunately for the interests of romance, stood the Indian. He was distinctive and he was American, and studied by men no longer in danger of being stalked and assassinated by him, he well fitted the romantic standard. Indeed, even now for many millions in Europe America is solely made up of Indians and cowboys. What in a dull world could be more thrilling than that incarnation of picturesque deviltry, the wild Indian as he has come down to us? Note the description of him by Philip A. Bruce: "The feeling of horror was made more intense by the noiselessness with which the enemy moved, the care with which they hid their tracks, the suddenness with which they appeared at unexpected points. The wildness of the Indian's physical aspect also added to this horror,—his naked and painted skin; his sinewy frame, as lithe and active as that of a panther or wild cat; his hawk-like eye; his scream of triumph, which curdled the blood far more than the cry of some fierce wild animal at midnight. The very image of the terrible creature stamped itself upon the imagination like some menacing figure conjured up from the region of devils." ([8])

This picture is fascinating to us; the reality was anything but pleasing to the provincials; and it is no great wonder that the dwellers in civilized America had no stomach for the obscure miseries of Indian warfare—the constant exposure, terrible fatigue, risk of starvation and danger of unseen death at the hands of skulking, filthy savages, who could be seldom brought to a stand-up fight. War is an exceedingly poor business without rations and glory; Indian war in the eighteenth century was a special art in which

---

([8]) Institutional History of Virginia, 1, 77.

courage and ordinary military knowledge in themselves were of small avail. Twenty years later the frontier had bred a sufficiently numerous race of woodsmen, who proved a match for the red man at his own game; in 1755 the company of gentlemen whom-Peyton Randolph raised for service on the frontier found themselves an incumbrance rather than a help.

The Virginia regiment, composed largely of borderers, steadily improved in discipline and finally took on the shape of a real military force. It was no longer a semi-civilian militia organization but was subject to the severe rules of military law and performed a most arduous service. In 1756 Virginia sent the "Sandy Creek expedition" against the Shawnees on the Ohio. Major Andrew Lewis was in command, and under him were Captains William Preston, Peter Hogg, John Smith, Archibald Alexander, Breckenridge, Woodson, and Overton, besides volunteer companies under Captains Montgomery and Dunlap and a handful of Cherokee Indians. (⁹)

The whole force amounted to 340 men, partly of the Virginia regiment and party militia and volunteers. The expedition proved a failure, and the troops nearly died of hunger.

This year, 1756, was a very harrassing one on the frontier. In April a severe Indian irruption drove Washington almost to despair, and Dinwiddie ordered out militia to his assistance. Probably several thousand men were in service along the border at some time or other during 1756, usually for brief periods.

In 1757 Lord Loudoun, the British commander-in-chief, required Virginia to send 400 men to South Carolina. The Virginia regiment was reduced to a thousand men, and Washington retired from command for a time owing to ill health. (¹⁰)

In 1758, the colony made greater military efforts. Volunteer companies were raised, some of them in the interior, and at one of such meetings, in Hanover on May 8, 1758, Samuel Davies preached with the view of stirring up recruits. The Virginia regulars, increased to 2,000 men, were divided into two regiments, one of which Washington continued to command, the other under Col. William Byrd, a planter turned soldier, who became a fairly efficient officer. Washington's command was sometimes called the first Virginia regiment, Byrd's the second. The latter organization at Fort Cumberland, on August 3, 1758, numbered 859 men. The officers were Lieutenant-Colonel George Mercer, Major William Peachey, Captains S. Mumford, Thomas Cocke, Hancock Eustace, John Field, John Posey, Thomas Fleming, John Roote, and Samuel Meredith. (¹¹)

Virginia troops formed an important contingent in Forbes's expedition against Fort DuQuesne in 1758. His army consisted of 1200 Highlanders, 350 Royal Americans, 2,700 Pennsylvanians, 1,600 Virginians, and several hundred men from Maryland and North Carolina—a total force of 6,000. (¹²) The Royal American regiment was organized in the colonies and received many recruits from Virginia, for the most part indented servants. The chief feature of Forbes's movement was Major Grant's engagement with the enemy near Fort DuQuesne. This officer, who had been sent in advance with

---

(⁹) Campbell, 490.
(¹⁰) Campbell, 497.
(¹¹) *Ibid.*, 500.
(¹²) Campbell, 501.

a force of 800 men, was totally defeated by the French and Indians, losing nearly half of his command. Major Andrew Lewis and 162 Virginians were present in this engagement; Lewis was taken prisoner and five of the eight other Virginia officers were killed. Captain Thomas Bullitt and his company, by their brave stand, enabled the survivors to get off. Of the 162 Virginians 62 were killed. Bradley says: "The small band of Virginians with Bullitt fought heroically, and were all killed except such as escaped by swimming the Alleghany River." ([13])

Upon Forbes's further advance the French abandoned Fort DuQuesne, and the Indians lost their great base of supplies for raids, which caused a speedy dwindling of hostilities on the English frontier. The year 1758 was the chief year of the war as far as Virginia was concerned, and a considerable force held the field. As the government raised four companies of rangers for defensive work, and as volunteers and militia companies along the whole exposed western and southern regions were in service, besides the 2,000 troops of the regular regiments, it is probable that between 3,000 and 4,000 men were in arms this year,—not a bad showing for a purely border war. Col. William Peachey commanded the newly raised battalion of rangers.

One-half of the 2,000 regulars had been enlisted to serve until December 1, 1758, and supplies had been voted by the assembly for the other thousand until May 1, 1759. This reduction was provided for on the theory that Forbes's expedition would end by December 1, 1758. But as the fall waned with Forbes still far from his goal, the assembly decided that the first regiment might be continued in service outside the colony until January 1, 1759, and that the second regiment, enlisted only until December 1, 1758, might also be used after the expiration of its term of service, provided the rank and file could be induced to continue with the colors. ([14])   Fort DuQuesne fell into the hands of the British on November 26, 1758, and the need for the continued service of the time-expired troops was passed. In 1758, Washington resigned his commission and took his seat as a member of the House of the Burgesses, whereupon the ranking officer of the Virginia forces became William Byrd. At the meeting of the assembly in February, 1759, it was determined to fill up the companies of the regiment then in service, and to raise an additional force of 500 men to take the place of the four ranger companies, disbanded. The greater part of this additional force was to remain within the limits of the colony. The assembly of November, 1759, continued the regiment in service until May, 1760.

The next trouble came from the Cherokee Indians, who in 1760 turned from the English alliance and began a war on their own account against the Carolinas and Virginia. Fighting centered around Fort Loudoun in the modern State of Tennessee, which the Cherokees closely beseiged. In March, 1760, the Virginia assembly continued the regiment in service until November 1, 1760, besides three companies of 100 men each to guard the frontier. At the hurriedly called session of May, 1760, the assembly resolved to raise 700 men, who, with the 300 already on the border, were to march to Fort Loudoun. Meanwhile Col. Montgomery, commanding a mixed force of British

---

([13]) Struggle with France for North America, 278.
([14]) Journals of the House of Burgesses, 1758-1761, xiii.

and Carolinians, had defeated the Cherokees and relieved Fort George, but abandoned the attempt to relieve Fort Loudoun, which surrendered to the Indians. The 700 extra troops were not raised, and the Virginia forces consisted only of the regiment already in service. The assembly provided for its maintenance until December, 1760, and allowed the governor to send it out of the colony. Amherst, the British commander in America, concerted an attack upon the Cherokees, to be carried out by Col. Grant from Charleston and the Virginia regiment under Byrd, together with North Carolina troops, from Virginia. Grant was successful, but Byrd did not manage to reach the enemy and resigned on account of the criticism, merited or unmerited, he ceived. He had under him 600 Virginians in this campaign. (15) Lieutenant-Colonel Adam Stephen succeeded Byrd in command of the regiment.

The Virginia regiment by 1760 had become an excellent military organization, whatever it may have been at the beginning. In March, 1760, the officers presented a petition to the House of Burgesses in which they mention its reputation: "That by close Application, and a steady Perseverance in the punctual Execution of their Duty, such good Order, Regularity, and strict Discipline (which can alone constitute good troops) have long been maintained in the regiment so as to have attracted the Particular Notice and Approbation of the best Judges; acquired a Superiority over all other Provincial Troops and rendered it universally admired by all with whom it did Duty: This Assertion is clearly evinced, by the behaviour of its officers in the many Actions it has been engaged in, and the Signal Bravery of several, whose gallant Conduct and glorious Deaths redound so much to the Honor of this Colony." (16) The regiment remained on the Cherokee frontier until early in 1762, when Governor Fauquier disbanded it on receiving word that peace had been concluded with the Indians.

The dying echoes of the Seven Years' War in Europe gave the colonies one more alarm. England had declared war on Spain, and Fauquier, at the meeting of the assembly in March, 1762, asked the colony to raise a regiment to be incorporated into the regiment on "British Capitol Establishments now in America." (17) The house of burgesses agreed, but the council demurred and only passed the bill creating a regiment of 1,000 men by a single vote. The regiment was raised, and remained for some time on duty in the west, but was disbanded in May, 1763.

It broke up just when needed, for in 1763 the Indians of the whole frontier, acting with a unity they never attained before or afterwards, attacked the British posts from Mackinaw to Fort Pitt, laying waste the settlements of New York, Pennsylvania, Maryland, and Virginia. The Virginia regiment had been disbanded chiefly because the board of trade would not allow the colony to issue the paper money needed for its maintenance, but in August, 1763, the governor and council called out 1,000 militia from Hampshire and the adjoining counties, half of them under the command of Col. Adam Stephen and half under Major Andrew Lewis, both of whom were now officers of the best quality. This force saw a good deal of service, and on one occasion a detachment was cut up by the Indians with heavy loss. (18)

---

(15) Virginia Magazine of History and Biography. 16, 136.
(16) Journals of the House of Burgesses, 1758-1761, 162.
(17) Journals of the House of Burgesses, 1761-1765, xv.
(18) Parkman's Conspiracy of Pontiac, 2, 105.

In the summer of 1764, Col. Bouquet, the most energetic and capable of the English officers in the colonies, prepared a retaliatory expedition against the Indian towns along the Ohio. In August, 1764, he wrote to Andrew Lewis to send him two hundred Virginia volunteers to take the place of his deserters. "A body of Virginians, accordingly, joined him at Fort Pitt, to his great satisfaction, for he set a high value on these backwoods riflemen." ([19]) The Virginia government, which was hard pressed for money, refused to pay the volunteers in Bouquet's army, attempting to make him responsible. Later, the Pennsylvania assembly assumed this debt, Pennsylvania being the great gainer by the suppression of the Ohio Indians. Virginia, indeed, had spent so much money in the French war that she suffered from a financial panic in 1765, for which reason her refusal to assume the obligation is excusable.

Between 1764 and 1774 there was no formal war on the border, though the whites were continually committing aggressions on the Indians and suffering retaliation. This state of affairs culminated in 1774 with a very brisk and stirring little war. On June 10, 1774, Lord Dunmore, the governor, issued a proclamation calling out the militia of the western counties, ([20]) and went to the frontier to take command in person. The southwestern militia concentrated at Lewisburg. It consisted of the Botetourt forces under William Fleming and those from Augusta under Charles Lewis, besides a company from Culpeper, one from Bedford, and two companies from the Holston; there were 14 companies in all. The veteran Col. Andrew Lewis commanded the whole force, numbering about 1100 men. Meanwhile Dunmore had raised the northwestern militia and found himself at the head of 1200 men.

Lewis advanced northward along the Kanawha to join Dunmore, until on October 6, 1774, he reached the Ohio. The Indians, seeing that the union of Dunmore and Lewis would make them overwhelmingly outnumbered, decided to attack one of the wings before it had joined the other. Accordingly, on October 9, 1774, they attempted to surprise Lewis's camp, but failed, and a fierce battle raged all day. At dark the Indians withdrew, leaving the field in the hands of the backwoodsmen, who made much of a rather indecisive victory. Soon after, Dunmore concluded peace with the red men, who had been disheartened by their failure to destroy Lewis at Point Pleasant. The troops of Dunmore's brigade, so called, continued in service on the frontier sometime longer and, indeed, almost until the colonial age blended into the Revolutionary. In the twenty years of frontier warfare in Virginia, from 1754 to 1774, the efficiency and reputation of the Virginia borderers grew apace. At the end of the colonial era they were considered the best rangers in the colonies, and as Morgan's riflemen won glory in the Revolutionary War wherever they appeared. In this struggle, in which for the first time civilized warfare was conducted in America on a large scale, the eastern Virginians served in large numbers and did well. Many of the best officers and troops in the Continental army came from that formerly inert tidewater section.

([19]) Parkman's Conspiracy of Pontiac, 2, 220.
([20]) Thwaites's Dunmore's War, xv.

This list of colonial soldiers of Virginia begins with a few of the names of the participants in the Cartagena expedition of 1740, recovered from the Journals of the House of Burgesses. The muster-rolls were probably never in the possession of the colonial government and are not now available, if they are in existence at all. A few other names represent the Canadian expedition and the Indian hostilities of the forties. It is not until 1754 that the list begins to be at all full, but starting with that year and running to 1758 the muster-rolls of the Virginia regiment are well preserved. Indeed, the rolls of the companies commanded by Washington and later by Stephen are singularly complete for a period comparatively so remote. For some of the other companies the rolls are not so good, and for the late period they hardly exist.

The rolls of the Virginia regiment are to be found in the Washington Papers in the Library of Congress, and some of them have been printed in the "Virginia Magazine of History and Biography." The other great source for a list of colonial soldiers is Hening's "Statutes at Large," which give, in the 7th and 8th volumes, a jumbled list of names of soldiers, provision providers, wagon drivers, and performers of various other services essential to the welfare of troops; it is with some difficulty that soldiers are detached from the mass of non-combatants. Furthermore, the Statutes are seriously deficient; they frequently mention captains of companies without giving the names of the soldiers, which are thus almost hopelessly lost. As the militia contingents in the Seven Years' War and the succeeding Indian troubles were large, it is probable that as many as several thousand militia-men remain unknown. From time to time, many of these names will be recovered in the county records and will go to swell the published list. It is believed, however, that few members of the Virginia regiment are un-accounted for, as in addition to the company rolls in the Washington Papers there are bounty applications in the Virginia land office, the bound volumes of which were used by Crozier in his "Virginia Colonial Militia," while the loose papers have been copied and made convenient for reference by the Virginia Historical Society. Other sources, such as the "Augusta County Records," and county histories, the "Journals of the House of Burgesses," and the "Journals of the House of Delegates," etc., have contributed some names. Lists of militia not known to have seen active service, a number of which are printed by Crozier, are omitted, as this list is limited to soldiers who actually served in war. The total number of entries is about 6700. Just what number of individuals these figures represent it is difficult to say, but beyond question the Virginia forces were much larger than has usually been supposed. In the present work the general form of the Revolutionary list has been followed, as it has been found convenient for reference purposes.

I wish to thank Miss Edmonia Blair Martin and Mrs. H. L. Goode for their assistance in arranging the cards.

The references are as follows:

Adam Stephen Ps.: Adam Stephen Papers. (Manuscript collection in the Library of Congress.)

Aug. Rec.: Abstracts from the Records of Augusta County. By Lyman Chalkley. 3 vols. Rosslyn, Va., 1912.

D. W.: R. G. Thwaites's Dunmore's War. Madison, Wis., 1905.

F. I. B. W.: French and Indian Bounty Warrants. 2 manuscript volumes. Copied from the loose applications for land bounties in the Virginia land office. (In the Virginia Historical Society Library.)

H. B.: Journals of the House of Burgesses. Successive volumes from 1740 to 1776. Published by the Virginia State Library.

H. D. M. (followed by year): Journal of the House of Delegates, May session, from 1776 on.

H. D. O. (followed by year): Journal of the House of Delegates, October session, from 1776 on.

Hist. of Frederick: History of Frederick County. (T. K. Cartmell's Shenandoah Valley Pioneer and their Descendants. Winchester, 1909.)

Hist. Orange: W. W. Scott's History of Orange County, Virginia. Richmond, 1907.

Hist. Rockingham: J. W. Wayland's History of Rockingham County. Dayton, Va., 1912.

Historic Shepherdstown: Danske Dandridge's Historic Shepherdstown. Charlottesville, 1910.

H. S.: Hening's Statutes at Large.

J.: Collection of manuscripts referred to by this numeral and consisting of pay accounts. (In the Virginia State Library.)

J. C. May, 1776: Journal of the Convention of May, 1776.

L. to Wash.: Letters to Washington. 3 vol. Boston and New York, 1898.

V. C. M.: W. A. Crozier's Virginia Colonial Militia. New York, 1905.

V. H. C.: Virginia Historical Collections.

Va. Mag.: Virginia Magazine of History and Biography. 21 vols.

Wash. Mss.: Washington Manuscripts. The great collection of letters and papers of Washington in the Library of Congress, consisting of a number of volumes referred to usually by folios but not always.

Withers's Chron.: Withers's Chronicles of Border Warfare.

A.

Abbott, George, H. S., 7, 206. ,

Abbott, Matthew, F. I. B. W., 2, 419.

Aberman, Jacob, H. S., 7, 184.

Aberman, John, H. S., 7, 184.

Abet George, H. S., 209.

Able, Jeremiah, D. W., 402.

Abney, William, H. S., 7, 201.

Abston, John, H. S., 7, 209.

Acres, James, F. I. B. W., 2, 408.

Acuff, John, H. S., 7, 224.

Acuts, John, F. I. B. W., 2, 534.

Adam, David, H. S., 7, 212.

Adams, Francis, Va. Mag., 1, 381; Wash. Mss., 112, 86, 89, 95; Wash. Mss., 1557.

Adams, George, H. S., 7, 207, 208, 209.

Adams, James, F. I. B. W., 2, 463; V. C. M., 48.

Adams, John, D. W., 400; F. I. B. W., 1, 189; F. I. B. W., 2, 381, 540; Va. Mag. 1, 378; Va. Mag., 2, 148, 150; Wash. Mss., 112, 87, 88; Wash. Mss., 1466.

Adams, Joseph, H. S., 7, 218.

Adams, Nathan, H. S., 7, 224.

Adams, Richard, H. S., 7, 224.

Adams, Thomas, Va. Mag., 2, 46.

Adams, William, Aug. Rec., 1, 478.

Adcock, Thomas, Va. Mag., 1, 37.

Adderson, Joseph, Va. Mag., 1, 384.

Adkins, Gardner, F. I. B. W., 1, 12; H. S., 7, 191.

Adkins, Joseph, F. I. B. W., 1, 170.

Adkins, Willinton, D. W., 398.

Afflack, Peter, Va. Mag., 1, 378; Wash. Mss., 112, 88, 94.

Aggnue, John, D. W., 411.

Ahorn, William, F. I. B. W., 1, 260; V. C. M., 31.

Alcorn, James, F. I. B. W., 2, 366; H. S., 7, 209; V. C. M., 39.

Alcorn, John, F. I. B. W., 2, 464; V. C. M., 48.

Alden, Andrew, D. W., 406.

Aldin, Wentworth, Aug. Rec., 1, 478.

Ale, Joseph, Va. Mag., 1, 378; Wash. Mss., 112, 88.

Alexander, Archibald (capt.), F. I.
B. W., 1, 36; V. C. M., 12; With-
ers's Chron., 81.
Alexander, Archibald, H. S., 7, 195.
Alexander, Francis, H. S., 7, 190.
Alexander, Hugh, H. S., 7, 203.
Alexander, James, D. W., 405, 407,
419; H. S., 7, 183, 185.
Alexander John (capt.) (Augusta),
Withers's Chron., 81.
Alexander, John, Va. Mag., 2, 144;
Wash. Mss., 1536.
Alexander, Robert, Wash. Mss., 1557.
Alexander, William, F. I. B. W., 1,
24; V. C. M., 11.
Alfort, Thomas, H. S., 7, 215.
Algier, Magis, H. S., 7, 186.
Alinthorp, John, Va. Mag., 2, 41.
Allan, John, Va. Mag., 1, 279; Wash.
Mss., 11, 111.
Allberry, Thomas, Va. Mag., 2, 41.
Allbury, Charles, Va. Mag., 1, 279;
Wash. Mss., 5, 8; Wash. Mss.,
11, 111.
Allden, Wentworth, Aug. Rec., 1, 478.
Allen, Charles, jr., H. S., 7, 226.
Allen, Francis, Wash. Mss., 112, 116.
Allen, Hugh (lt.), V. C. M., 89.
Allen, Hugh, Aug. Rec., 1, 184; H. S.,
7, 190, 191; V. C. M., 89.
Allen, James (capt.), Aug. Rec., 1,
317; H. B., 1752-58, 484.
Allen, James, H. S., 7, 190.
Allen, John (lt.), H. S., 7, 216.
Allen, John (en.), H. S., 7, 216;
Wash. Mss., 5, 4.
Allen, John (cadet), Wash. Mss.,
112, 95.
Allen, John, Wash. Mss., 5, 8.
Allen, Malcom, H. S., 7, 203.
Allen, Robert, H. S., 7, 196.
Allen Robert, jr., H. S., 7, 196.
Allen, Samuel, F. I. B. W., 2, 531.
Allen, Thomas, H. .S., 7, 216.
Alley, Thomas, Va. Mag., 2, 143.
Alliet (Eliott), Robert (en.), D. W.,
408.
Allison, Charles, H. S., 7, 196.
Allison, Robert, Wash. Mss., 1557.
Ally, Nicholas, H. B., 1758-61, 28, 31.
Alsberry (Alsbury), Thomas, Aug.
Rec., 2, 68; D. W.. 408.
Alsop (Alsup), John, F. I. B. W.,
2, 463; V. C. M., 48.
Alston, John, H. S., 7, 204.
Ambries, Freeman, Va. Mag., 2, 153.
Amons, Absalom, Wash. Mss., 1432.
Amos, Absalom, Va. Mag , 2, 49, 150;
Wash. Mss., 112, 87.

Amos, Francis, F. I. B. W., 1, 30;
V. C. M., 12.
Amox, James, H. S., 8, 129.
Anderson, ———, H. B., 1742-49, 94.
Anderson, Alexander, Va. Mag., 2,
145.
Anderson, Andrew, J., 8.
Anderson, George, Aug. Rec., 1, 339;
H. S., 7, 185.
Anderson, Henry (capt.), V. H. C.,
4, 157.
Anderson, Henry, H. S., 7, 201.
Anderson, Isaac, Wash. Mss., 1477.
Anderson, Jacob, H. S., 7, 205, 210.
Anderson, James, D. W., 402; F. I.
B. W., 1, 17; H. S., 7, 179, 187,
188; Va. Mag., 1, 379.
Anderson, John, F. I. B. W., 1, 94;
H. S., 7, 195, 208, 214; V. C. M.,
17; Va. Mag., 2, 43; Wash. Mss.,
5, 4; Wash. Mss., 1555.
Anderson, Matthew, F. I. B. W., 2,
383; H. B., 1770-72, 16, 84; V. C.
M., 41.
Anderson, Robert, H. S., 7, 187.
Anderson, Thomas, H. B., 1752-58,
273.
Anderson, William, F. I. B. W., 2,
425; H. S., 7, 190, 195, 209, 224.
Anderton, James, Wash. Mss., 112,
88, 94.
Andrews, Richard, H. S., 7, 206.
Andrews, Robert, H. B., 1761-65, 219,
220.
Andrews, Samuel, D. W., 407.
Ankor, William (lt.), Historic Shep-
herdstown, 25.
Annet, Joseph, F. I. B. W., 2, 401;
V. C. M., 42.
Anon, James, H. S., 7, 191.
Anthony, Emanuel, Aug. Rec., 1, 478.
Anthony, John (lt.), H. S., 7, 206.
Anthony, John, F. I. B. W., 2, 507;
V. C. M., 51.
Appling, John, H. S., 201
Arbuckle, James, Aug. Rec.. 1, 336,
498; H. S., 8, 129.
Arbuckle, John, D. W., 423; H. S.,
8,129; V. C. M., 89.
Arbuckle, Matt (capt.), V. C. M., 89.
Arbuckle, Matthew, H. S., 8, 129.
Arbuckle, William, D. W., 423; V.
C. M., 89.
Archer, Sampson (lt.) (Augusta), H.
S., 7, 183.
Archer, Sampson (lt.) (Augusta), H.
58, 484; H. S., 7, 179.
Archer, Sampson, H. S., 7, 180.
Ard, James, D. W., 409.

Armentrout, George, Aug. Rec., 2, 366.

Armfield, David, H. B., 1766-69, 314.

Armistead, Robert (maj.), Wash. Mss., 1479.

Armontrout, Christopher, H. S., 7, 187.

Armstrong, George, D. W., 412.

Armstrong, John, H. B., 1761-65, 239; H. S., 7, 187, 195, 199; H. S., 8, 127.

Armstrong, Lanty, Aug. Rec., 1, 344; H. B., 1761-65, 239; H. S., 8, 127.

Armstrong, Paul, J., 9.

Armstrong, Robert, H. B., 1761-65, 254, 259; H. S., 7, 191, 192.

Armstrong, Thomas (capt.), L. to Wash., 1, 305.

Armstrong, Thomas, Aug. Rec., 1, 75; D. W., 407; Wash. Mss., 5, 15, 1.

Armstrong, William, D. W., 407; F. I. B. W., 2, 394; H. S., 7, 199; V. C. M., 41.

Arnold, Anthony, Va. Mag., 2, 150; Wash. Mss., 112, 87.

Arnold, Humphrey, V. C. M., 8, 97; Va. Mag., 7, 305.

Arnold, James, D. W., 406; F. I. B. W., 1, 168; H. S., 7, 201.

Arnold, Jeremiah, J., 116.

Arnold, Moses, Va. Mag., 2, 153.

Arnold, Stephen, D. W., 406, 419.

Arrans, Jacob, Va. Mag., 1, 279, 283; Wash. Mss., 1490.

Arrans, John, Wash. Mss., 11, 111.

Arrel, David, Wash. Mss., 1557.

Arrenton, Samuel, H. S., 7, 205.

Arskins, John, Wash. Mss., 1311.

Arthington, Jeptha (en.), H. S., 7, 211.

Arthur, Barnabas, H. S., 7, 206.

Arthur, Barnaby, jr., H. S., 7, 206.

Arthur, John, D. W., 408.

Arthur, William, H. S., 7, 206, 207.

Artus, John, Aug. Rec., 1, 344.

Asbery, Thomas, Wash. Mss., 1460.

Ashby, Hankerson, J., 191.

Ashby, Henry (lt.), H. B., 1766-69, 71.

Ashby, John (capt.), H. B., 1752-58, 459.

Ashby, Nimrod (capt.), H. B., 1761-65, 281, 346.

Ashby (Ashbey), William, Va. Mag. 2, 45; Wash. Mss., 112, 90.

Asher, William, H. S., 7, 220.

Ashford, Butler, Wash. Mss., 1460.

Ashley, Richard, Wash. Mss., 112, 85, 1, 96.

Ashley, William, H. S., 7, 225.

Ashwell, Richmond, Va. Mag., 1, 390; Wash. Mss., 112, 100.

Ashworth, Isaac, H. S., 7, 223.

Ashworth, John, H. S., 7, 223.

Ashworth, Samuel, H. S., 7, 223.

Askins, John, Aug. Rec., 1, 208; Va. Mag., 2, 149.

Askins, Philemon, Va. Mag., 2, 149.

Atherton, James, H. B., 1752-58, 339, 346.

Atkins, Edward, H. S., 7, 224.

Atkins, Frass, H. S., 7, 224.

Atkins, John, Aug. Rec., 1, 68.

Atkins, William, F. I. B. W., 1, 275.

Atkinson, James, Va. Mag., 1, 389; Wash. Mss., 112, 85.1, 96.

Auberry, James, Wash. Mss., 111, 110.

Aulburey, Charles, Wash. Mss., 112, 0.

Austin, Benjamin, F. I. B. W., 1, 141.

Austin, Edward, Adam Stephen Ps.; Wash. Mss., 112, 114.

Austin, Francis, Aug. Rec., 2, 505; Hist. of Fred., 90; Va. Mag., 1, 385; Wash. Mss., 112, 82; Wash. Mss., 1311.

Austin, Henry, F. I. B. W., 2, 535; Wash. Mss., 1479.

Austin, Henry, jr., F. I. B. W., 1, 141.

Austin, John, Va. Mag., 2, 43; Wash. Mss., 1479.

Austin, William, Va. Mag., 1, 388; Wash. Mss., 112, 85.1, 96, 116.

Avery, John, H. S., 7, 201.

Avery, William, F. I. B. W., 2, 327; V. C. M., 36; Wash. Mss., 5, 4.

Awbrey, Francis, H. S., 7, 218.

Ayres, Thomas, F. I. B. W., 1, 116; V. C. M., 19.

B.

Baber, Josias, Wash. Mss., 112, 89.

Backley, John, J. C., May, 1776, 57.

Bacon, Edmund, F. I. B. W., 2, 489, 551; V. C. M., 50.

Bailer, Stephen, V. C. M., 97.

Bailey, Carr, V. C. M., 97; Va. Mag., 7, 306.

Bailey, David, Wash. Mss., 112, 114.

Bailey, Edward, Wash. Mss., 111, 15.

Bailey, Henry, Aug. Rec., 2, 49, 51, 170.

Bailey, James, V. C. M., 97; Va. Mag., 7, 306.

Bailey, John, D. W., 422, 423.

Bailey, Nathaniel, H. S., 7, 215.

Bailey, Peter, H. S., 7, 215.

Bailey, Roger Cock, F. I. B. W., 2, 430.

Bailey, Stephen, Va. Mag., 7, 306.

Bailey, Thomas, Va. Mag., 1, 389; Wash. Mss., 112, 85.1, 96.

Bailey, William, Aug. Rec., 2, 49, 51; J., 130; Wash. Mss., 5, 8; Wash. Mss., 111, 15.
Baillie, Thomas, H. B., 1761-65, 39, 42.
Baily, Campbell, D. W., 399.
Baisey, John, V. C. M., 97; Va. Mag., 7, 305.
Baisley, Edmund, V. C. M., 97; Va. Mag., 7, 305.
Baisley, John, V. C. M., 97.
Baker, Christopher, H. D., May, 1777, 16.
Baker, Edward, H. S., 7, 214.
Baker, Humphrey, H. S., 8, 129.
Baker, James (lt.), F. I. B. W., 1, 68; H. B., 1761-65, 115; L. to Wash., 2, 89; V. C. M., 15; Va. Mag., 1, 287.
Baker, James, F. I. B. W., 1, 69; Wash. Mss., 5, 4.
Baker, John, Wash. Mss., 1490.
Baker, Josias, Va. Mag., 1, 279; Wash. Mss., 11, 111.
Baker, Martain, D. W., 411.
Baker, Samuel (en.), D. W., 411.
Baker, Thomas, D. W., 419; H. S., 7, 210; Wash. Mss., 1555.
Baker, William, F. I. B. W., 1, 132; H. S., 7, 213; Va. Mag., 2, 144.
Baldock, Levy, F. I. B. W., 1, 76; V. C. M., 16.
Baldock, Richard, F. I. B. W., 1, 75; V. C. M., 16; Va. Mag., 1, 390; Va. Mag., 2, 40; Wash. Mss., 112, 85.1, 96, 100; Wash. Mss., 1467.
Baldwin, John, H. S., 7, 201.
Baley, Robert, Wash. Mss., 1557.
Ball, Edward, V. C. M., 97; Va. Mag., 7, 305.
Ball, William, V. C. M., 97; Va. Mag., 7, 306.
Ballard, Edmond, H. S., 7, 202.
Ballen, Edward, Va. Mag., 2, 42.
Ballenger, John, H. S., 7, 213; Wash. Mss., 1555.
Baller, John, F. I. B. W., 1, 33; V. C. M., 12.
Ballot, John, Aug. Rec., 1, 340.
Baltimore, Christopher, F. I. B. W., 2, 444.
Bambrige, James, D. W., 406.
Banger, John, H. S., 7, 214; Wash. Mss., 1555.
Banner, Peter, Va. Mag., 2, 149; Wash. Mss., 1478.
Bannister, ———, H. B., 1742-49, 101.
Banton, William, V. C. M., 38.
Barber, Philip, H. B., 1766-69, 88.
Barden, John, H. B., 1742-49, 169, 174.

Bardin, James, H. S., 7, 223.
Bare, William, Wash. Mss., 112, 90.
Barecraft, William, Wash. Mss., 112, 82.2.
Barefoot, William, F. I. B. W., 1, 158; Wash. Mss., 1472.
Baret, Edward, D. W., 411.
Barker, Edmunds, H. S., 7, 212.
Barker, Lewis, H. S., 7, 212.
Barker, Moses, F. I. B. W., 2, 434.
Barker, Thomas, F. I. B. W., 2, 471; V. C. M., 49.
Barkley, George, H. S., 7, 198.
Barkly, John, D. W., 406.
Barlow, Benjamin, Va. Mag., 2, 152.
Barlow, William, F. I. B. W., 1, 214.
Barnes, Bartholomew, Wash. Mss., 11, 111.
Barnes, Francis, F. I. B. W., 1, 293.
Barnes, Thomas, J. C., May, 1776, 49.
Barnet, John, H. S., 7, 212; Va. Mag., 1, 386; Wash. Mss., 112, 84.
Barnet, William, Wash. Mss., 1472.
Barnett, James, D. W., 422; F. I. B. W., 2, 451; Va. Mag., 2, 45.
Barnett, William, Va. Mag., 2, 43.
Barns, William, Wash. Mss., 1542.
Barrack, John, Va. Mag., 2, 144.
Barret, Lemuel, F. I. B. W., 2, 304.
Barret, Nathaniel, Aug. Rec., 1, 478.
Barret, S. L., D. W., 425.
Barrett, Benjamin, L. to Wash., 1, 299; Va. Mag., 2, 147.
Barrett, Charles, F. I. B. W., 1, 230; V. C. M., 29.
Barrett, John, L. to Wash., 1, 300; Va. Mag., 2, 46.
Barrett, Nathaniel, Aug. Rec., 2, 51; Va. Mag., 1, 279; Va. Mag., 2, 149; Wash. Mss., 11, 111; Wash. Mss., 111, 15.
Barringer, Isaac, L. to Wash. 1, 299; Va. Mag., 2, 40.
Barrow, Thomas, H. S., 7, 185.
Bartee, William, F. I. B. W., 2, 534.
Barton, Samuel, D. W., 408.
Barton, William, F. I. B. W., 1, 169; Wash. Mss., 1467.
Basdel, John, D. W., 419.
Bashford, Alexander, Wash. Mss., 1477.
Baskin, William, H. B., 1766-69, 63.
Baskine, John, H. S., 7, 187.
Baskine, Thomas, H. S., 7, 187.
Baskins, William, Aug. Rec., 1, 73, 329, 476.
Basset, John, Va. Mag., 1, 388.
Bassett (Basset), Robert, Wash. Mss., 5, 4; Wash. Mss., 112, 114; Wash. Mss., 1485.

Bewtoole, Gasper, H. S., 7, 216.
Bibb, Thomas (lt.), V. C. M., 37.
Bibb, Thomas, F. I. B. W., 2, 333.
Bibb, William, F. I. B. W., 1, 139.
Bickley, Humphrey, H. S., 7, 222.
Bickley, Joseph, F. I. B. W., 2, 538.
Biddlecome, John, Va. Mag., 1, 279; Wash. Mss., 11, 111.
Bidgood (Bedgood), Joseph, Va. Mag., 2, 47.
Bigger, James, Wash. Mss., 112, 83.
Biggers, James, Va. Mag., 1, 386.
Bigham, George, H. B., 1752-58, 484.
Bigs, John, H. S., 7, 204.
Billot, James, Aug. Rec., 2, 506.
Bingaman, Christian (lt.), H. S., 7, 186.
Bingaman, John, H. S., 7, 186.
Bins, James, Va. Mag., 2, 145.
Bird, Thomas, Wash. Mss., 111, 15.
Bishop, John, Aug. Rec., 2, 49, 505; Va. Mag., 1, 279; Wash. Mss., 11, 111.
Bishop, Levi, D. W., 403.
Bishop, William, Wash. Mss., 1485.
Bissell, John, Wash. Mss., 112, 85.1.
Bisset, John, Wash. Mss., 112, 96.
Bist, Abraham, H. S., 7, 199.
Black, Anthony, H. S., 7, 190.
Black, James, F. I. B. W., 1, 241; V. C. M., 29; Va. Mag., 1, 279; Wash. Mss., 5, 8; Wash. Mss., 11, 111; Wash. Mss., 111, 15; Wash. Mss., 112, 0.
Black, John, Aug. Rec., 2, 63; H. B., 1773-76, 197; H. S., 7, 179, 190, 191.
Black, Matthew, H. S., 7, 181, 184, 186.
Black, Robert, H. S., 7, 186, 188.
Black, Samuel, Aug. Rec., 1, 68, 518.
Black, William, Aug. Rec., 1, 212; F. I B.. W., 2, 566; H. S., 7, 181.
Blackbourn (Blackborn), Edward, Va. Mag., 1, 378; Wash. Mss., 112, 94.
Blackburn, Andrew, H. S., 7, 216.
Blackburn, Arthur, D. W., 412.
Blackburn, Benjamin, H. S., 7, 216.
Blackburn, Christopher, F. I. B. W., 1, 122.
Blackburn, Edward, Wash. Mss., 112, 88.
Blackburn, Robert, J., 237.
Blackburn, William, H. S., 7, 216.
Blackford, Joseph, D. W., 421; V. C. M., 88.
Blackstone, Richard, J., 39.
Blackwell, John, V. C. M., 97; Va. Mag., 7, 306.

Blackwood, William, H. S., 7, 179, 190.
Blagg (Blagge), John (capt.), Aug. Rec., 1, 97, 340, 343, 477, 493; H. B., 1761-65, 102; V. C. M., 15.
Blagg, John (lt.), V. H. C., 3, 423.
Blagg, John, V. H. C., 4, 401.
Blair, Daniel, D. W., 406.
Blair, James, H. S., 7, 195.
Blair, John, Aug. Rec., 1, 215; H. S., 7, 195.
Blair, William, H. S., 7, 185, 187.
Blakeley, William, Va. Mag., 2, 143.
Blakey, William, Wash. Mss., 112, 90.
Blanchet, Robert, H. S., 7, 201.
Bland, Richard, jr. (capt.), H. S., 7, 229.
Blankenship (Blanketship), Henry, Wash. Mss., 112, 95.
Blankenship (Bankenship, Blankinship), Stephen, F. I. B. W., 2, 344; H. B., 1761-65, 324, 328; H.. S., 8, 128; Va. Mag., 1, 390; Wash. Mss., 112, 85.1, 96.
Blankenship, William, F. 1. B. W., 2, 404.
Blanket, Henry, Wash. Mss., 112, 86.
Blankinship, Henry, Va. Mag., 1, 381.
Blanks, William, H. S., 7, 223.
Blanton, William, F. I. B. W., 1, 79; H. B., 1761-65, 249, 259; V. C. M., 16; Va. Mag., 1, 382; Wash. Mss., 112, 86, 89, 95.
Bledcer, Abraham, Va. Mag., 1, 381; Wash. Mss., 112, 89.
Bledsoe (Bledso), Abraham, H. B., 1752-58, 460, 461; Wash. Mss., 112, 86.
Bledsoe, Anthony (capt.), J. C., May, 1776, 28.
Bledsoe, Joseph, F. I. B. W., 1, 161; L. to Wash., 1, 300; V. C. M., 129.
Bleeker, Abraham, Wash. Mss., 5, 4.
Blesly, Jacob, D. W., 400.
Blesly, John, D. W., 400.
Bletcher, Abraham, Wash. Mss., 112, 95.
Blevins, James, H. S., 7, 220.
Blevins, John, H. S., 7, 220.
Blevins, William, jr., H. S., 7, 220.
Blewford, Jeremiah, F. I. B. W., 2. 350; V. C. .M., 38.
Blor, John, H. S., 7, 183.
Bludoe, Joseph, Va. Mag., 2, 143.
Blue, Abraham (scout), H. B., 1766-69, 294.
Blunkall (Bluntkall), William, F. I. B. W., 1, 274; V. C. M., 32; Wash. Mss., 1472.

Bradbeary, James, Wash. Mss., 5, 4.
Bradberry, Joseph, F. I. B. W., 1, 46; V. C. M., 13.
Bradbury, James, Aug. Rec., 1, 478.
Bradford, John, F. I. B. W., 1, 212.
Bradford, Thomas, Va. Mag., 1, 382.
Bradley, John, D. W., 412; H. S., 7, 214; Wash. Mss., 1555.
Bradley, Joseph, H. S., 7, 218.
Bradly, William, D. W., 406.
Bradshaw, James, H. S., 7, 185.
Braffit, William, H. B., 1758-61, 68, 70.
Bragg, William, V. C. M., 97; Va. Mag., 7, 306.
Brakin, Matt (en.), V. C. M., 89.
Bramham, Richard, F. I. B. W., 1, 166.
Bramlett, Ambrose (Ambus), H. S., 7, 205, 209.
Bramlitt, William, H. S., 7, 209.
Branan, Thomas, H. B., 1761-65, 179, 185.
Branfoot, William, Wash. Mss., 112, 90.
Branham, Nathaniel, F. I. B. W., 1, 136.
Braning, Thomas, Wash. Mss., 112, 90.
Brann, Jacob, Va. Mag., 2, 144.
Brannan, Peter, F. I. B. W., 2, 487, 553.
Brannin, Thomas, Va. Mag., 1, 383.
Brannon, Thomas, Aug. Rec., 1, 97.
Branstead, Andrew, D. W., 404.
Brashear, Joseph, J., 123.
Brassfield, John, H. S., 7,201.
Bratchy, William, H. S., 7,203.
Bratton, Robert, Aug. Rec., 1, 72.
Bratton, William, H. S., 7, 181.
Braughton, William, Va. Mag., 1, 279; Wash. Mss., 11, 111.
Braxley, Baron, Wash. Mss., 111, 15.
Bray, John, H. S., 7, 226.
Breadsell, Edward, Wash. Mss., 1471.
Breckenridge, Robert (maj.), Aug. Rec., 1, 354, 463.
Breckenridge (Breckinridge), Robert (capt.), F. I. B. W., 2, 316; H. B. 1752-58, 484; L. to Wash., 1. 305; V. H. C., 4, 531; Withers's Chron., 81.
Breckinridge, Alexander, D. W., 422.
Breckinridge, Robert (capt. Augusta m.), Wash. Mss., 5, 15, 1.
Breden, John, D. W., 405.
Breeze, Richard, D. W., 401.
Breeze, Robert, D. W., 401.
Breken, Matthew (en.), D. W., 410.

Brennon, Thomas, Wash. Mss., 112, 95.
Brenton, Henry, H. S., 7, 203.
Brenton, James, J., 1.
Brewer, George, H. S., 7, 212.
Briant, James, Wash. Mss., 112, 115.
Briant, Jesse, Wash. Mss., 112, 85.1, 96, 100.
Briant, John, Wash. Mss., 112, 115.
Brickner, Rudolph, Va. Mag., 1, 279; Wash. Mss., 11, 111.
Bridge, John, F. I. B. W., 2, 330; V. C. M., 36.
Bridge, Joseph, Va. Mag., 1, 389.
Bridge, Joshua, Wash. Mss., 112, 96.
Bridgells, James, Aug. Rec., 1, 213.
Bridges, Joseph, Wash. Mss., 112, 85.1.
Bridgetts, James, F. I. B. W., 2, 411.
Bridgman, Roger, Va. Mag., 2, 40.
Briggs, John, Wash. Mss., 1483.
Briggs, Joseph, Va. Mag., 2, 146.
Briggs, Thomas, H. S., 7, 211.
Bright, Charles, H. S., 7, 207, 210.
Bright, Edward, H. S., 7, 210.
Bright, Thomas, F. I. B. W., 2, 355; Wash. Mss., 1543.
Brinton, Henry, D. W., 421.
Brinton, James, D. W., 421.
Bristoe, Henry, Va. Mag., 1, 279; Wash. Mss., 11, 111.
Bristol, —— H. B., 1742-49, 101.
Bristol, Henry, Wash. Mss., 111, 15; Wash. Mss., 112, 0.
Brittaine, John, Wash. Mss., 112, 88.
Britton, John, Va. Mag., 1, 379; Wash. Mss., 112, 94.
Broadwaters, C., Wash. Mss., 1557.
Brock, Elias, H. S., 8, 131.
Brock, William, Aug. Rec. 1, 478; F. I. B. W., 1, 137; F. I. B. W., 2, 572; Hist. Orange, 60; Va. Mag., 2, 42.
Broil, Jacob, H. S., 7, 214.
Broke, William, Aug. Rec. 1, 478.
Brokenborough, Augustine (1t.), Va. Mag., 1, 287.
Bromlett, James, H. S., 7, 210.
Bromley, Augustine, F. I. B. W., 2, 555.
Bromley, Thomas, F. I. B. W., 1, 130.
Bromley, William, Va. Mag., 1, 384.
Bronstetter, Andrew, D. W., 399.
Brook (Brooke), Bibby, Va. Mag., 1, 279; Wash. Mss., 11, 111.
Brook, Thomas, D. W., 405.
Brooke, George (1t.), F. I. B. W., 1, 1.

Brooks, Bibby, Va. Mag., 1, 385; Va. Mag., 2, 144.
Brooks, Francis, Va. Mag., 2, 150.
Brooks, George, D. W., 412.
Brooks, John, Va. Mag., 1, 381; Wash. Mss., 112, 86, 95.
Brooks, William, Wash. Mss., 112, 88, 94.
Broomley, Augustine, F. I. B. W., 2, 482; V. C. M., 49.
Bronaugh, William (capt.), Wash. Mss., 5.
Bronaugh, William (en.), Va. Mag., 1, 279.
Bronaugh, William, Aug. Rec., 2, 168; V. H. C., 3, 111.
Brothers, Francis, L. to Wash., 2, 163; Va. Mag., 2, 45.
Broughton, William, Aug. Rec., 2, 49; Va. Mag., 2, 38; Wash. Mss., 112, 0.
Brown, Charles, D. W., 405.
Brown, Christopher, Wash. Mss., 112, 90, 95.
Brown, Coleman (Colman), D. W., 421; H. D., 1776, 42, 48.
Brown, Combes, Wash. Mss., 112, 88.
Brown, Edward, F. I. B. W., 2, 580; H. S., 7, 214; Va. Mag., 2, 150; Wash. Mss., 112, 87, 115; Wash. Mss., 1555.
Brown, Francis, H. S., 7, 213.
Brown, Isaac, H. S., 7, 206, 209.
Brown, Jacob, H. S., 7, 203.
Brown, Jesse, H. S., 7, 211.
Brown, John (maj. Augusta m.), Wash. Mss., 5, 15.1.
Brown, John (maj.), H. S., 7, 191; L. to Wash., 1, 305.
Brown, John, H. S., 7, 190, 205, 206; Va. Mag., 1, 279, 382; Wash. Mss., 5, 8; Wash. Mss., 112, 86, 95.
Brown, John Windell, H. B., 1758-61, 16.
Brown, Low, D. W., 422.
Brown, Peter, H. B., 1752-58, 282.
Brown, Philip Combs, Va. Mag., 1, 379.
Brown, Robert, D. W., 396, 401, 403; H. S., 7, 191.
Brown, Samuel, H. S., 7, 207, 210; Va. Mag., 2, 40.
Brown, Thomas, D. W., 407; H. B., 1761-65, 343; J., 234; Va. Mag., 1, 379; Va. Mag., 2, 45, 146, 150; Wash. Mss., 112, 87, 88, 90, 94; Wash. Mss., 1311.

Brown, William (capt.), H. B., 1752-58, 461.
Brown, William (doctor), Wash. Mss., 1557.
Brown, William, D. W., 406.
Brown, Winsor, Wash. Mss., 1557.
Browning, James, H. S., 7, 213; Wash. Mss., 1555.
Bruce, Alexander, Wash. Mss., 112, 96.
Bruce, Charles, Va. Mag., 1, 380; Wash. Mss., 112, 88, 94, 114.
Brumley, Austin, Aug. Rec., 1, 479.
Brumley, John, V. C. M., 32.
Brumley (Brumly), Thomas, Aug. Rec., 1, 479; D. W., 401, 403.
Brumley, William, Aug. Rec., 1, 479; H. B., 1758-61, 188; Va. Mag., 2, 147; Wash. Mss., 5, 4.
Brundige, Solomon, D. W., 406.
Bryan, Ambrose, H. S., 7, 207.
Bryan, James, H. S., 7, 205; H. S., 8, 128.
Bryan, Jesse, H. S., 7, 206.
Bryan, John, H. S., 7, 203; Va. Mag., 1, 279; Wash. Mss., 11, 111.
Bryan, William, H. S., 7, 211.
Bryans, David, H. S., 7, 196.
Bryans, James, H. S., 7, 191.
Bryans, John, Va. Mag., 1, 279; Wash. Mss., 11, 111.
Bryans, William, D. W., 408.
Bryant, Ambrose, H. S., 7, 204.
Bryant, Jesse, Va. Mag., 1, 389.
Bryant, John, Va. Mag., 1, 283; Va. Mag., 2, 150; Wash. Mss., 111, 15.
Bryant, William, D. W., 409.
Buchanan, Alexander, H. S., 7, 196.
Buchanan, Andrew, H. S., 7, 196, 198.
Buchanan, Archibald (lt.), H. S., 7, 196.
Buchanan, Archibald, F. I, B. W., 2, 461; V. C. M., 48.
Buchanan, James, F. I. B. W., 2, 545; H. S., 7, 196; Va. Mag., 2, 38.
Buchanan, John (col. Augusta m.), V. H. C., 3, 268; Wash. Mss., 5, 15.1.
Buchanan, John (col.), L. to Wash., 1, 305.
Buchanan, John (capt.), (Augusta), H. S., 7, 182.
Buchanan, John (capt.) F. I. B. W., 423.
Buchanan, John, D. W., 407; Wash. Mss., 1472.
Buchanan, William, H. S., 7, 196.

Buckles, Robert, F. I. B. W., 2, 417; Historic Shepherdstown, 26.
Buckley, Butler, F. I. B. W., 1, 143; V. C. M., 21.
Buckley, John, Va. Mag., 2, 41.
Buckner, Mordecai (capt.), F. I. B. W., 1, 239, 290.
Buckner, Mordecai (lt.), Aug. Rec., 1, 346.
Buckridge, James, Va. Mag., 2, 48.
Bucksy, John, Wash. Mss., 112, 115.
Buckus, Robert, H. S., 7, 216.
Budge, Joshua, Wash. Mss., 1472.
Buffen, Joseph, Va. Mag., 2, 47.
Buford, James, V. C. M., 31.
Buford, John, F. I. B. W., 2, 371.
Buford, Thomas (capt.), V. C. M., 88.
Buford, Thomas, Aug. Rec., 2, 170; F. I. B. W., 1, 263; H. B., 1766-69, 88.
Bullard, John, F. I. B. W., 1, 170.
Bullet (Bullitt), Thomas (capt.), Aug. Rec., 1, 333; L. to Wash., 1, 114.
Bullitt, Thomas (lt.), Withers's Chron., 71.
Bullitt, Thomas, V. H. C., 4, 401.
Bullock, James (en.), V. C. M., 29.
Bullock, James, F. I. B. W., 1, 232.
Bullock, Richard, F. I. B. W., 1, 157; Wash. Mss., 112, 90.
Bullock, Samuel, Wash. Mss., 112, 90.
Bullock, William, Hist. Orange, 59.
Bumpass, William, H. S., 7, 204.
Bunch, Joseph, D. W., 409.
Bunshell, John, D. W., 399.
Bunton, James, H. S., 7, 198.
Burck, Richard, D. W., 412.
Burcks, Samuel, D. W., 409.
Burford, William, Va. Mag., 2, 43.
Burgess (Burges) John, Va. Mag., 2, 46; Wash. Mss., 112, 90.
Burgess, Joseph, H. S., 7, 201.
Burgh, William, H. S., 7, 202.
Burk, James, H. S., 7, 183.
Burk, John, Va. Mag., 1, 279; Wash. Mss., 5, 4; Wash. Mss., 11, 111; Wash. Mss., 111, 15; Wash. Mss., 1460.
Burk, Thomas, Va. Mag., 1, 279; Wash. Mss., 11, 111.
Burke, John, D. W., 410.
Burke, Thomas, F. I. B. W., 1, 44; V. C. M., 13.
Burkem, Solomon, H. S., 7, 215.
Burkham, Roger, Va. Mag., 1, 379; Wash. Mss., 112, 88, 94.
Burks, Boling, H. S., 7, 210.
Burks, John Patrick, H. S., 7, 210.
Burks, Richard, H. S., 7, 210.

Burks, Richard, Jr., H. S., 7, 210.
Burks, William, H. S., 7, 210.
Burn, Aquilla (Equilia), Va. Mag., 1, 387; Va. Mag., 2, 145.
Burn, Joheph, Va. Mag., 2, 145; Wash. Mss., 1535.
Burnes, Thomas, D. W., 409.
Burnett, James, F. I. B. W., 1, 75; V. C. M., 16.
Burney (Burny) Thomas, D. W, 406; H. B., 1752-58, 364; Va. Mag., 1, 279; Wash. Mss., 11, 111; Wash. Mss., 111, 15.
Burnley, Zachariah, H. S., 7, 206.
Burns, Aquilla, Wash. Mss., 112, 82.
Burns, Bartholomew, Va. Mag., 1, 279; Wash. Mss., 11, 111.
Burns, John, Va. Mag., 2, 38.
Burns, Michael, Va. Mag., 1, 381; Wash. Mss., 112, 86, 89, 95.
Burns, Robert, Aug. Rec. 1, 479; Va. Mag., 1, 279; Wash. Mss., 11, 111.
Burns, Thomas, J., 235.
Burnsides, James, D. W., 408; H. S., 7, 198.
Burrens, James, D. W., 411.
Burrill (Burrel) Philip, Va., Mag., 1, 379; Wash. Mss., 112, 88.
Burris, Thomas, Va. Mag., 1, 279; Wash. Mss., 11, 111.
Burroughs, John, J. C., Dec., 1775, 71.
Burson, Joseph, H. B. 1752-58, 374.
Burtchfield, James, D. W., 408.
Burton, Caleb, H. S., 7, 203.
Burton, John, Aug. Rec., 1, 251; F. I. B. W., 2, 413; H. B., 1770-72, 266, 270.
Burton, Joshua, Va. Mag., 1, 279; Wash. Mss., 11, 111; Wash. Mss., 111, 15.
Burton, Peter, H. S., 7, 201.
Burton, Samuel (Prince Edward), Va. Mag., 21, 89.
Burton, Samuel, F. I. B. W., 1, 299; Va. Mag., 2, 149; Wash. Mss., 111, 110.
Bush, Edward, H. S., 7, 214.
Bush, John, Aug. Rec., 1, 97; H. S., 7, 211.
Bush. Michael (scout), H. B., 1766-69, 294.
Bush. William, D. W., 405.
Bushby, William, Wash. Mss., 1557.
Bustar, David, D. W. 403.
Bustar. William, D. W., 402.
Buster, John, Aug. Rec., 1, 213.
Butcher. Samuel, Va., Mag., 1, 388; Wash. Mss., 112, 85.1, 96, 116.

Butler, James, Aug. Rec., 1, 479; Va.
Mag., 1, 390; Wash. Mss., 112,
85.1.
Butler, Joseph, D. W., 405.
Butler, Shadrich, D. W., 405.
Butterworth (Buterworth), Isaac.
H. S., 7, 205, 206.
Butts, Peter (capt.), H. S., 7, 230.
Buyers, William, H. S., 7, 195.
Byerly, Christian, Va. Mag., 1, 279.
Byerly, Christopher, Wash. Mss.,
5, 8.
Bynn, Aquilla, Wash. Mss., 1432.
Byrd, Richard, D. W., 402.
Byrd, Thomas, Va. Mag., 1, 279;
Wash. Mss., 11, 111.
Byrd, William (col.), F. I. B. W., 1,
199,
Byrne, Charles, D. W., 407.

C.

Cabell, Edward, Va. Mag., 1, 279.
Cadon, Thomas, H. S., 7, 197.
Cage, Benjamin, F. I. B. W., 2, 420;
H. B., 1758-61, 192; V. C. M., 44.
Caghey, James, H. S., 7, 191.
Caillian, Charles, Va. Mag., 2, 43.
Cain (Caine), John, H. S., 7, 198; J.,
220, 228.
Cakeh, Edward, Wash. Mss., 11, 111.
Calbreath, Thomas, F. I. B. W., 1, 14.
Caldwell, George, H. S., 7, 204, 206.
Caldwell, James, H. S., 7, 224.
Caldwell, John, D. W., 421; H. S., 7,
224.
Caldwell, Robert, H. S., 7, 224.
Caldwell, Thomas, H. B., 1766-69,
261; H. S., 8, 129.
Caldwell, William (maj.), H. S., 7,
223.
Caldwell, William, D. W., 421.
Calinex, ——, Wash. Mss., 112, 0.
Callan, John, Aug. Rec., 1, 479.
Callaway, Dudley, D. W., 411.
Callaway, James, H. S., 7, 204, 210.
Callaway, Richard (lt.), H. S., 7,
204.
Callaway, Richard, H. B., 1752-58,
484; H. S., 7, 207.
Callaway, Thomas (capt.), H. S., 7,
219.
Callaway, Thomas, H. S., 7, 219.
Callaway, William (col.), V. H. C.,
4, 582.
Callaway, William, V. H. C., 4, 109.
Calmer, Davis (chap.), Aug. Rec., 1,
335, 500.
Calston, William, Aug. Rec., 1, 479.
Calton, John, H. S., 7, 212.

Calvin, William, H. S., 7, 217.
Camble, James, H. S., 7, 183, 185.
Cameron, Hugh, D. W., 423.
Cameron, John (lt.), Aug. Rec., 1,
331.
Cammock, James, Va. Mag., 1, 283;
Wash. Mss., 111, 13.
Camp, James, H. S., 7, 217.
Camp, John, Wash. Mss., 112, 88,
94.
Camp, William, F. I. B. W., 1, 66;
V. C. M., 15.
Campbell, Absalom, Va. Mag., 1, 380;
Wash. Mss., 112, 88, 94.
Campbell, Aeneas (lt.), H. S., 7,
222.
Campbell, Alexander, J. C., May,
1776, 57.
Campbell, Archibald, H. S., 7, 205,
208.
Campbell, Arthur, D. W., 420; F. I.
B. W., 1, 87; H. B., 1761-65, 324,
328; H. S., 8, 129; V. C. M., 88.
Campbell, Dougal (Dugald, Dow-
gald), H. B. 1761-65, 240, 259;
Va. Mag., 1, 388; Wash. Mss.,
112, 85.1, 96
Campbell, George, Aug. Rec., 1, 72;
Va. Mag. 1, 283; Va. Mag., 2, 150;
Wash. Mss., 112, 87.
Campbell, Hugh, L. to Wash., 1, 300;
Wash. Mss., 112, 115.
Campbell, James, H. S., 7, 187, 201;
J., 221, 225; Va. Mag., 2, 146;
Wash. Mss., 1311.
Campbell, John (lt.), Va. Mag., 1,
287.
Campbell, John (en.), D. W., 403.
Campbell (Camble), John, Aug. Rec.,
1, 72; D. W., 409; H. S., 7, 187;
V. C. M., 89; Va. Mag., 1, 280,
378, 383; Wash. Mss., 5, 4, 8;
Wash. Mss., 11, 111; Wash. Mss.,
112, 86, 88, 89, 95.
Campbell, Joseph, D. W., 410.
Campbell (Camble), Matthew, H. S.,
7, 195, 196.
Campbell, Robert, D. W., 423; F. I. B.
W., 2, 368; H. D. Oct., 1777, 10,
38; H. S., 7, 198; V. C. M., 39.
Campbell (Campble), Samuel, D. W.,
399; F. I. B. W., 1, 30; V. C. M.,
12.
Campbell, Thomas (capt.), V. H.
C., 4, 570.
Campbell, William (capt.), J. C.,
May, 1776, 28.
Campbell, William, D. W., 399, 409,
420; V. C. M., 88, 89.

Campole, Dougle, Wash. Mss., 112, 116.
Canaday (Kanady), Thomas, D. W., 408.
Canady, William, D. W., 411.
Candfield, William, Wash. Mss., 1543.
Cannafax (Carnifax), Edward, Wash. Mss., 112, 114; Wash. Mss., 1485.
Cannon, William, H. S., 7, 201.
Cantley, John, H. S., 7, 198.
Caperton, Adam, D. W., 409.
Caperton, Hugh, D. W., 409.
Capham, John, Va. Mag., 1, 283.
Caphaw, John, Wash. Mss., 111, 13.
Capliner, George, H. S., 7, 184.
Capper, John, H. S., 7, 216.
Capshaw, John, Wash., Mss., 5, 2; Wash. Mss., 111, 15; Wash. Mss., 112, 0.
Car, John, H. S., 7, 218.
Care, John, H. S., 7, 214; Wash. Mss., 1555.
Care, Thomas, Wash. Mss., 112, 94.
Cargil, Cornelius, Jr., (lt.), H. S., 7, 223.
Cargill, Daniel, H. S., 7, 223.
Cargill, John (capt.), H. S., 7, 223.
Cargill, John, Jr., H. S., 7, 223.
Cargon, Patrick, H. S., 7, 197.
Cargyle, John, Wash. Mss., 1460.
Carlile, John, Aug. Rec., 1, 211; F. I. B. W., 2, 566; H. S., 7, 212.
Carlile, Robert, H. S., 7, 192.
Carlyle, John (comm.), L. to Wash., 1, 4; V. H. C., 3, 53; Wash. Mss., 111, 15.
Carmack, John, D. W., 412.
Carmichael, James, Va., Mag. 2, 48, 150; Wash. Mss., 112, 87; Wash. Mss., 1465.
Carnax, James, Aug. Rec., 2, 51.
Carnes (Carns), William, Aug. Rec., 2, 49; Va. Mag., 1, 279; Wash. Mss., 11, 111.
Carnev, Martin, D. W., 408.
Carpenter, Jeremiah, D. W., 408.
Carpenter, John, D. W., 409; Va. Mag., 2, 46; Wash. Mss., 112, 95.
Carpenter, Solomon, D. W., 408; F. I. B. W., 1, 234.
Carpenter, Thomas, D. W., 419; F. I B. W., 1, 82; V. C. M., 17.
Carpenter, William, Wash. Mss., 1465.
Carr, Dabney, F. I. B. W., 2, 328; V. C. M., 36.
Carr, George, D. W., 400, 422.
Carr, Henry, H. S., 7, 184.

Carr, James, D. W., 400.
Carr, John, D. W., 400; H. S., 7, 199.
Carr, Richard, H. S., 7, 199.
Carr, Samuel, H. S., 7, 195.
Carr, Thomas, Va. Mag., 1, 379; Va. Mag., 2, 37; Wash. Mss., 112, 88.
Carr, William, D. W., 400.
Carrier, Henry, L. to Wash., 1, 300; Va. Mag., 1, 390; Va. Mag., 2, 41; Wash. Mss., 112, 85.1, 96.
Carrier, Thomas, Va. Mag., 1, 390; Va. Mag., 2, 42; Wash. Mss., 112, 85.1, 96.
Carrigan, Patrick, F. I. B. W., 1, 83; V. C. M., 17.
Carroll, John, Va. Mag., 1, 279; Va. Mag., 2, 149; Wash. Mss., 11, 111; Wash. Mss., 1478.
Carroll, Joseph, H. S., 7, 216.
Carroll, Matthew, Va. Mag., 2, 49, 150; Wash. Mss., 112, 87.
Carson, James, H. S., 7, 208; Va. Mag., 1, 279; Va. Mag., 2, 43; Wash. Mss., 11, 111.
Carson, John (drum-maj.), Wash. Mss., 111, 15.
Carson, William, H. S., 7, 208.
Carter, Charles (capt.), V. C. M., 107.
Carter, Edward, Aug. Rec., 1, 478.
Carter, John, D. W., 409; F. I. B. W., 2, 303; Wash. Mss., 112, 96.
Carter, Joseph, V. C. M., 97; Va. Mag., 7, 306.
Carter, Merry, H. S., 7, 206, 225.
Carter, Peter, Wash. Mss., 1460.
Carter, Solomon, H. S., 7, 203.
Carter, Thomas (en.), Va. Mag,, 1, 287.
Carter, Thomas, H. R., 1758-61, 24; L. to Wash., 1, 299; Va. Mag., 1, 280; Va. Mag., 2, 40; Wash. Mss., 5, 8; Wash. Mss., 11, 111.
Carter, William (Prince Edward), Va. Mag;, 21, 89.
Carter, William, Va. Mag., 1, 280; Wash. Mss., 5, 8; Wash. Mss., 11, 111.
Carther, Edward, D. W., 411.
Cartie, William, H. S., 7, 204.
Cartmill, Edward (lt.), H. R., 1766-69, 71.
Cartmill, James, H. S., 7, 197.
Cartmill, John, H. S., 7, 198.
Cartwright, Thomas, H. S., 7, 218.
Caruthers (Crurothers), William, H. S., 7, 196.
Carvin, Edward (scout), H. B., 1761-65, 253, 259.
Carvin, Edward, H. S., 8, 127.

Carvin, William, Aug. Rec., 1, 331;
H. S., 7, 199; V. C. M., 48.
Carwick, John, Wash. Mss., 112, 85.1,
100.
Cary, Edward, F. I. B. W., 1, 108; V.
C. M., 18.
Casady, Thomas, V. C. M., 14.
Casdale, Samuel, Wash. Mss., 112,
89.
Casey, John, H. S., 7, 205.
Casey, William, D. W., 412, 422.
Cash, Stephens, H. S., 7, 203.
Cashaday, Thomas, H. S., 7, 191.
Cashiah, Sandiver, H. S., 7, 206.
Cason, Edward, H. S., 8, 131.
Cason, Larkin, H. S., 8, 131.
Cassady, Thomas, F. I. B. W., 1, 61.
Casterson, Joseph, Va. Mag., 1, 279;
Wash. Mss., 11, 111; Wash. Mss.,
112, 0.
Castle, Valentine, H. S., 7, 183.
Cathrim, John, Va. Mag., 2, 145.
Caton, Thomas (capt.), H. B., 1752-
58, 452, 461.
Catron, Francis, D. W., 400.
Catron, Jacob, D. W., 399, 400.
Catron, Michael, D. W., 400.
Catron, Peter, D. W., 400.
Catron, Philip, D. W., 400.
Cats, Roger, D. W., 400.
Catt (Cat), Jacob, Va. Mag., 1, 282.
283; Wash. Mss., 5, 2; Wash.
Mss., 111, 13.
Cattes, John, D. W., 400.
Cave, William, F. I. B. W., 1, 201;
Hist. Orange, 60.
Cawood, John, Historic Shepherds-
town, 26.
Cawood, Moses, Historic Shepherds-
town, 26.
Caygill, Edward, Wash. Mss., 111, 15.
Cellars, Thomas, Wash. Mss., 111, 15.
Celly, Isaac, Wash. Mss., 1543.
Cempt, William, F. I. B. W., 1, 167.
Cenney, Edward, H. S., 7, 196.
Chaddock, Thomas, Va. Mag., 1, 279;
Wash. Mss., 11, 111.
Chaine (Chain, Chane), Francis, J.,
19, 134, 222.
Chainey, Thomas, Wash. Mss., 1432.
Chalmore (Chalmor). William, H. S.,
7, 205, 208.
Chamberlayne, Thomas, F. I. B. W.,
2, 326; V. C. M., 36.
Chambers, John, Wash. Mss., 5, 4.
Champain, John, H. S., 7, 216.
Champion, Henry, Va. Mag., 2, 47.
Chandler, Abraham, H. S., 7, 205.
Chandler, John, Va. Mag., 2, 49.
Chandy, Greenberry, J., 161.
Chane, Thomas, J., 224.

Chaplain, William, Va. Mag., 1, 283;
Wash. Mss., 111, 13.
Chapline, Abraham, D. W., 421; V.
C. M., 88.
Chapline, William, Historic Shep-
herdstown, 25.
Chapman, Cornelius, Va. Mag., 2, 45.
Chapman, John, Va. Mag., 1, 279;
Wash. Mss., 11, 111; Wash. Mss.,
111, 15.
Chapman, Nathan, Aug. Rec., 2, 49;
H. B., 1770-72, 45, 49; Va. Mag.,
1, 279; Wash. Mss., 11, 111.
Chapman, Paris, Wash. Mss., 111, 15.
Chapman, Richard, F. I. B. W., 1,
127; V. C. M., 20.
Chapman, William (capt.), J. C.,
May, 1776, 20.
Chapple, Edward, Va. Mag., 1, 379.
Charlton, James, D. W., 408.
Chatt, ———, H. B., 1742-49, 320.
Cheatham, James, H. S., 7, 201.
Checok, James, Wash. Mss., 5, 4.
Chesher, Justanor, Wash. Mss., 5, 4.
Chew, Coleby (Colby, Colesby), F.
I. B. W., 1, 239; H. B., 1761-65,
122; Withers's Chron., 81.
Chew, James (lt.), H. B., 1761-65,
297.
Chew, Larkin (lt.), H. B., 1761-65,
122, 124.
Chew, Larkin, F. I. B. W., 1, 205; F.
I. B. W., 2, 402; V. C. M., 129.
Chewe, Roger, Wash. Mss., 1557.
Chick, James, F. I. B. W., 2, 579.
Childers, Abram, Aug. Rec., 1, 478.
Childers, Edward, Aug. Rec., 1, 478.
Childers, John, H. S., 7, 219.
Childers, Philemon, Wash. Mss., 1485
Childers, Philip, Wash. Mss., 112,
114.
Childre, William, H. S., 7, 201.
Childs, Edward, H. B., 1758-61, 188;
H. B., 1761-65, 179, 185; Va. Mag.,
2, 39; Wash. Mss., 5, 4; Wash
Mss., 112, 114.
Chilton, Mark, H. B., 1752-58, 374.
Chinworth, John, J., 219.
Chinworth, Thomas, J., 226.
Chisum (Chism), John, D. W., 405;
F. I. B. W., 2, 397; H. S. 7, 214;
Wash. Mss., 1555.
Chisum (Chism), William, H. B.,
1761-65, 7, 10; Wash. Mss., 112,
82.
Chiswell, William, Va. Mag., 1, 387.
Chizem, James, H. B., 1766-69, 88.
Choat, Augustine, H. S., 7, 207.
Choat, Edward, H. S., 7, 207.
Christian, Gilbert, H. S., 7, 181; H.
S., 8, 129.

Christian, Israel (capt.), L. to Wash., 1, 305.
Christian, Israel, Aug. Rec., 1, 72; F. I. B. W., 2, 524, 542; V. C. M., 53; Wash. Mss., 5, 15-1.
Christian, William (col.), D. W., 429.
Christian, William (capt. Augusta m.), Wash. Mss., 5, 15.1.
Christian, William (capt.), D. W., 423; H. B., 1758-61, 194; H. S., 7, 190; L. to Wash., 1, 305; V. C. M., 89.
Christian, William, Aug. Rec., 1, 80, 85, 120, 341.
Christy, William, F. I. B. W., 1, 19.
Chumley, John, H. S., 7, 201.
Cincaid, John, Aug. Rec., 2, 49.
Cisko, Thomas, J., 44.
Cissel, Henry, F. I. B. W., 1, 145.
Cissel, James, F. I. B. W., 1, 145.
Cissel, William, F. I. B. W., 1, 146.
Clancy, George, Va. Mag., 2, 38.
Clapham, Josias (lt.), H. S., 7, 217.
Clark (Clarke), Andrew, Va. Mag., 1, 280; Wash. Mss., 11, 111; Wash. Mss., 112, 0.
Clark, Charles, F. I. B. W., 1, 167.
Clark, George, H. S., 7, 199; Va. Mag., 1, 388; Wash. Mss., 112, 85.1, 96, 116.
Clark, George Rogers (capt.), J., 54.
Clark, James (lt.), H. S., 7, 201.
Clark (Clarke), James, D. W., 410; Va. Mag., 1, 378; Wash. Mss., 112, 88, 114.
Clark, John, Aug. Rec., 1, 210, 344; D. W., 421; F. I. B. W., 1, 100; F. I. B. W., 2, 337; H. B., 1773-76, 122, 128; H. S., 7, 192; V. C. M., 18, 88; Va. Mag., 1, 389; Va. Mag., 2, 48, 150; Wash. Mss., 112, 85.1, 87, 88
Clark, Samuel, D. W., 410.
Clark, William, H. S., 7, 181.
Clarke, John, Va. Mag., 1, 379.
Clarkson, Absalom (Ansolum), F. I. B. W., 1, 260; V. C. M, 31.
Clarkson, Peter, F. I. B. W., 2, 576.
Clatterbuck, John, Va. Mag., 2, 148.
Clay, George, J., 18.
Clay, Henry, H. S., 7, 202
Claypole, Joshua, H. S., 7, 218.
Cleek, Jacob, F. I. B. W., 1, 142.
Cleeke, Matthias, H. S., 7, 198.
Cleet, Jacob, V. C. M., 21.
Clemens, Joseph, J., 46.
Clement, Christian, H. S., 7, 181.
Clements, Benjamin, F. I. B. W., 1, 187.
Clements, John, Va. Mag., 1, 280; Va. Mag., 2, 47; Wash. Mss., 11, 111

Clemons (Clemonds), John, Wash. Mss., 112, 0; Wash. Mss., 1543.
Clendenin, Charles, V. C. M., 90.
Clendennin, Alexander, D. W., 423.
Clendennin, George, D. W., 423.
Clendennin (Clendennen, Clendenning, Clendinin), John, Aug. Rec., 1, 342, 349, 490; H. S., 7, 198; J., 223.
Clendennin (Clandening, Clendenin), Robert, D. W., 423; H. B., 1761-65, 214, 220; V. C. M., 90.
Clendennin, William, D. W., 423.
Clendinin, Arsbel, H. S., 7, 198.
Clerk, Andrew, Wash. Mss., 111, 15.
Clerk, Gerrard, Va. Mag., 1, 279; Wash. Mss., 11, 111.
Clerk, John, D. W., 411; H. S., 7, 197.
Clerk, Joseph, H. S., 7, 191.
Clifton (Cliftton), William, Aug. Rec., 1, 478; D. W., 408.
Clifts, James, Va. Mag., 2, 46.
Clinding, George, D. W., 410.
Clindining, William, D. W., 410.
Cloud, Daniel, H. S., 7, 187.
Cloyd, James, H. S., 7, 199.
Cloyd, Michael, Aug. Rec., 1, 344; H. S., 7, 199.
Cloyne, Nicholas, D. W., 399.
Cobb, John, Wash. Mss., 112, 116.
Cobb, Stratton, Wash. Mss., 1477.
Cochran, Edward, F. I. B. W., 2, 471; V. C. M., 48.
Cochran, William, D. W., 406.
Cock, Robin, Wash. Mss., 112, 87.
Cockburn, Martin, Wash. Mss., 1557.
Cocke, Thomas (capt.), Wash. Mss., 5.
Cocke, Thomas, V. H. C., 3, 271.
Cockeril, John, Va. Mag., 2, 47.
Cockeril, Thomas, Wash. Mss., 1460.
Cockren, Thomas, Va. Mag., 2, 153.
Cockrill (Cockrell), Joseph, Va. Mag., 2, 49, 150; Wash. Mss., 112, 87.
Codare, John, F. I. B. W., 2, 529; V. C. M., 53.
Coe, Barnard, Va. Mag., 2, 47.
Coen, John, Va. Mag., 1, 280.
Coffield, Joseph, H. B., 1742-49, 276.
Coffield, Philip, Va. Mag., 2, 39; Wash. Mss., 112, 114.
Coffill, Willis, Wash. Mss., 112, 83.
Coffland, William, Aug. Rec., 2, 49; Va. Mag., 1, 279; Va. Mag., 2, 40; Wash. Mss., 11, 111.
Cofflin, John, Va. Mag., 2, 145.
Coffman, Henry, J., 121.
Cogh, Phelty, H. S., 7, 196.
Coghel, Edward, Wash. Mss., 112, 95.
Coiler, John, D. W., 406.
Coiler, Moses, D. W., 406.

Coine (Coin), John, Va. Mag., 2, 148; Wash. Mss., 5, 8; Wash. Mss., 11, 111; Wash. Mss., 1432.
Coker, Bryan, H. S., 7, 223.
Coker, Joseph, H. S., 7, 223.
Colbert (Coltbert), William, Va. Mag., 1, 380; Va. Mag., 2, 39; Wash. Mss., 112, 88, 94, 114.
Cole, John, H. B., 1761-65, 52; Va. Mag., 1, 385; Va. Mag., 2, 40; Wash. Mss., 112, 83.1; Wash. Mss., 1467.
Cole, William, Aug. Rec., 1, 478.
Colebythew, ——, Wash. Mss., 5, 4.
Coleman, Cornelius, Wash. Mss., 112, 87.
Coleman, George, V. C. M., 26.
Coleman, Hezekiah (Prince Edward), Va. Mag., 21, 89.
Coleman, John, H. S., 7, 226.
Coleman, William, Aug Rec., 2, 49; Va. Mag., 1, 279; Wash. Mss., 11, 111.
Coler, Henry, H. S., 7, 186.
Coles, John, Wash. Mss., 112, 82.
Coller, John, Wash. Mss., 1460.
Collet, Thomas, D. W., 422.
Colley, Christopher, H. S., 7, 185.
Colley, John, H. S., 7, 185.
Collier, Daniel, H. S., 7, 212.
Collier, Moses, F. I. B. W., 2, 399; V. C. M., 42.
Collier, Samuel, H. S., 8, 129.
Collier, Vines (en.). H. S., 7, 211.
Collieux, Charles, L. to Wash., 1, 300.
Collin, William, H. S., 7, 214.
Collins, Achilles, Wash. Mss., 1467.
Collins, David, Wash. Mss., 112, 114.
Collins, John, F. I. B. W., 2, 505; Wash. Mss., 112, 90, 95, 114.
Collins, Luke (capt.), H. B., 1761-65, 248, 253; H. S., 8, 129.
Collins, Richard, D. W., 407.
Collins, Thomas, V. C. M., 128.
Collins, William, Wash. Mss., 1555.
Collis, Killis, Va. Mag., 2, 40.
Collom, Jeremiah, Va. Mag., 1, 387; Va. Mag., 2, 145.
Colman, Cornelius, Va. Mag., 2, 150.
Colmer, Davis (chap.), H. B., 1761-65, 247.
Colquhond, James, F. I. B. W., 1, 14.
Colson, Charles, H. S., 7, 215.
Colson, John (en.), H. S., 7, 225.
Colson, William, Aug. Rec., 1, 478.
Colston, John, H. S., 7, 216.
Colston, William, Va. Mag., 2, 147.
Colter, James, H. S., 7, 196.
Colton, Thomas, Wash. Mss., 112, 94.

Colven, Joseph, Aug. Rec., 1, 358.
Colvin, James (en.), V. C. M., 45.
Colvin, James, F. I. B. W., 2, 437; H. B., 1766-69, 88.
Colyer, Isaac, J., 140.
Combo, William, Wash. Mss., 112, 82.2.
Combs, Josiah, H. S., 7, 216.
Combs, Thomas, Va. Mag., 2, 147.
Combs, William, Va. Mag., 1, 386.
Comer, William, H. S., 7, 226.
Commack, James, Aug. Rec., 2, 49.
Combsbrown, Phil, Wash. Mss., 112, 94.
.Conaway (Conoway), Timothy, Va. Mag., 1, 387; Va. Mag., 2, 145; Wash. Mss., 112, 82.
Condon, David, D. W., 411.
Condrow, Richard, H. S., 7, 202.
Connally, Thomas, H. S., 7, 212.
Connell (Connel), William, Va. Mag., 2, 46; Wash. Mss., 112, 82.2.
Connelly (Connerly), Phil, Va. Mag., 1, 279; Wash. Mss., 11, 111; Wash. Mss., 111, 15.
Conner, Bryan, Va. Mag., 1, 282; Wash. Mss., 5, 2; Wash. Mss., 111, 13, 15.
Conner, John, F. I. B. W., 1, 164; F. I. B. W., 2, 381; J., 227; V. C. M., 129; Va. Mag., 1, 379; Va. Mag., 2, 44; Wash. Mss., 5, 4; Wash. Mss., 112, 88, 94.
Conner, Patrick, D. W., 407.
Conner, Samuel, F. I. B. W., 2, 364; V. C. M., 39.
Conner, Stephen, Aug. Rec., 1, 479.
Connolly, Herman, J., 132.
Connor, William, D. W., 406; J., 61.
Conoly, Thomas, H. S., 7, 215.
Constantine, Edward, L. to Wash., 2, 163.
Constantine, Edward Tully, Va. Mag., 2, 45.
Constantine, Patrick, D. W., 411; L. to Wash., 2, 163; Va. Mag., 2, 45.
Conway, Darby, H. S., 7, 179.
Conway, Philip, Wash. Mss., 112, 95.
Conway, Richard, Wash. Mss., 1557.
Conway, Thomas, Jr., H. B., 1752-58, 462.
Conway, Timothy, Aug. Rec., 2, 49, 170; H. B., 1773-76, 105, 113; Va. Mag., 1, 280; Va. Mag., 2, 153; Wash. Mss., 11, 111; Wash. Mss., 111, 15.
Conway, Withers (capt.), H. S., 7, 231.
Cook, David, D. W., 408.
Cook, Henry, D. W., 405.

Cook, John, D. W., 409; H. S., 7, 216, 217.
Cook, Reuben, Va. Mag., 2, 150.
Cook, Thomas, Va. Mag., 2, 47.
Cook, William, D. W., 409.
Cooke, John, H. S., 7, 201.
Cooke, Shem, H. S., 7, 201.
Cooke, William, H. S., 7, 212.
Coolley (Cooley), Francis, Wash. Mss., 112, 90, 95.
Coonrod, Woolsey, H. S., 7, 179.
Cooper, Abraham, D. W., 402.
Cooper, Francis, D. W., 402.
Cooper, James, F. I. B. W., 1, 149; F. I. B. W., 2, 486, 556; H. S., 7, 224; Va. Mag., 1, 389; Wash. Mss., 112, 85.1, 96.
Cooper, Jeremiah, H. S., 7, 184.
Cooper, Job, Va. Mag., 2, 153.
Cooper, John, H. S., 7, 216, 217; Wash. Mss., 112, 85.1, 96.
Cooper, Leonard, D. W., 423; H. S., 7, 216; V. C. M., 90.
Cooper, Nathaniel, D. W., 409.
Cooper, Samuel, Va. Mag., 1, 383; Wash. Mss., 112, 86, 89, 95.
Cooper, Spencer, D. W., 410.
Cooper, Thomas, D. W., 411; F. I. B. W., 1, 215; H. S., 7, 204; J. C., May, 1776, 57; V. C. M., 27.
Cooper, Valentine, Aug. Rec., 2, 169.
Cooper, William, F. I. B. W., 1, 215; V. C. M., 27.
Cope, James, Va. Mag., 2, 49.
Copland, William, Wash. Mss., 111, 15.
Corbin, Peter, Wash. Mss., 112, 95.
Corder, James, H. B., 1752-58, 462; H. S., 7, 214; Wash. Mss., 1555.
Cormick, John, D. W., 419.
Corn, David, H. B., 1766-69, 294.
Corn, Edward, Jr., H. B., 1766-69, 294.
Cornelius, Richard, Wash. Mss., 112, 116.
Cornelius, Robert, Va. Mag., 2, 38.
Cornet, Martin, H. S., 7, 179.
Cornwell, Adman, D. W., 409.
Cornwell, Charles, H. B., 1758-61, 24.
Corrie, David, Wash. Mss., 112, 86.
Corser, James, H. S., 7, 208.
Corvin, Samuel, Va. Mag., 2, 148.
Cosby, John, H. S., 7, 179.
Cosby, Philip, F. I. B. W., 1, 232; V. C. M., 29.
Cosby, Zaccheus, F. I. B. W., 2, 306.
Cotham, Thomas, Va. Mag., 1, 387.
Cothron (Cothran), Thomas, Wash. Mss., 111, 110; Wash. Mss., 112, 83.
Cotling, John, Va. Mag., 2, 149.
Cotrell, Thomas, H. S., 7, 203.

Cotril (Cotrel), John, Aug. Rec., 1, 341, 490.
Cotter, John, Aug. Rec., 1, 479; Wash. Mss., 112, 114.
Cotton, Benjamin, L. to Wash., 1, 300; Va. Mag., 2, 47.
Cotton, Thomas, Va. Mag., 1, 379; Wash. Mss., 112, 88.
Cottrill, William, H. S., 7, 218.
Couch, Tetrarch, H. S., 7, 186.
Couden, James, H. S., 7, 195.
Coughlin, John, Wash. Mss., 111, 110; Wash. Mss., 1432.
Coughron, Thomas, Wash. Mss., 112, 82.2.
Coulter, Michael, J. C., May, 1776, 25.
Counsel, Michael, F. I. B. W., 2, 515; V. C. M., 52.
Coupper, Cyrus, Wash. Mss., 1557.
Courtney, John, D. W., 396.
Covey, Durret (Durrett), Va. Mag., 1, 389; Wash. Mss., 112, 85.1, 96.
Cowan, Alexander, J., 55.
Cowan, Jared, D. W., 421; V. C. M., 88.
Cowan, John, D. W., 420; V. C. M., 88.
Cowden, Henry, Aug. Rec., 1, 478.
Cowdown, James, H. S., 7, 198.
Cowen, John, H. S., 7, 203; J., 12.
Cowen, Samuel, Va. Mag., 2, 150; Wash. Mss., 112, 87.
Cowherd, James (en.), Hist. Orange, 59.
Cowherd, James, H. B., 1766-69, 88.
Cowper, James, F. I. B. W., 2, 308.
Cox, Charles, H. S., 7, 208.
Cox, David, H. S., 8, 129.
Cox, George, D. W., 421.
Cox, Gabriel (lt.), D. W., 425.
Cox, Isaac, H. B., 1766-69, 88.
Cox, John, H. S., 7, 201, 213, 214; H. S., 8, 129; Wash. Mss., 111, 15; Wash. Mss., 1555.
Cox, Joshua, F. I. B. W., 2, 484, 558.
Cox, Josiah, H. S., 7, 220.
Cox, Matthew, Aug. Rec., 2, 49, 50; Va. Mag., 1, 279; Wash. Mss., 11, 111.
Cox, William (capt.), H. B., 1752-58, 459.
Cox, William. H. S., 7, 220; Va. Mag., 2, 40.
Coyl, James, D. W., 402.
Coyle, Patrick, Va. Mag., 1, 279; Wash. Mss., 11, 111.
Crabtree, William, D. W., 404; H. S., 7, 208.
Craddock, John, Wash. Mss., 1538.
Craddock, Richard, H. S., 7, 201.

Craddock, Thomas, F. I. B. W., 1, 272; V. C. M., 32.
Crafford, Barnod, D. W., 405.
Crafford (Craford), John, D. W., 404, 407.
Craig, Alexander, H. S., 7, 180, 187, 195.
Craig, George, D. W., 407.
Craig, John, Va. Mag., 2, 38.
Craig, Robert, H. S., 7, 195.
Craig, William, D. W., 410.
Craighead, Robert, Va. Mag., 2, 45.
Craik, James (lt.), F. I. B. W., 2, 502.
Craik, James (en.), Va. Mag., 1, 279.
Craik, James (surg.), Aug. Rec. 2, 49; L. to Wash., 2, 246; V. H. C., 3, 115; Va. Mag., 1, 279.
Crain, John, D. W., 410.
Cram, Peter, Va. Mag., 2, 40.
Crane, Thomas, H. B., 1758-61, 38.
Craton, William, F. I. B. W., 1, 84.
Craven, William, H. S., 7, 187.
Cravens, James, D. W., 403.
Cravens, John, D. W., 403.
Cravens, Joseph, D. W., 403.
Cravens, Robert, D. W., 403.
Cravens, William, H. S., 7, 180, 187.
Crawford, Charles, H. S., 7, 204.
Crawford, John, D. W., 400; H. S., 8, 127; J., 229.
Crawley (Croly), James, D. W., 406, 408.
Crawley, John, Va. Mag., 2, 46.
Crayton, William, V. C. M., 17.
Creagh, John, F. I. B. W., 2, 324; H. B., 1761-65, 259.
Creak, John, Wash. Mss., 112, 82.
Creaugh, John, Aug. Rec., 1, 478; Wash. Mss., 112, 83.1.
Creed, Matthew, D. W., 409.
Creekmore, Jonas, Wash. Mss., 112, 82.2, 83.
Cremone, Henry, F. I. B. W., 2, 493.
Cremore, Henry, V. C. M., 50.
Crenshaw, Joseph, Wash. Mss., 5, 4.
Creock, John, Va. Mag., 1, 385.
Cresop, Daniel, J., 230.
Cresop, Daniel, Jr., J., 232.
Cresop (Cresap), Joseph, D. W., 425; J., 233.
Cresop, Michael, Jr, J., 17.
Creswell, Michael, J., 37.
Creswell, Robert, Va. Mag., 2, 46.
Crevens, John, H. S., 7, 188.
Crews, David, F. I. B. W., 2, 508; V. C. M., 51.
Crickmore, James, Va. Mag., 1, 386.
Crisman, Isaac, D. W., 402.
Crittendon (Crittenden), Abraham, L. to Wash., 1, 300; Va. Mag., 2, 43; Wash. Mss., 1432.

Crocket, Hugh, H. S., 7, 210.
Crocket, Walter (capt.), J. C., May, 1776, 28.
Crockett, Alexander, Aug. Rec., 1, 331.
Crockett, John, Aug. Rec., 1, 344; F. I. B. W., 2, 459; H. S., 7, 191; V. C. M., 47.
Crockett, Joseph, D. W., 423.
Crockett, Samuel, Aug. Rec., 1, 342, 490.
Croford, George, H. S., 7, 191.
Croghan, George (capt.), V. H. C., 3, 184.
Croley, Benjamin, H. S., 7, 220.
Croley, Samuel, D. W., 408; H. B., 1773-76, 211, 225, 263.
Cromwell, William, Wash. Mss., 111, 15.
Crosby, John, H. S., 7, 185.
Crosby, John, Jr., H. S., 7, 184.
Cross, John, Va. Mag., 2, 46.
Cross, William, F. I. B. W., 2, 503; H. S., 7, 215.
Crosslin, William, Wash. Mss., 112, 90.
Crosthwait, Isaac, F. I. B. W., 2, 390; Hist. Orange, 59.
Crosthwait, Jacob, F. I. B. W., 1, 34; Hist. Orange, 59.
Croswell (Crosswell), William, Va. Mag., 1, 389; Wash. Mss., 5, 4; Wash. Mss., 112, 85.1, 96.
Crouch, Jacob, Va. Mag., 2, 44.
Croucher, Charles, Aug. Rec., 2, 170; F. I. B. W., 1, 105; V. C. M., 18.
Crow, Isam, F. I. B. W., 1, 191; V. C. M., 25.
Crow, John, D. W., 421; V. C. M., 88.
Crow, William, D. W., 421; V. C. M., 88.
Crowley, ——, H. D., Oct., 1780, 31.
Croxton, Thomas, Va. Mag., 2, 49.
Crump, Charles (capt.), H. S., 7, 228.
Crump, Edward, H. S., 7, 198.
Crump, William, Wash. Mss., 1460.
Cull, James, Aug. Rec., 1, 80; H. S., 7, 191.
Cullin (Culin), Jeremiah, Wash. Mss., 112, 82.2.
Cullom (Culom), Jeremiah, Wash. Mss., 5, 4; Wash. Mss., 112, 83.
Culpeper, John, H. S., 7, 201.
Culton, James, H. S., 7, 196.
Culton (Cultin), Joseph (capt.), H. B., 1752-58, 484; L. to Wash., 1, 305.
Culwell, Alexander, D. W., 411.
Cumbo, William, Wash. Mss., 112, 83.
Cummings, Josiah, F. I. B. W., 1, 12.

Cummings (Cumings), Samuel, Va. Mag., 2, 39; Wash. Mss., 112, 114.
Cummins, George, D. W., 406.
Cumpton, Ambrose, H. S., 7, 202.
Cundiff, ——— (en.), V. C. M., 89.
Cundiff, Jonathan (en.), D. W., 409.
Cuningham, Jacob, H. S., 7, 191.
Cunningham, Andrew, Jr., H. S., 7, 179.
Cunningham, James, D. W., 406.
Cunningham, John, D. W., 411; H. S., 7, 179, 184.
Cunningham, John, Jr., H. S., 7, 185.
Cunningham (Cuningham), Robert, H. S., 7, 181, 185.
Cunningham, Walter (capt.), Aug. Rec., 1, 342, 349; H. B., 1761-65, 254, 332.
Cunningham, Walter, H. B., 1766-69, 63; H. S., 7, 195.
Cunningham, William (lt.), Aug. Rec., 1, 209; H. S., 7, 181.
Cunningham, William. H. S., 7, 179, 185, 223.
Cunrod, John, H. S., 7, 184.
Cunrod, Walter, H. S., 7, 185.
Cunrod, Willry, H. S., 7, 187.
Curll, John, Wash. Mss., 112, 95.
Curls (Curles), John, Va. Mag., 1, 382; Wash. Mss., 112, 86.
Current, Joseph, D. W., 410.
Currey, William, H. S., 7, 192.
Currie (Curry), David, Va. Mag., 1, 382, Wash. Mss., 112, 89, 95.
Curtis, Christopher (capt.), H. S., 7, 226.
Curtis (Curtas), George, Wash. Mss., 112, 88.
Curvin, William, F. I. B. W., 2, 461.
Cusan, William, Wash. Mss., 1543.
Custer, William, D. W., 411.
Custis, Thomas (maj.), H. S., 7, 200.
Cutlip, David, D. W., 411.
Cuttan, Joseph (capt. Augusta m.), Wash. Mss., 5, 15.1.

D.

Dabord, David, Wash. Mss., 112, 86.
Dacres, John, Va. Mag., 2, 47.
Dailey (Daily), James, Va. Mag., 1, 280; Wash. Mss., 11, 111.
Daingerfield, William (capt.), F. I. B. W., 1, 18, 238.
Daingerfield, William, F. I. B. W., 1, 207.
Dair, William, Wash. Mss., 1471.
Dale James, D. W., 409.
Dalley, Thomas, F. I. B. W., 2, 497; V. C. M., 50.

Dallis, Denis, Wash. Mss., 1460.
Dallowe (?), Claud, Wash. Mss., 11, 111.
Dalton, Claud, Va. Mag., 1, 280.
Dalton, David, Wash. Mss., 1466.·
Dalton, John, F. I. B. W., 1, 150; F. I. B. W., 2, 575; V. C. M., 56.
Dalway, Henry (lt.), F. I. B. W., 1, 2.
Danaldson, James, Wash. Mss., 112, 96.
Dandridge, Nathaniel West, V. C. M., 107.
Dandy, Thomas, H. S., 7, 223.
Daniel, John, Wash. Mss., 112, 86.
Daniel, Samuel, F. I. B. W., 2, 447.
Dansey, Joseph, Wash. Mss., 5, 4.
Danson, David, Wash. Mss., 112, 90.
Darby, Edward, H. S., 7, 223.
Darke, Henry, Historic Shepherdstown, 26.
Darke, William, F. I. B. W., 2, 417.
Darling, William, H. B., 1752-58, 429, 433.
Darnal, John, H. B., 1752-58, 462.
Darns, William, H. S., 7, 218.
Darr, George, H. B., 1761-65, 236, 238.
Dashforan (Dastforan), John, F. I. B. W., 2, 352; V. C. M., 38.
Daugherty, Edward, Va. Mag., 2, 49; Wash. Mss., 112, 87.
Daugherty Thomas, H. S., 7, 223.
Daulton, James, H. S., 7, 225.
Daunn, John, H. S., 7, 208.
Daves, William, Wash. Mss., 112, 0.
Davice, John, H. S., 7, 192.
Davice, Samuel, H. S., 7, 196.
David, John, Aug. Rec., 1, 183.
Davidson, John, Va. Mag., 2, 45.
Davies, Benjamin, H. S., 7, 191.
Davies, David, F. I. B. W., 2, 539.
Davies, Samuel, F. I. B. W., 2, 540.
Davis, Azariah, D. W., 420; V. C. M., 88.
Davis, Charles, D. W., 407.
Davis, David, H. S., 7, 203; Va. Mag., 1, 389; Wash. Mss., 112, 85.1, 96.
Davis, Edward, H. S., 7, 208; Va. Mag., 1, 385; Wash. Mss., 112, 82, 83.1
Davis, George, D. W., 411; Va. Mag., 2, 40; Wash. Mss., 5, 4.
Davis, Henry, F. I. B. W., 2, 477.
Davis, Isham, H. S., 7, 203.
Davis (Daviss), James, F. I. B. W., 2, 492; H. B., 1758-61, 24; H. S., 7, 191; V. C. M., 88; Va. Mag., 1, 387; Va. Mag., 2, 48, 146; Wash. Mss., 112, 82 2.

34   REPORT OF THE STATE LIBRARIAN

Davis, John, F. I. B. W., 1, 7; H. S.,
7, 185, 198, 208, 218; V. C. M.,
9; Va. Mag., 1, 283, 379, 382;
Wash. Mss., 5, 4; Wash. Mss.,
111, 13; Wash, Mss., 112, 86, 94,
95; Wash. Mss., 1460.
Davis, Leonard, H. B., 1752-58, 462.
Davis, Richard, L. to Wash., 1, 300;
L. to Wash., 2, 163; Va. Mag.,
2, 45.
Davis, Robert, D. W., 404, 409.
Davis, Samuel, D. W., 409.
Davis, Thomas, Aug. Rec., 1, 212;
F. I. B. W., 1, 213; H. B., 1770-72,
31; Va. Mag., 1, 384; Wash. Mss.,
112, 86, 89, 95.
Davis, Tudor, H. B., 1752-58, 273.
Davis, William, F. I. B. W., 2, 490;
H. S., 7, 208.
Davison, George, H. S., 7, 196.
Davison, James, H. S., 7, 196.
Davison, John, H. S., 7, 191.
Daviss, Amos, Wash. Mss., 112, 90.
Daviss, George, Wash. Mss., 112, 90.
Daviss, John, Wash. Mss., 112, 88.
Daws, Thomas, H. S., 7, 209.
Dawson, Andrew, Aug. Rec., 1, 184.
Dawson, David, Va. Mag., 2, 45.
Dawson, Henry, F. I. B. W., 1, 16;
V. C. M., 11.
Dawson, John, H. B., 1752-58, 374.
Dav, Joseph, D. W., 410.
Day, William, H. S., 7, 214; Wash.
Mss., 1555.
Dayley, James, Wash. Mss., 111, 15.
Deadman, Nathaniel, Va. Mag., 1,
283, 383; Wash. Mss., 111, 13;
Wash. Mss., 112, 89, 95.
Deal, William, D. W., 409.
Dean, John (en.), Va. Mag., 1, 287.
Dean, John, H. S., 8, 130; J., 16.
Dean, William, Va. Mag., 1, 280; Va.
Mag., 2, 150; Wash Mss, 11, 111;
Wash. Mss, 111. 15
Deane ——, (en.), L. to Wash. 1,
298.
Debord, David, Va. Mag., 1, 382;
Wash. Mss., 112, 95.
Dedder, John, Wash. Mss., 112, 90.
Deek, John, D. W., 405.
Deekens. Thomas, Va. Mag , 2, 40
Deer, William, Va. Mag , 2, 48.
Degell, Edward, H. S., 7, 216.
Degranch, John Abraham, H. S., 7,
224.
Dehay, David, Va. Mag., 1, 381.
Dehority, James, D. W., 411.
Deigs, Thomas, Aug. Rec., 1, 341,
490.
De Keyser, —— (en.), L. to Wash.,
1, 171; Wash. Mss , 5.

Delancey, John, H. B., 1758-61, 26.
Delaney (Delany), Thomas, Va.
Mag., 1, 389; Wash. Mss., 112,
85.1, 96.
Delany, Benjamin, Wash. Mss., 1557.
Delloy, Henry (scout), H. B., 1766-69,
294.
Deloack, Michael, Va. Mag., 2, 48.
Demonse, Abraham, D. W., 407.
Demovil, Sampson, H. B., 1752-58,
375.
Dempsey, William, F. I. B. W., 1,
60; V. C. M., 14.
Deniston, John, D. W., 408.
Dennochy, John, Wash. Mss., 112, 114.
Denny, Richard, Va. Mag., 2, 150;
Wash. Mss., 112, 87, 115.
Dent, Arthur, Aug. Rec., 2, 505; H.
B., 1773-76, 88, 97, 123; Va. Mag.,
2, 146.
Denton, Abraham (capt.), H. B., 1766-
69, 71.
Denton, Thomas, H. S., 7, 212.
Denton, William, H. S., 7, 212.
Depay, David, Wash. Mss., 112, 86.
Depriest, John, H. S., 7, 204.
Depriest, Langsdon, H. S., 7, 204.
Deskin, Daniel, J., 136.
Deveeny, William, Va. Mag., 1, 280;
Wash. Mss., 11, 111.
Devey, James, Wash. Mss., 11, 111.
Devoy, James, Va. Mag., 1, 280;
Wash. Mss., 111, 15.
Dew, Arthur, H. B., 1752-58, 346.
Dew, Robert, H. S., 7, 195.
Dewitt. Peter, J., 145.
Dexter, Samuel, Va. Mag., 1. 387;
Wash. Mss., 112, 82.2.
Diaper, William, Va. Mag., 2, 153.
Dice, Matthias, H. S., 7, 187.
Dick, Charles (comm.), F. I. B. W.,
1, 288.
Dick, Jacob, J., 122.
Dicken, Thomas, Wash. Mss., 1465.
Dickenson, Henry, H. S., 7, 222.
Dickenson, John (capt.) (Augusta),
H. S., 7, 182.
Dickenson, John (capt.), Aug. Rec.,
1, 213; H. B., 1752-58, 462; H.
B., 1761-65, 215, 220.
Dickenson, Thomas, Wash. Mss., 112,
90.
Dickinson, John (capt.), Aug. Rec.,
1, 183, 342, 490; V. C. M., 89.
Dickinson, John, Aug. Rec., 1, 72,
249.
Dickinson, Thomas, F. I. B. W., 1,
184.
Dickinson, William, Wash. Mss.,
1479.
Dickison, John, V. C M., 88.

LIST OF COLONIAL SOLDIERS OF VIRGINIA   35

Dickison, John, V. C. M., 88.
Diell, Terrence, J., 165.
Dier, John, H. S., 7, 201.
Dikton, Joseph, H. S., 7, 185.
Dilenham, William, H. S., 7, 208.
Dillard, James (capt.), V. H. C., 4, 619, 620.
Dillard, James (lt.), H. S., 7, 219.
Dillard, Joseph, Va. Mag., 2, 148.
Dillard, Robert, Histroic Shepherdstown, 26.
Dillingham, Vachel, H. S., 7, 226.
Dillinham, William, H. S., 7, 226.
Dillon, —— (lt.), D. W., 423.
Dinnally, John, Wash. Mss., 112, 86.
Diver, Hugh, H. S., 7, 180.
Diver, John, D. W., 400.
Divinny, William, Wash. Mss., 111, 15.
Dixon, John, Historic Sheperdstown, 26; Wash. Mss., 111, 15.
Dixon, William, H. S., 7, 223.
Dixton, John, H. S., 7, 209.
Dixton, Joseph, H. S., 7, 188.
Doack, David, Jr., D. W., 399.
Doack, Robert (capt.), D. W., 399.
Doack, Samuel, D. W., 399, 404.
Dobbins, Richard, H. S., 7, 212.
Dobins, Abner, Wash. Mss., 112, 90.
Dohler, Jacob, D. W., 399.
Dodd, John, D. W., 407.
Dodd, Richard, Aug. Rec., 1, 341, 490.
Dodd, Zachariah, H. S., 7, 225.
Dodson, William, Va. Mag., 2, 145, 148, 152; Wash. Mss., 111, 110.
Doggett, Miller, Wash. Mss., 1470.
Doggett, Richard, H. S., 7, 213.
Doherty, James, H. S., 7, 224.
Doherty, John, D. W., 410.
Dohorty, George, D. W., 403.
Dollarhide, Samuel, D. W., 396.
Donahough (Donahugh, Donnahough, Donnoho, Donohow), Thomas, Va. Mag., 1, 280; Va. Mag., 2, 149; Wash. Mss., 5, 8; Wash. Mss., 11, 111; Wash. Mss., 112, 0; Wash. Mss., 1311; Wash. Mss., 1432.
Donald, John, Va. Mag., 1, 381; Wash. Mss., 112, 95.
Donaldson, James, Va. Mag., 1, 388; Wash. Mss., 112, 85.1, 100, 116.
Donaldson (Donelson), Robert, D. 7, 217; Wash. Mss., 1483.
Donaldson, Joseph (surg. mate), H. B., 1761-65, 119, 135.
Donaldson, Robert, H. B., 1766-69, 44, 52.
Donaley, James, D. W., 410

Donally (Donnelly), John, D. W., 408; F. I. B. W., 1, 128; H. S., 8, 128; Va. Mag., 1, 383; Va. Mag., 2, 143; Wash. Mss., 112, 89.
Donally (Donolly), Mark, Va. Mag., 1, 383; Wash. Mss., 112, 89, 95.
Donaldson (Donelson), Robert, D. W., 396, 401.
Donaway, Charles, Wash. Mss., 1432.
Donelly, Dudley, Wash. Mss., 112, 87.
Donelson, Thomas, D. W., 401.
Donlap, Nathaniel, H. S., 7, 190.
Donnelson, Joseph, F. I. B. W., 1, 11; V. C. M., 10.
Dony, John, H. B., 1761-65, 7, 10.
Doolen, Thomas, Va. Mag., 2, 152.
Dooley, Abraham, H. S., 8, 129.
Dooley (Dooly), Henry, Aug. Rec., 1, 342; F. I. B. W., 1, 128; H. S., 8, 129; V. C. M., 20.
Dooley, Jacob, D. W., 409.
Dooley, James, H. S., 8, 129.
Dooley, Thomas (lt.), D. W., 409.
Doran, Matthew, Aug. Rec., 2, 49, 170; H. B., 1752-58, 236, 273; Wash. Mss., 111, 15; Wash. Mss. 112, 0.
Doran, Patrick, D. W., 421; V. C. M., 88.
Doran, Thomas, H. B., 1761-65, 252; Wash. Mss., 5, 4.
Dorens, James, F. I. B. W., 2, 526; V. C. M., 53.
Doss, Joel, D. W., 411.
Dotherty, Edmund, Va., Mag., 2, 150.
Doughty, John, Wash. Mss., 112, 114.
Douglas (Douglass), James. D. W., 400, 403; Wash. Mss., 5, 4.
Douglas, Thomas, Va. Mag., 2, 143.
Douglas, William, F. I. B. W., 2, 513.
Douglass, George, D. W., 400.
Dounaway, William, V. C. M., 13.
Downand, James, D., 197.
Downey, Cornelius, J., 162.
Downey (Downy), James, Aug Rec., 1, 479, D. W., 399.
Downey (Downy), John, D. W., 399; Va. Mag., 2, 151; Wash. Mss., 112, 87.
Downing, John, Wash. Mss., 112, 115.
Downs, Henry, H. S., 7, 188.
Dowrant, Matthew, H. B., 1761-65, 265.
Draper. John (capt.), V. C. M., 89.
Draxeller (Draxilla), Bernard, Va. Mag., 1, 280. 283; Wash. Mss., 5, 8: Wash. Mss., 11, 111.
Drennon, Jacob, D. W., 421.
Drighouse, ——. H. B., 1742-49, 101

Driscole, Stephen, Wash. Mss., 111, 15.
Driver, Charles, H. S., 7, 179.
Druggers, Thomas, V. C. M., 40.
Drummon, Aaron, H. S., 7, 224.
Duckworth, John, H. S., 7, 217.
Dudding, John, Va. Mag., 2, 47.
Dudgeon, Richard (lt.), H. S., 7, 223.
Dudgeon, William, H. S., 7, 223.
Due, Thomas, Va. Mag., 2, 145; Wash. Mss., 1535.
Duffey, Patrick, Wash. Mss., 112, 0.
Dulin, James, D. W., 408.
Duly, James, H. S., 7, 210.
Duly, Thomas, H. S., 7, 210.
Duncan, John H,. S., 7, 214; Wash. Mss., 1555.
Duncan, John, Jr., V. C. M., 97; Va. Mag., 7, 306.
Duncan, Joseph, H. S., 7, 214; Wash. Mss., 1555.
Duncan, Robert, H. B., 1758-61, 26.
Duncan, William, F. I. B. W., 1, 33; V. C. M., 12; Wash. Mss., 112, 95.
Duncanson, James (lt.), H. B., 1761-65, 152, 154.
Duncklebery, Abraham, H. S., 7, 191.
Dunkerton, John, Wash. Mss., 112, 90, 95.
Dunkin, John, D. W., 402.
Dunkle, George, H. S., 7, 185, 187.
Dunkle, John, H. S., 7, 185, 187.
Dunlap, Robert, D. W., 423.
Dunlevy, Anthony, H. S., 7, 217.
Dunlop, ——— (capt.), Aug. Rec., 1, 212.
Dunlop, Adam, H. S., 7, 179, 195.
Dunlop (Dunlap), James (capt.), Aug. Rec., 1, 321, 335; Aug. Rec., 3, 80; F. I. B. W., 2, 457; H. B., 1752-58, 484; H. S., 7, 197; V. C. M., 47.
Dunlop (Dunlap), James (lt.), Aug. Rec., 1, 211; V. C. M., 18.
Dunlop (Dunlap), James, Aug. Rec., 1, 72; F. I. B. W., 1, 99.
Dunlop, John, H. S., 7, 196.
Dunn, Abram Mashaw, Va. Mag., 2, 48.
Dunn, Charles, Va. Mag., 1, 280; Wash. Mss., 5, 8; Wash. Mss., 11, 111; Wash. Mss., 111, 15.
Dunn, John, D. W., 407.
Dunn, Richard, Va. Mag., 2, 144.
Dunnaway, William, Wash. Mss., 112, 90.
Dunnowho, James, D. W., 411.
Dunwoody, John, Aug. Rec., 3, 152.
Durbin, Daniel, H. S., 7, 220.
Durham, James, F. I. B. W., 2, 435.

Durham, John, H. B., 1752-58, 290, Va. Mag., 1, 280; Wash. Mss., 11, 111, Wash. Mss., 111, 15.
Durham, Matthew, Va. Mag., 1, 280; Wash. Mss., 11, 111.
Durphy, Patrick, Va. Mag., 1, 280; Wash. Mss., 11, 111.
Dutton, Philip, D. W., 400, 403.
Dyer, John, H. S., 8, 131.
Dyer, Roger, H. S., 7, 185.
Dyer, Thomas, Va. Mag., 2, 44; Wash. Mss., 112, 90.
Dyer, William, D. W., 410; H. S., 7, 184, 185.

E.

Eager, John, D. W., 406.
Ealey, Thomas, F. I. B. W., 2, 370; V. C. M., 11.
Earhart, Abraham, H. S., 7, 183.
Earhart, Michael, H. S., 7, 183.
Earhart, Michael, Jr., H. S., 7, 184.
Earle, John, H. B., 1770-72, 63, 75.
Earles, Thomas, F. I. B. W., 2, 533; V. C. M., 53.
Earley, Jeremiah (lt.), H. S., 7, 210.
Early (Earley), Jeremiah, H. S., 7, 207.
Early, John, H. S., 7, 186.
Earnest, Henry, Va. Mag., 1, 280; Wash. Mss., 11, 111.
Earwig (Carwig, Earwigg), John, Va. Mag., 1, 389; Wash. Mss., 112, 96, 116.
Easdale, Samuel, Va. Mag., 1, 382; Wash. Mss., 112, 86.
Easley, William, V. C. M., 39.
East, John, H. S., 7, 223.
East, Josiah, Va. Mag., 2, 151; Wash. Mss., 112, 87.
East, Talton, H. S., 7, 223.
East, William, H. S., 7, 223.
Eastey, Thomas, L. to Wash., 1, 273.
Eastham, Robert (col.), V. H. C., 4, 289.
Eastham (Easthom), William, D. W., 423; V. C. M., 90.
Eastis, William, H. S., 7, 224.
Eaton, Thomas, Va., Mag., 2, 44.
Eberman, Jacob, H. S., 7, 185.
Eberman, John, H. S., 7, 185.
Eberman, Michael, H. S., 7, 184, 185.
Edemston, Samuel, H. S., 7, 198.
Edemston, William, H. S., 7, 198.
Edger, Joseph, Va. Mag., 2, 43.
Edger, Thomas, D. W., 408.
Edlington, William, F. I. B. W., 2, 438; V. C. M., 46.

Edmiston, David, H. S., 7, 196.
Edmiston (Edmistone), Moses, H. S., 7, 196.
Edmiston, William, Aug. Rec., 1, 80.
Edmond, William (capt.), V. C. M., 97.
Edmondson (Edmonson), Thomas, L. to Wash., 1, 300; Va. Mag., 2, 43.
Edmonston, Thomas, F. I. B. W., 2, 359.
Edson, Joseph, Wash. Mss., 1476.
Edwards, Frederick, H. S., 8, 131.
Edwards, Ignatius, Va. Mag., 2, 147.
Edwards, James, D. W., 403.
Edwards, Jeremiah, Aug. Rec., 1, 213; F. I. B. W., 2, 421.
Edwards, John, F. I. B. W., 2, 364; H. S., 7, 220; Va. Mag., 2, 147.
Edwards, Jonathan, D. W., 404.
Edwards, Joseph, Aug. Rec., 1, 349, 488; Wash. Mss., 5, 4.
Edwards, Richard, H. S., 7, 206.
Edwards, Thomas, H. S., 7, 219; Va. Mag., 1, 388; Wash. Mss., 5, 4; Wash. Mss., 112, 85.1, 96, 116.
Edwards, William (lt.), H. S., 7, 219.
Edwards, William, F. I. B. W., 2, 307; H. S., 7, 204, 206, 212, 213; Va. Mag., 1, 382; Wash. Mss., 112, 86, 95; Wash. Mss., 1555.
Effleck, Peter, Va. Mag., 1, 280; Wash. Mss., 11, 111.
Eger, Crosby, H. B., 1758-61, 66, 68.
Egins, Edward, D. W., 408.
Ehrmantrout, George, F. I. B. W., 2, 340.
Eister, Frederick, H. S., 7, 187.
Elam, Joel, H. S., 7, 223.
Elate, William, H. S., 7, 197.
Eldas, Ephraim, Wash. Mss., 1432.
Eleonar, John, Va. Mag., 2, 38.
Eley, Artker, Wash. Mss., 112, 90.
Eliot (Aliot), Robert, Va. Mag., 1, 382; Wash. Mss., 112, 89.
Elkin, James, H. S., 7, 220.
Ellenburgh, Peter, D. W., 408.
Ellias, Thomas, D. W., 411.
Elliot (Elliott), Robert, Va., Mag., 1, 280; Wash. Mss., 112, 83.1, 86, 95.
Elliot, William, Aug. Rec., 1, 212; H.' S., 7, 191.
Elliott, Peter, Wash. Mss., 11, 111.
Elliott, Thomas (p. m.), F. I. B. W., 1, 23.
Elliott, Thomas, F. I. B. W., 1, 86.
Ellis, Bartlett, F. I. B. W., 1, 55.
Ellis, Charles (capt.), H. S., 7, 203.
Ellis, James, H. S., 7, 226.
Ellis, Nathan, H. S., 7, 226.
Ellis, Richard, F. I. B. W., 1, 55; F. I. B. W., 2, 451.

Ellison (Ellisson), Charles, D. W., 411; F. I. B. W., 2, 527.
Ellison, James, D. W., 408, 423.
Ellot, Robert, Va. Mag., 1, 385.
Ellzey, Lewis (capt.), H. B., 1752-58, 375.
Emacks, James, Aug. Rec., 1, 330, 340.
Emberson, Henry, Aug. Rec., 1, 478.
Emmerson, Henry, H. B., 1761-65, 179, 185; Va. Mag., 2, 42.
Englebury, George, Wash. Mss., 112, 114.
English, Patrick, Aug. Rec., 1, 518.
English, William (capt.), Aug. Rec., 1, 332.
Eppes, Francis (lt.), F. I. B. W., 1, 62, 78.
Eppes, Richard, V. C. M., 107.
Erhart, Michael, H. S., 7, 180.
Ersdale, Samuel, Wash. Mss., 112, 95.
Ervin, Edward, H. S., 7, 187.
Ervin, William, H. S., 7, 187.
Erwin, Charles, Aug. Rec., 1, 518.
Erwin, Samuel, Aug. Rec., 1, 215.
Esham, Hezekiah, Wash. Mss., 112, 115.
Estil, Samuel, D. W., 408.
Estis, John, H. S., 7, 201.
Estis, Moses, H. S., 7, 201.
Estis, Thomas (capt.), H. S., 7, 231.
Estis, William, H. S., 7, 201.
Estle, Bond, F. I. B. W., 1, 13.
Estle, John, F. I. B. W., 1, 73.
Eustace, Hancock (capt,), H. B., 1761-65, 207.
Eustace, Hancock (lt.), V. H. C., 4, 401.
Eustace, Hancock, F. I. B. W., 1, 280.
Evans, Abram, Va. Mag., 1, 381.
Evans (Evins), Adam, Wash. Mss., 112, 86, 89.
Evans, Amos, F. I. B. W., 1, 46; V. C. M., 13.
Evans, Barnaby, Wash. Mss., 1490.
Evans (Evins), Edward, Aug. Rec., 2, 49, 506; J., 43; Va. Mag., 1, 280; Va. Mag., 2, 147; Wash. Mss., 11, 111; Wash. Mss., 111, 15.
Evans (Evins), John, Va. Mag., 1, 379; Wash. Mss., 112, 88, 94; Wash. Mss., 1467.
Evans, Joseph, H. B., 1758-61, 21, 26.
Evans, Nathaniel, H. S., 7, 195.
Evans (Evins), Philip, Wash. Mss, 112, 90, 95.
Evans, Richard, F. I. B. W., 1, 235.
Evans, Thomas, Va. Mag., 2, 49, 150; Wash. Mss., 112, 87.

Evans, William, F. I. B. W., 1, 8; V.
  C. M., 9; Va. Mag., 2, 48, 151;
  Wash. Mss., 112, 87.
Evens (Evins), Daniel, H. S., 7, 184,
  187.
Evens, Even, D. W., 411.
Evington, Morris, F. I. B. W., 1, 110;
  V. C. M., 18.
Evins, Andrew, D. W., 406.
Evins, Stamp, Aug. Rec., 1, 341, 490.
Ewing, Alexander, D. W., 400.
Ewing, Alexander, Jr., D. W., 400.
Ewing, Robert, D. W., 409.
Ewing, Samuel, D. W., 400.
Ewing, William, D. W., 400, 407, 410,
  423.
Ewings, Joshua, H. S., 7, 215.

F.

Fain, John, D. W., 412.
Fain, Samuel, D. W., 412.
Fair, Edmund, H. S., 7, 210.
Fair, James, H. S., 7, 207, 210.
Fairfax, Bryan (capt.), Wash. Mss.,
  1460.
Fairfax, George William (col.), H.
  B., 1752-58, 374.
Fairly, George, Wash. Mss., 112, 115.
Falling, William, H. S., 8, 131.
Fann, John, H. S., 7, 226.
Farah, Thomas, F. I. B. W., 1, 192;
  V. C. M., 26.
Farguson, Bryan, H. S., 7, 201.
Farguson, Edward, H, S., 7, 201.
Farguson, Richard, H. S., 7, 201.
Farguson (Fargison), Thomas, D.
  W., 410; H. S., 7, 201.
Farguson, William, H. S., 7, 201.
Faris, Benjamin, F. I. B. W., 2, 445.
Farley, George (en.), H. S., 7, 201;
  V. H. C., 4, 157.
Farley, John James, H. S., 7, 201.
Farmer, Charles, Va. Mag., 2, 150.
Farmer, Francis, F. I. B. W., 1, 127.
Farmer, Frederick, H. S., 7, 131.
Farmer, Job, Va. Mag., 1, 386; Wash.
  Mss., 112, 82.2.
Farmer, John, Va. Mag., 1, 280;
  Wash. Mss., 11, 111; Wash. Mss.,
  111, 15.
Farmer, Nathan, D. W., 409.
Farmour, Francis, Va. Mag., 2, 147.
Farrar, Abel (lt.), H. S., 8, 128.
Farrar, Abel, H. B., 1758-61, 218.
Farrar, John, F. I. B. W., 2, 326; V.
  C. M., 36.
Farrar, William, H. S., 7, 225.
Farrel, Samuel, Va. Mag., 2, 153.
Farrell (Farroll), John, H. S., 7, 183;
  Wash. Mss., 111, 15.

Farrow, Thomas, Va. Mag., 1, 389;
  Wash. Mss., 112, 85.1, 96, 100.
Farses, Edward, H. S., 7, 191.
Faubous, William, Va. Mag., 1, 382.
Fauster, James, H. S., 7, 224.
Fauster, John, H. S., 7, 202.
Fauster, Richard, H. S., 7, 201.
Fauster, Robert, H. S., 7, 201.
Faver, John, Jr., H. S., 7, 214.
Fear (Feer), William, Va. Mag., 2,
  48; Wash. Mss., 1538.
Fearis, Robert, Aug. Rec., 1, 209.
Feavil, William, D. W., 405.
Felton, George, Wash. Mss., 1465.
Felts, Aaron, Wash. Mss., 112, 90, 95.
Fendall, Nehemiah, Va. Mag., 1, 282.
Fendby, Barnaby, Wash. Mss., 112,
  87.
Fendley, Briant, Va. Mag., 2, 151.
Fenley (Fendly, Fenly), Patrick, Va.
  Mag., 1, 387; Va. Mag., 2, 144;
  Wash. Mss., 112, 82, 84; Wash.
  Mss., 1432.
Fennell, Nicholas, H. S., 7, 211.
Fent, Joseph, H. B., 1752-58, 479; Va.
  Mag., 2, 150; Wash. Mss., 1477.
Ferguson   (Fergusson),   Duncan
  (drummer), V. H. C., 3, 471.
Ferguson, Duncan, Va. Mag., 1, 381;
  Va. Mag., 2, 48; Wash. Mss., 11,
  111.
Ferguson, James, Wash. Mss., 11,
  111; Wash. Mss., 112, 115; Wash.
  Mss., 1485.
Ferguson, John, Va. Mag., 1, 280;
  Wash. Mss., 11, 111.
Ferguson, Thomas, Wash. Mss., 1485.
Ferguson, William, Wash. Mss., 112,
  115.
Fern, Thomas, H. S., 7, 220.
Ferrell (Ferrall, Ferrel), John, H.
  S., 7, 186; Va. Mag., 2, 151; Wash.
  Mss., 112, 87.
Ferril, Robert, D. W., 411.
Ferrill, Gabriel, H. S., 7, 224.
Ferrill, William, D. W., 402.
Ferry, George, J., 163.
Fhares, John, H. S., 7, 184.
Ficker, Richard, Wash. Mss., 112, 94.
Fie, Charles, H. S., 7, 186.
Field, Abram, H. B., 1773-76, 189,
  204.
Field, John (maj.), V. C. M., 40.
Field, John (capt.), V. C. M., 89.
Field, John, H. B., 1766-69, 88; H.
  S., 7, 213; Va. Mag., 1, 280;
  Wash. Mss., 11, 111.
Field, William, F. I. B. W., 1, 179; Va.
  Mag., 2, 153; Wash. Mss., 11, 111.
Fielder, Charles, D. W., 412.
Fielding, Christian, Va. Mag., 1, 387.

Fielding, Christopher, F. I. B. W., 1, 278; Wash. Mss., 112, 82.2.

Fields, Henry, Va. Mag., 2, 151; Wash. Mss., 112, 87.

Fields, John, D. W., 409; Wash. Mss., 111, 15.

Fields, Stephens, Va. Mag., 1, 380; Wash. Mss., 112, 88, 94.

Fields, William, D. W., 420; V. C. M., 88.

Fiell, William, H. S., 7, 216.

Fienquay, Isham, D. W., 411.

Fillbrick (Filbrick, Fillbricks), Henry, Aug. Rec., 1, 333, 339, 475; H. S., 8, 129.

Finch, Henry, F. I. B. W., 1, 195; V. C. M., 26.

Findley, George, D. W., 423.

Findley, John, D. W., 412.

Findley, Robert, D. W., 411.

Finegin, Terrence, J., 22.

Fines, William, Va. Mag., 2, 42.

Finley, James, Historic Shepherdstown, 26.

Finley, John, H. S., 7, 190, 191; Wash. Mss., 1465.

Finley, John, Jr., H. S., 7, 190, 191.

Finley, Robert, H. S., 7, 195.

Finnie, Alexander (recruiting-officer), H. B., 1752-58, 367.

Finnie (Finney), Christopher, F. I. B. W., 2, 503; H. S., 7, 192; V. C. M., 51.

Fishback, Josiah, H. B., 1752-58, 462.

Fisher, Isaac, D. W., 408.

Fisher, John, Va. Mag., 2, 151; Wash. Mss., 112, 87.

Fisher, Moses, F. I. B. W., 1, 12; Wash. Mss., 112, 87.

Fisher, Patrick, F. I. B. W., 2, 574; Hist. Orange, 60.

Fisher, Richard, Va. Mag.. 1, 387; Wash. Mss., 112, 82.2, 83; Wash. Mss., 1465.

Fisher, Thomas, Va. Mag., 1, 280; Wash. Mss., 11, 111; Wash. Mss. 111, 15.

Fitzgarrell, James, F. I. B. W., 1, 66.

Fitzgeffries (Fitchgeffreys), William, Va. Mag., 1, 386; Wash. Mss., 112, 82.2, 83.

Fitzgerald (Fitzgirl), Bartley, J., 112.

Fitzgerald, Frederick, F. I. B. W., 1, 77; V. C. M., 16.

Fitzgerald, Thomas, Hist. Orange, 59.

Fitzgerrald, John, Wash. Mss., 1557.

Fitzhugh, John, D. W., 411.

Fitzpatrick, Andrew, H. S., 7, 196.

Fitzpatrick, John (en.), H. S., 7, 201.

Fitzpatrick, John, H. B., 1761-65, 7, 10; J., 138; Va. Mag., 2, 151; Wash. Mss., 112, 87, 115.

Flanders, William, F. I. B. W., 1, 271; V. C. M., 32.

Fleming, John (lt.), V. C. M., 9.

Fleming, John, F. I. B. W., 1, 3; Wash. Mss., 112, 90, 95.

Fleming, Joseph, H. S., 7, 216.

Fleming, William (col.), D. W., 428.

Fleming, William (lt.), H. B., 1773-76, 202, 222; V. H. C., 4, 335.

Fleming, William (en.), L. to Wash., 1, 130.

Fleming, William (surg.), Aug. Rec., 1, 355; Aug. Rec., 2, 170.

Fleming (Flemin), William, F. I. B. W., 1, 90; H. S., 7, 185.

Fleshman, Peter, H. S., 7, 214.

Fletcher, Joseph, Va. Mag., 2, 144.

Flimon (Fleming), John, Aug. Rec., 1, 343, 493.

Flin, James, H. S., 7, 223.

Flin, John, H. S., 7, 223.

Fling, Matthew, Va. Mag., 2, 147.

Flintham, John, D. W., 403.

Fliping, Thomas, D. W., 409.

Flowers, John, Va. Mag., 2, 43.

Floyd, James, V. C. M., 25.

Flurity, Stephen, J., 32.

Fogg, Obediah, Va. Mag., 2, 41.

Foley, Edward, H. B., 1766-69, 106; V. C. M., 128.

Folk, Ludwig, H. S., 7, 184.

Follas, William, H. S., 8, 131.

Fontaine, Peter (p. m.), H. B., 1758-61, 234, 237.

Foolam, Benjamin, H. S., 7, 215.

Forbes, Duncan, Wash. Mss., 112, 86.

Forbes, William, Wash. Mss., 112, 86, 95.

Ford, Bartlet, F. I. B. W., 1, 272; V. C. M., 32.

Ford, James, Aug. Rec., 2, 49; H. B., 1770-72, 31, 49; Wash. Mss., 11, 111; Wash. Mss., 111, 15.

Ford, Samuel, H. S., 7, 191.

Ford, Thomas, H. S., 7, 191.

Ford, William, H. S., 7, 201.

Foreman, John, J., 176.

Forster, William, H. S., 7, 201.

Fossett, Francis (lt.), Historic Shepherdstown, 25.

Foster, Edmund, F. I. B. W., 1, 216.

Foster, James (Prince Edward), Va. Mag., 21, 89.

Foster, James, F. I. B. W., 1, 255.

Foster, Nicholas, Va. Mag., 1, 280; Wash. Mss., 11, 111.

Foster, Richard (Prince Edward), Va. Mag., 21, 88.

G.

Gahagan, Bryant, Wash. Mss., 112, 90.
Gahagan, John, Aug. Rec., 1, 478.
Gaile, John, Va. Mag., 2, 148.
Gailor, Edward, Va. Mag., 1, 383; Wash. Mss., 112, 89.
Gaines, James, F. I. B. W., 1, 162; Hist. Orange, 60.
Gale, John, Wash. Mss., 112, 87; Wash. Mss., 1466.
Gale, Richard, Va. Mag., 1, 385; Va. Mag., 2, 144; Wash. Mss., 112, 82.2.
Gales, John, Va. Mag., 2, 151.
Galespie, Alexander, Aug. Rec., 1, 341.
Gallard, John, Va. Mag., 2, 146.
Gallaspy, Alexander (armorer), H. B., 1773-76, 108.
Gallaw, David, Jr., H. S., 7, 198.
Gallihorn (Gallahorn), John, Va. Mag., 1, 280; Wash. Mss., 11, 111; Wash. Mss., 111, 15.
Galloway, David, H. S., 7, 197.
Galloway, David, Jr., F. I. B. W., 1, 61; V. C. M., 14.
Galloway (Gallaway), John, H. S., 7, 208.
Galloway (Gallaway, Galoway), Patrick, Aug. Rec., 2, 49, 51; Va. Mag., 1, 280; Wash. Mss., 5, 8; Wash. Mss., 11, 111; Wash. Mss., 111, 15; Wash. Mss., 1485.
Gambell, David, J., 135.
Garcer, John, H. S., 7, 220.
Gardener, John, Va. Mag., 1, 387; Wash. Mss., 112, 83.
Gardner, Andrew, D. W., 410.
Gardner, John, Wash. Mss., 112, 82.2.
Gardner, Thomas, Va. Mag., 2, 43; Wash. Mss., 1535.
Gardner, William, Va. Mag., 1, 280; Wash. Mss., 11, 111.
Garland, John, Va. Mag., 2, 143.
Garner, Charles, V. C. M., 97; Va. Mag., 7, 306.
Garner, Clement, H. B., 1752-58, 374.
Garner, James, Wash. Mss., 1483.
Garrett, James, F. I. B. W., 2, 309; H. S., 7, 214; Wash. Mss., 1555.
Garrett, William, D. W., 421; V. C. M., 88; Wash. Mss., 112, 0.
Garsnell, Mordecai, Va. Mag., 2, 45.
Garvine (Garvin), Moses, Va. Mag., 1, 383; Wash. Mss., 112, 89, 95.
Gaskins, John, Va. Mag., 2, 144.
Gasman, David, Aug. Rec., 2, 51.
Gass, David, H. S., 7, 203.

Gatewood, Joseph, Aug. Rec., 2, 49, 169; F. I. B. W., 1, 124; Va. Mag., 1, 280.
Gatewood, Joshua, Wash. Mss., 11, 111, Wash. Mss., 111, 15.
Gatewood, Philip, Aug. Rec., 2, 49.
Gatliff, Samuel, Aug. Rec., 1, 344.
Gatlive, James, H. S., 7, 199.
Gaudilock, Adam, H. S., 7, 203.
Gaulding, John (Prince Edward), Va. Mag., 21, 89.
Gaulding, John, F. I. B. W., 1, 255.
Gaultney, Robert, H. S., 7, 212.
Gause, Jacob, Va. Mag., 1, 280; Wash. Mss., 11, 111.
Gay, James, H. S., 7, 198.
Gay, John, H. S., 7, 197.
Gayes, Richard, Wash. Mss., 1432.
Gaylor, Edward, Wash. Mss., 112, 86, 95.
Gee, Robert, Jr., H. S., 7, 212.
Gender, John, L. to Wash., 1, 300; Va. Mag., 2, 41; Wash. Mss., 112, 96.
Gerrard, Elias, H. B., 1766-69, 107, 111.
Gerrard, William, Va. Mag., 1, 280; Wash. Mss., 5, 8; Wash. Mss., 11, 111.
Getty (Gettey), Dennis, H. S., 7, 199.
Gholson, John, Aug. Rec., 2, 49; Wash. Mss., 111, 15.
Gibbons, George, Va. Mag., 1, 280; Wash. Mss., 11, 111; Wash. Mss., 111, 15.
Gibbs, Francis, F. I. B. W., 1, 59; Hist. Orange, 60; V. C. M., 14.
Gibbs, Joseph, Wash. Mss., 111, 15.
Gibbs, Joshua, Va. Mag., 1, 280; Wash. Mss., 11, 111.
Gibson, George (lt.), D. W., 424.
Gibson, John (comm.), F. I. B. W., 1, 54.
Gibson, John, D. W., 411.
Gibson, Joseph, D. W., 406.
Gibson, Josiah, H. S., 7, 206.
Gibson, Nathan, F. I. B. W., 1, 257.
Gibson, Robert, H. S., 7, 181, 190, 191.
Gibson, William, F. I. B. W., 1, 162; V. C. M., 97; Va. Mag., 7, 305.
Gifins, James, H. S., 7, 191.
Gilbert, Acquiller, H. S., 7, 206.
Gilbert, Benjamin, H. S., 7, 206.
Gilbert, Daniel, H. S., 7, 205, 206.
Gilbert, John, F. I. B. W., 1, 135.
Gilbert, Samuel, H. S., 7, 205.
Gilbert, Thomas (en.), H. S., 7, 206.
Gilberts, Thomas, D. W., 407.
Giles, Richard, Wash. Mss., 1472.

Gilespy, Hugh, H. S., 7, 198.
Gilfillin, Alexander, J., 40.
Gilihan, John, D. W., 399.
Gilkeson, Archibald, Aug. Rec., 1, 518.
Gilkeson, James, D. W., 411.
Gilkson, Archibald, H. S., 7, 191.
Gill, Edward, F. I. B. W. 2, 503; Va. Mag., 1, 390; Va. Mag., 2, 42, 148; Wash. Mss., 112, 85.1, 96.
Gill, John, Va. Mag., 2, 37.
Gill, Michael, Aug. Rec., 1, 478.
Gill, Presly, D. W., 406.
Gill, William, F. I. B. W., 2, 506; Wash. Mss., 112, 90, 95.
Gillam, Joseph, H. B., 1752-58, 273.
Gillans, Brandon, Wash. Mss., 112, 95.
Gillaspey, James, H. S., 7, 191.
Gilleland, Thomas, J., 117.
Gillespie, Robert, V. C. M., 17.
Gillespy, Alexander (armorer), Aug. Rec., 1, 213.
Gillespy (Gillespie) Alexander, F. I. B. W., 2, 530; V. C. M., 53.
Gillespy, Thomas, D. W., 410.
Gillett (Gillet), Simon, F. I. B. W., 1, 29; F. I. B. W., 2, 370; V. C. M., 12.
Gilliam, William, Va. Mag., 2, 144.
Gillions, Brandin, Va. Mag., 1, 382; Wash. Mss., 112, 86.
Gillions, Elijah, Va. Mag., 1, 384.
Gillispie, Robert, F. I. B. W., 1, 82.
Gilliss, William, D. W., 411.
Gills, Edward, Aug. Rec., 1, 479.
Gilmer (Gilmore), James, D. W., 406.
Gilmore, James, H. S., 7, 195.
Gilmore (Gilmor), John, D. W., 406, 424; H. D., May, 1777, 44; H. S., 7, 191; Va. Mag., 1, 382; Wash. Mss., 112, 86, 89, 95.
Gilmore, Robert, J. C., May, 1776, 57.
Gilmore, Thomas, H. S., 7, 191, 196.
Gimber, James, F. I. B. W., 1, 163; V. C. M., 23.
Ginnings, Jonathan, H. S., 7, 209.
Gipson, Benjamin, F. I. B. W., 2, 404.
Gipson, George, H. S., 7, 191.
Girty, Simon, J., 15; V. C. M., 89.
Gist, Christopher, F. I. B. W., 1, 208; L. to Wash., 1, 4.
Gist, Nathaniel, F. I. B. W., 1, 210; L. to Wash., 1, 4; V. C. M., 128.
Gist, Thomas (lt.), H. B., 1761-65, 52, 54.
Gist, Thomas, Wash. Mss., 5, 4.
Githings, John, H. S., 7, 201.
Givin, James, Aug. Rec., 2, 49.
Gladdis, Richard, Wash. Mss., 112, 115.

Glaisbrook, Richard, Wash. Mss., 1483.
Glascum, David., D. W., 419.
Glass, Samuel, D. W., 408; H. S., 7, 226.
Glass, William, D. W., 411.
Glaves, Michael, D. W., 403.
Glen, James, H. S., 7, 204.
Glenn, Davis, D. W., 421; V. C. M., 88.
Glinn, Patrick, Va. Mag., 1, 378; Wash. Mss., 112, 88.
Glover, Frederick, H. S., 7, 211.
Gobell, (George, Va. Mag., 1, 280; Wash. Mss., 5, 8; Wash. Mss., 11, 111.
Gobley, George, Wash. Mss., 111, 15.
Goburn (Gobourn), John, Wash. Mss., 112, 86, 95.
Godfrey, Anthony, Va. Mag., 1, 389; Wash. Mss., 112, 85.1, 96.
Godfrey, Thomas, F. I. B. W., 2, 362.
Goff, Andrew, D. W., 412.
Goff, John, H. S., 8, 131.
Goggins, George, H. S., 7, 213.
Going, James (drummer), Wash. Mss., 1543.
Going, Moses, F. I. B. W., 2, 532.
Goings, Zadock, Wash. Mss., 112, 90.
Gold, Edward (en.), V. C. M., 128.
Golden, George, Wash. Mss., 112, 88.
Golding, George, Va. Mag., 1, 379.
Goldman, Edward, F. I. B. W., 1, 132.
Goldon, George, Va. Mag., 2, 37.
Goldsbarry, Robert, Va., Mag., 2, 153.
Goldsbarry, William, Va. Mag., 2, 153.
Goldson, John, Va. Mag., 1, 280; Wash. Mss., 11, 111.
Gooch, William, F. I. B. W., 1, 78.
Good, James, H. B., 1752-58, 245; Va. Mag., 1, 280; Wash. Mss., 11, 111; Wash. Mss., 112, 0.
Good, Richard, L. to Wash., 1, 300; Va. Mag., 2, 143.
Goodall, John, D. W., 405.
Gooddin, John, Va. Mag., 1, 382; Wash. Mss., 112, 89.
Goode, McKemess, H. S., 7, 223.
Goode, Philip, H. S., 7, 223.
Goodin, John, Wash. Mss., 112, 86.
Gooding, Jacob (capt.), V. C. M., 12.
Gooding, Jacob, F. I. B. W., 1, 33.
Goodman, Bartlett (Bartelott), F. I. B. W., 1, 134; F. I. B. W., 2, 574.
Goodman, George, H. S., 7, 184.
Goodman, Jacob, H. S., 7, 184.
Goodman, Joseph, H. S., 7, 201.
Goodrich, Edward (capt.), H. S., 7, 211, 212.

Goodrich, Edward, H. B., 1758-61, 28.
Goodwin, Daniel, H. S., 7, 195.
Goodwin, Edward, Aug. Rec., 2, 49;
Va. Mag., 1, 280; Wash. Mss., 11,
111.
Goodwin, Peter (Robert), H. B., 1761-
65, 211, 221.
Goodwin, Robert, F. I. B. W., 1, 231.
Goosberry, Robert, H. S., 7, 216.
Gorden, Gilbert, H. S., 7, 215.
Gordon, George (en.), Va. Mag., 1,
287.
Gordon, John, H. S., 7, 188.
Gordon, Moses, D. W., 399.
Gore, —— (lt.), H. B., 1761-65, 248,
253; H. S., 8, 132.
Gorman, David, Aug. Rec., 2, 49, 51;
H. B., 1752-58, 258, 273; Va. Mag.,
1, 280; Wash. Mss., 11, 111; Wash.
Mss., 111, 15; Wash. Mss., 112, 0.
Goss (Ghoss), Benjamin, F. I. B. W.,
2, 362; V. C. M., 39; Va. Mag.,
1, 382; Wash. Mss., 112, 86, 89, 95.
Gouldman Edward (lt.), D. W., 411.
Govern, John, Va. Mag., 1, 381.
Gowen, Daniel, Wash. Mss., 112, 96.
Gowen (Gowan, Gowin), Jacob, Va.
Mag., 1, 280; Wash. Mss., 11,
111; Wash. Mss., 112, 95.
Gowen, Zadock, Va. Mag., 2, 45.
Gower, Richard, H. S., 7, 211.
Gowing, Daniel, Va. Mag., 1, 388;
Wash. Mss., 112, 85.1, 116.
Gowings, Zadoc, Wash. Mss., 112, 95.
Gown, John, Wash. Mss., 1460.
Gragg, Robert, H. S., 7, 181.
Gragg, William, H. S., 7, 180, 185.
Graham, David, F. I. B. W., 2, 349;
V. C. M., 38.
Graham, Edward, Wash. Mss., 112,
82.2, 94.
Graham, Jacob, H. S., 7, 191.
Graham, John, Aug. Rec., 1, 213;
H. S., 7, 192; L. to Wash., 1, 299;
Va. Mag., 2, 40; Wash. Mss., 1557.
Graham, Robert, Aug. Rec., 1, 212;
F. I. B. W., 2, 567; Va. Mag., 1,
283; Wash. Mss., 111, 13, 15.
Grainger, Edward, Wash. Mss., 1476.
Grammer, John J. Peter, Va. Mag.,
2, 45.
Grana, Alexander, Va. Mag., 1, 385.
Grant, Alexander, D. W., 403; Wash.
Mss., 112, 0, 82.2.
Grant, John (drummer), Wash. Mss.,
112, 85.1.
Grant, John, Aug. Rec., 1, 478; Va.
Mag., 1, 388; Wash. Mss., 112,
96, 116.
Grant, William, Aug. Rec., 1, 329,
476; L. to Wash., 1, 299.

Graves, Edward, Va. Mag., 1, 280;
Wash. Mss., 11, 111; Wash, Mss.,
111, 15.
Gray, David, H. S., 7, 196.
Gray, James, H. S., 7, 181.
Gray, Richard, Wash, Mss., 1483.
Gray, Thomas, H. B., 1758-61, 12.
Grayum (Graham), Benjamin, D. W.,
412.
Greagh (Creagh), John, H. B., 1761-
65, 240, 259.
Greathouse, Daniel, J., 24.
Green, Burril (Burrel), Wash. Mss.,
112, 90, 95.
Green, James, H. S., 7, 214.
Green, Jeremiah, H. S., 7, 199.
Green, John, Va. Mag., 1, 383; Wash.
Mss., 112, 86, 89, 95.
Green, Lewis, Va. Mag., 1, 378; Wash.
Mss., 112, 88.
Green, Richard, Adam Stephen Ps.
Green, Thomas (lt.), H. S., 7, 218.
Green, Thomas, Jr., F. I. B. W., 1,
29; V. C. M., 12.
Greenfield, —— (capt.), Adam Ste-
phen Ps.
Greenlee, James, H. S., 8, 129.
Greenlee, John, H. S., 8, 129.
Greenway, Joseph, H. S., 7, 217.
Greer, Andrew, H. S., 7, 203.
Greer, Arthur, H. S., 7, 187.
Gregory, John, H. S., 7, 224; H. S.,
8, 129.
Gregory, Richard, Aug. Rec., 2, 505.
Gregory, Thomas, Wash. Mss., 1467.
Greiner, David, Aug. Rec., 1, 213.
Greir, Arthur, H. S., 7, 195.
Grenway, John, Wash. Mss., 5, 4.
Griffin, Richard, F. I. B. W., 2, 326;
V. C. M., 36.
Griffin, Richard, Jr., H. S., 8, 131.
Griffin, Robert, D. W., 396.
Griffin, William, F. I. B. W., 2, 429.
Griffis, Robert, Wash. Mss., 1460.
Griffith, Thomas, J., 23.
Grigger, Michael, D. W., 399.
Grigger, Peter, D. W., 399.
Grigs, John, D. W., 406.
Grigsby, John, D. W., 405.
Grigson, James, H. S., 7, 215.
Grim. John, D. W., 424.
Grimes, Edward, Va. Mag., 1, 386.
Grimes, James, H. S., 7, 198.
Grimes, Nicholas, H. B., 1752-58, 374.
Grimes, Philip, H. B., 1752-58, 375.
Grimes, Robert, H. S., 7, 198.
Grimsley, Joseph, V. C. M., 32.
Grinnan, John, L. to Wash., 1, 299.
Grinnaway (Grinaway), John, Va.
Mag., 2, 149; Wash. Mss., 1472.
Grinup, John, D. W., 404.

Growter, David, Va. Mag., 2, 144.
Grub, Humphrey, H. B., 1758-61, 24.
Grub, Jacob, H. S., 7, 185.
Grubb, Daniel, F. I. B. W., 2, 341;
V. C. M., 37.
Grubs, Thomas, H. S., 7, 203.
Grundy, George, H. S., 7, 207.
Grymes, Benjamin (cty.-lt. Spotsyl-
vania), V. H. C., 3, 265.
Grymes, Edward, Wash. Mss., 112, 83.
Grymes, John, H. S., 7, 205.
Grymes, Robert, Va. Mag., 1, 280;
Wash. Mss., 11, 111.
Guffey, Henry, H. S., 7, 203.
Guffy, James, D. W., 411.
Guile, Gabriel, Aug. Rec., 1, 518.
Guile, George, Aug. Rec., 1, 518.
Guile, Jacob, Aug. Rec., 1, 518.
Guillin, James M., D. W., 407.
Guillum, James (en.), H. S., 7, 224.
Guin, David, H. S., 7, 196.
Guin, John, H. S., 7, 181.
Guinnon, John, Va. Mag., 2, 147.
Gullion, Barney, D. W., 399.
Gullion, Duncan, D. W., 399, 422.
Gullion, John, D. W., 399.
Gunn, George, H. S., 7, 199.
Gunn, James (capt.), H. B., 1758-61,
175, 206; H. B., 1761-65, 195.
Gunn (Gun), James, F. I. B. W., 1,
195; H. B., 1752-58, 372; V. C.
M., 26.
Gunn, Thomas, H. S., 7, 202.
Gunnell, John, F. I. B. W., 2, 537.
Gunson, Jacob, H. S., 7, 225.
Gunter, Charles, H. S., 7, 212.
Gurden, Michael, D. W., 405.
Gupton, William, Va., Mag., 2, 49;
Wash. Mss., 112, 87.
Guptor, William, Va. Mag., 2, 151.
Gutridge (Gutrige), James, Va. Mag.,
2, 144; Wash. Mss., 112, 83;
Wash. Mss., 1432.
Guttere, John, Wash. Mss., 112, 90.
Guttroy (Guttry), James, Va. Mag.,
1, 387; Wash. Mss., 112, 82.
Guy, ——, H. B., 1742-49, 101.
Gwilliams, Edgcumb, F. I. B. W., 1,
69.
Gwin, Pearce, H. S., 7, 220.
Gwin (Guin), Peter, Va. Mag., 1,
381; Wash. Mss., 112. 86, 95.
Gwinn (Gwin), James, Va. Mag., 1,
280; Wash. Mss., 11, 111.
Gwinn (Gwin), Robert, Aug. Rec.,
1, 212; F. I. B. W., 2, 565.

H.

Hack, Spencer, Wash. Mss., 1542.
Hackley, Francis, Hist. Orange, 59.
Hackworth, Augustine, D. W., 409.
Hackworth, George, H. S., 7, 206.

Hackworth, William, D. W., 409.
Hagan, William, Aug., Rec., 2, 49;
Va. Mag., 2, 43.
Hagerly, Matthew, Va. Mag., 2, 46.
Haggerty, Patrick, D. W., 421.
Haggoman, John (capt.), H. S., 7,
228.
Hagler, Benjamin, H. S., 7, 184.
Hagler, Jacob, H. S., 7, 184.
Hagler, John, H. S., 7, 184.
Hagler, Postine, H. S., 7, 184.
Haile, Meshack, H. S., 7, 205.
Hailes, John, H. S., 7, 212.
Hains (Haines), James, Va. Mag.,
2, 47; Wash. Mss., 1466.
Hains, John, H. S., 7, 225.
Hairston, Andrew, H. S., 7, 208.
Hairston, Robert, H. S., 7, 204, 208.
Hairston, Samuel (lt.), H. S., 7, 208.
Hairston, Samuel (en.), H. S., 7, 204.
Haislop, Abner, Wash. Mss., 112,
85.1, 100.
Haiter, James, H. B., 1752-58, 236,
273.
Halbe, Richard, V. C. M., 129.
Halbert, Richard, F. I. B. W., 1,
177; V. C. M., 24.
Hale, Edward, D. W., 398.
Hale, Thomas, D. W., 398.
Hall, Aquilla, H. S., 7, 225.
Hall, Andrew, H. S., 7, 195.
Hall, Bowling, H. S., 7, 201.
Hall, Hezekiah, H. S., 7, 225.
Hall, James, D. W., 406.
Hall, John (lt), L. to Wash., 1, 299;
Va. Mag., 1, 287.
Hall, John, H. S., 7, 206, 224, 225,
226; Va. Mag., 2, 46.
Hall, Moses, H. S., 7, 180.
Hall, Richard, Va. Mag., 1, 389;
Wash. Mss., 112, 85.1, 96.
Hall, Robert, Aug. Rec., 1, 213, 354,
463; F. I. B. W., 1, 140; F. I. B.
W., 2, 422; H. S., 7, 201, 226.
Hall, Thomas, Aug. Rec., 1, 478; D.
W., 409; H. S., 7, 224; Va. Mag.,
1. 389; Va. Mag., 2, 42; Wash.
Mss., 112, 85.1, 96, 116.
Hall, William, F. I. B. W., 1, 201; H.
S., 7, 215.
Hallaway, Bennett, H. S., 7, 225.
Halliard, William, F. I. B. W., 1,
223; V. C. M., 28.
Hallis, James, H. S., 7, 202.
Halloguan, Patrick, H. S., 7, 209.
Halloway, John, Va. Mag., 1, 389.
Hamblet (Hamblett), Jesse, F. I. B.
W., 2, 440; V. C. M., 46.
Hamblet, Richard, H. S., 7, 226.
Hambleton, Francis, D. W., 404.
Hambleton, Isaiah, D. W., 404.

Hambleton, John, D. W., 403; Wash. Mss., 1557.
Hambleton, Moses, H. S., 7, 199.
Hambleton, Robert, H. S., 7, 191.
Hambleton, William, H. S., 7, 191.
Hamby, David, H. S., 8, 131.
Hamby, Jonathan, H. S., 8, 131.
Hamer, George, H. S., 7, 183.
Hames, Edmund, H. S., 7, 226.
Hamilton, Alexander (lt.), H. S., 7, 197.
Hamilton, Audly, H. S., 7, 195.
Hamilton, Benjamin, Va. Mag., 1, 280; Wash. Mss., 11, 111; Wash. Mss., 112, 0.
Hamilton, Francis, D. W., 400.
Hamilton, Isaiah, D. W., 400.
Hamilton, Jacob, D. W., 400.
Hamilton, James (capt.), H. S., 7, 218.
Hamilton, James, D. W., 424; H. S., 7, 187.
Hamilton, John (lt.), H. B., 1761-65, 255.
Hamilton, John, Aug. Rec., 1, 332, 340, 341, 490; Aug. Rec., 2, 49; H. B. 1752-58, 245, 273; H. B., 1766-69, 269; H. S., 7, 193, 198; Va. Mag., 1, 280, 283; Wash. Mss., 5, 2; Wash. Mss., 11, 111; Wash. Mss., 111, 13; Wash. Mss., 112, 116.
Hamilton, Joseph, Va. Mag., 1, 386; Wash. Mss., 112, 82.2.
Hamilton, Samuel, F. I. B. W., 2, 560; V. C. M., 55.
Hamilton, Thomas, D. W., 400; H. S., 7, 196.
Hamilton, William, F. I. B. W., 2, 547; H. S., 7, 197.
Hamlin, Peter, H. S., 7, 224.
Hamm, Robert, H. S., 7, 201.
Hamm, William, H. S., 7, 201.
Hammock, John, H. S., 7, 201.
Hammond (Hammon), Philip, D. W., 408, 424; V. C. M., 89.
Hammond, Thomas, Va. Mag., 2, 45.
Hammons, John, H. S., 7, 225, 226.
Hampton, John, H. S., 7, 215, 216; H. S., 8, 131.
Hamrick, Thomas, D. W., 409.
Hamrick, William, D. W., 409.
Hamton, John, H. S., 7, 201.
Hanburgher, Stephen, H. S., 7, 186.
Hancock, Daniel, H. S., 7, 224.
Hand, Philip, H. B., 1770-72, 210, 290.
Handcock, Joseph, Va. Mag., 2, 148.
Handcock, Stephen, F. I. B. W., 2, 569.

Handley (Handly), Samuel, D. W., 399, 422.
Handley, Thomas Kelley, Aug. Rec., 1, 124.
Handy, John, H. S., 7, 207.
Handy, William, H. B., 1761-65, 278; H. B., 1766-69, 57, 60; H. S., 7, 208.
Hanee, Philip, D. W., 411.
Hankins, John, H. S., 7, 224, 227.
Hankins, Joseph, Aug. Rec., 1, 211.
Hankins, Richard, H. S., 7, 217.
Hannah (Hanna, Hanner), John, Va. Mag., 1, 385; Wash. Mss., 112, 82.2, 94.
Hansburger, Adam, D. W., 405.
Hansley, —— (lt.), Aug. Rec., 1, 341.
Hansley, Benjamin, H. S., 7, 191.
Hansley, William, D. W., 407.
Hara, Patrick, Aug. Rec., 1, 97.
Harbet, Thomas, H. S., 7, 203.
Harbinson, William, Va. Mag., 1, 280; Wash. Mss., 11, 111; Wash. Mss., 111, 15.
Harbison, Matthew, H. S., 216.
Harclip, Suthard, Wash, Mss., 1311.
Harden, Simon, Wash. Mss., 112, 90.
Harden, Thomas, Aug. Rec., 1, 478.
Hardie, Benjamin, Wash. Mss., 1460.
Hardiman, John, H. S., 7, 206.
Hardin, Edward, H. B., 1752-58, 374; H. S., 7, 217.
Hardin, John (capt.), H. B., 1752-58, 484.
Hardin, John, H. S., 7, 198.
Hardin, John, Jr., D. W., 421; H. D., 1776, 88.
Hardin, Mark, H. S., 7, 214, 215; Wash. Mss., 1555.
Hardin, Peter, Va. Mag., 2, 49.
Hardman, John, H. S., 7, 205.
Hardy, Thomas, Aug. Rec., 1, 478.
Harfield, David, F. I. B. W., 2, 439; V. C. M., 46.
Hargrove, James, H. S., 7, 211.
Harlan, Elijah, D. W., 421; V. C. M., 88.
Harlan, Silas, D. W., 420; V. C. M., 88.
Harlow, Joel, F. I. B. W., 1, 95; V. C. M., 17.
Harman, Edward, Wash. Mss., 1311.
Harman, Richard, Wash. Mss., 1476.
Harmon, Caleb, Aug. Rec., 1, 334, 494.
Harmon, Dangerfield, D. W., 411.
Harmon, Edward, Wash. Mss., 5, 4.
Harmon, George, D. W., 405.
Harmon, John, D. W., 411.
Harmon, Richard, Va. Mag., 2, 43.
Harper, Adam, H. S., 7, 179, 183.
Harper, Edmund, Wash. Mss., 112, 114.

Harper, Jacob, H. S., 7, 183.
Harper, Jeduthan, H. S., 7, 222.
Harper, Leonard, Va. Mag., 2, 152.
Harper, Matt, Aug. Rec., 1, 344.
Harper, Michael, Aug. Rec., 1, 351, 475.
Harper, Philip, H. S., 7, 183.
Harres, William, Va. Mag., 2, 148.
Harrie, William, H. B., 1761-65, 334.
Harriman, Skidr, D. W., 410.
Harring, Leonard, H. S., 7, 188.
Harrington, Jeremiah, Aug. Rec., 1, 478.
Harris, Benjamin, F. I. B. W., 1, 229.
Harris, Charles, H. D., May, 1777, 16; H. S., 7, 206.
Harris, David, H. B., 1758-61, 26.
Harris, Edward, F. I. B. W., 1, 39.
Harris, Hugh (en.), H. S., 7, 219.
Harris, Isham, H. S., 7, 211.
Harris, James, F. I. B. W., 2, 383; H. S., 7, 201.
Harris, John, D. W., 410; H. B., 1758-61, 24; H. S., 7, 202, 220.
Harris, John, Jr., H. S., 7, 202, 220.
Harris, Nathan, H. S., 7, 212.
Harris, Reuben, Va., Mag., 2, 43.
Harris, Samuel (capt.), H. B., 1770-72, 50.
Harris, Stephen, D. W., 406.
Harris, Thomas, Va., Mag., 1, 280; Wash. Mss., 11, 111; Wash. Mss., 111, 15.
Harris, William, H. S., 7, 201.
Harrison, ——, H. B., 1742-49, 245.
Harrison, Andrew, D. W., 411.
Harrison, Benjamin (capt.), H. S., 8, 127.
Harrison, Benjamin, V. C. M., 89.
Harrison, Charles, H. S., 7, 201.
Harrison, Daniel (capt.), Aug. Rec., 1, 324.
Harrison, Gideon, H. S., 7, 188.
Harrison, Henry (capt.), F. I. B. W., 1, 88; L. to Wash., 1, 299.
Harrison, Henry (lt.), V. H. C., 3, 219; V. H. C., 4, 401.
Harrison, John (lt.), D. W., 421.
Harrison, John, H. S., 7, 188.
Harrison, Laurence, J., 205.
Harrison, Nathan, H. S., 7, 181.
Harrison, Nathaniel, H. S., 7, 186, 188.
Harrison, Richard, Wash. Mss., 1557.
Harrison, Robert, Wash. Mss., 1557.
Harrison, Thomas (cnty-lt.), Va. Mag., 7, 306.
Harriss, Griffith, D. W., 407.
Harriss, John, Va. Mag., 2, 44.
Harriss, Joseph, Wash. Mss., 1460.
Harrod, James (capt.), V. C. M., 88.

Harrod, James, D. W., 420.
Harrup, William, Wash. Mss., 1483.
Hart, John, Va. Mag., 1, 283, 383; Wash. Mss., 111, 13.
Hart, Thomas, D. W., 422.
Hart, .William, Wash. Mss., 112, 89.
Hartley, Thomas, Wash. Mss., 1465.
Hartwell, David, L. to Wash., 1, 300; Va. Mag., 1, 378; Wash. Mss., 112, 88, 94, 114.
Harvey, John, F. I. B. W., 1, 122, 214; V. C. M., 19, 27.
Harvey, William, H. B., 1758-61, 26; H. S., 7, 225.
Harwood, James (capt.), J. C., May, 1776, 28.
Harwood, John, H. B. 1766-69, 24, 32; Va. Mag., 1, 283; Va. Mag., 2, 43, 49; Wash. Mss., 111, 13.
Haslip, Abner, Va. Mag., 1, 280; Wash. Mss., 112, 96; Wash. Mss., 1311.
Haslip, Southy, Va., Mag., 1, 280.
Haslop (Haeslop), Abram, Va., Mag., 1, 389.
Hasting, George, H. S., 7, 201.
Hasty, John Baptist, Va. Mag., 1, 283; Wash. Mss., 111, 15.
Hatcher, Benjamin (en.), H. S., 7, 206, 207.
Hatchill, Stephen, H. S., 7, 225.
Hatfield, James, Va. Mag., 1, 378; Wash. Mss., 112, 88.
Hathaway, Francis, Va. Mag., 2, 145; Wash. Mss., 1535.
Hathaway, Philip, J., 141.
Hathaway, William, H. B., 1752-58, 454.
Haul, John, Wash. Mss., 1460.
Haulcom, Thomas, H. S., 7, 212.
Havely, Jacob, Va. Mag., 1, 282; Wash. Mss., 5, 2; Wash. Mss., 111, 13.
Haven, Edward, H. S., 7, 216.
Havener, Jacob, H. S., 7, 185.
Havener, Nicholas, H. S., 7, 184, 185.
Hawes, James, Wash. Mss., 111, 15.
Hawkes, Henry, H. B., 1752-58, 339, 346.
Hawkins, Benjamin, Aug. Rec., 1, 344.
Hawkins, John, H. B., 1761-65, 151; Wash. Mss., 1555.
Hawkins, Jonathan, Aug. Rec., 1, 478.
Hawkins, Philemon (Prince Edward), Va. Mag., 21, 89.
Hawkins, Philemon, F. I. B. W., 1, 44; V. C. M., 13.
Hawkins, Pinkithman (capt.), H. S., 7, 225.
Hawkins, William, H. B., 1758-61, 38.

Hawks, Richard, H. S., 7, 202.
Hawks, Uriah, H. S., 7, 202.
Hawl, John, H. S., 7, 195.
Hawley, John, Wash. Mss., 112, 82.
Hay, Andrew (capt.), H. S., 7, 196.
Hay, James, H. S., 8, 129.
Hayden, Samuel, Va. Mag., 1, 280.
Hayes, William, H. B., 1752-58, 374.
Hayle, Thomas, Aug. Rec., 2, 505;
   F. I. B. W, 1, 48; V. C. M., 13.
Haymand, William, F. I. B. W., 2,
   495; V. C. M., 50.
Haynes, Benjamin, D. W., 422.
Haynes, George, H. S., 7, 205.
Haynes, Henry, H. B., 1761-65, 278;
   H. B., 1766-69, 60.
Haynes, James, H. S., 8, 129.
Haynes, John, F. I. B. W., 2, 490; H.
   S., 7, 210.
Haynes, Joseph (capt.), Aug. Rec.,
   1, 183; J. C., May, 1776, 63; V.
   C. M., 89.
Haynes, William, H. S., 7, 201, 205,
   206.
Hays, Andrew (capt.), H. S., 7, 196.
Hays (Hayes), John, Aug. Rec., 1,
   97; D. W., 424; F. I. B. W., 2,
   470; H. S., 7, 196.
Hays, Nicholas, H. S., 7, 204, 208.
Hays, Samuel, D. W., 404.
Hazel, David, Va. Mag., 2, 41.
Hazlip (Heaslup), Abner, Va. Mag.,
   2, 41; Wash. Mss., 11, 111.
Hearbert, William, Wash. Mss., 1557.
Hearper, Robert, Wash. Mss., 1557.
Hearst, George, Wash. Mss., 5, 2;
   Wash. Mss., 111, 13.
Heart, John, Wash. Mss., 112, 86, 95.
Heasleys, Abner, Wash. Mss., 112, 0.
Heaslup, Albert, Va. Mag., 2, 41.
Heath, John, H. S., 7, 228.
Heath, William, F. I. B. W., 1, 171;
   Va. Mag., 2, 49, 151; Wash. Mss.,
   112, 87.
Hebdon, James, F. I. B. W., 1, 93;
   V. C. M., 17.
Hecks, Henry, H. S., 7, 191.
Hedden, Thomas, D. W., 406.
Hedgcocke (Hidgcocks), Thomas,
   F. I. B. W., 1, 158; V. C. M., 22.
Hedge, Joseph, F. I. B. W., 2, 356.
Hedges, Silas, D. W., 421.
Hedgman, John, Va. Mag, 2, 147;
   Wash. Mss., 5, 4.
Hedrick, Adam, H. S., 7, 186.
Pedrick, George, H. S., 7, 185.
Hedrick, Peter, D. W., 400.
Heffley, Jacob, Va. Mag, 1, 283.
Heland, John, V. C. M., 35.
Helling, James, F. I. B. W., 1, 108.
Helm, Leonard, D. W., 421.

Helphinstone, Peter (capt.), D. W.,
   421.
Helsley, Christian, Va. Mag., 1, 280
Helsley, Christopher, Wash. Mss., 11,
   111.
Helsley, Jacob, Va. Mag., 1, 283.
Hemphill, Samuel, H. S., 7, 188.
Henacry, Thomas, Wash. Mss., 111,
   15.
Henderson, Alexander, D. W., 404;
   Wash. Mss., 1557.
Henderson, Daniel, D. W., 400; H. S.,
   7, 180.
Henderson, Jacob, H. S., 7, 207.
Henderson, James (lt.), H. S., 7, 190.
Henderson, James (en.), H. S., 7,
   179.
Henderson, James, H. S., 7, 226.
Henderson, John (lt.), D. W., 408,
   424; V. C. M., 89.
Henderson, John (en.), H. S., 7, 195.
Henderson, John, Aug. Rec., 1, 85;
   D. W., 400.
Henderson, Michael, H. S., 7, 190.
Henderson, Samuel, D. W., 400; H.
   S., 7, 190.
Henderson, William, Aug. Rec., 1,
   210; F. I. B. W., 1, 113; V. C.
   M., 19.
Hendley, Nathaniel, H. S., 7, 220.
Hendon, James, Wash. Mss., 5, 4.
Hendrick, Ezekiel (Prince Edward),
   Va. Mag., 21, 89.
Hendrick, Humphrey, H. S., 7, 201.
Hendrick, John, H. S., 7, 201.
Hendrin (Hendren), John, Va. Mag.,
   2, 44; Wash. Mss., 1535.
Hendrix, Peter, D. W., 408.
Henley, Cornelius, Va. Mag., 1, 280;
   Va. Mag., 2, 44; Wash. Mss., 11,
   111.
Henly, George, D. W., 400.
Henly, William, D. W., 400.
Hennesey, Thomas, Va. Mag., 1, 280;
   Wash. Mss., 5, 8; Wash. Mss.,
   11, 111.
Henry, Michael, Adam Stephen Ps.
Henry, Robert, H. S., 7, 196.
Hensey, Patrick, H. S., 7, 208.
Henshaw, Joseph, Wash. Mss., 112,
   86.
Henshaw, Joshua, Wash. Mss., 112,
   95.
Henshaw, William, D. W., 425.
Hensley, Benjamin, H. S., 7, 203.
Hensley (Handley), Samuel, D. W.,
   412; H. S., 7, 214; Wash. Mss.,
   1555.
Henslie, Benjamin (lt.), F. I. B. W.,
   2, 477.

Hogshead, Michael, H. S., 7, 185, 187.
Holland, William, Va. Mag., 1, 280, 382; Wash. Mss., 11, 111; Wash. Mss., 112, 86, 89, 95, 114.
Holley, William, D. W., 411; F. I. B. W., 2, 487; V. C. M., 50.
Hollin, William, Wash. Mss., 111, 15.
Hollis, Mark, Aug. Rec., 2, 49; Va. Mag., 1, 280; Wash. Mss., 11, 111.
Holliss, Burr, Wash. Mss., 1460.
Holliway, Richard, D. W., 412.
Holloway, James, Va. Mag., 1, 390; Wash. Mss., 112, 85.1, 96.
Holloway, John, Wash. Mss., 112, 85.1, 96, 100.
Holloway, Nathan, F. I. B. W., 1, 296.
Holloway, William, F. I. B. W., 2, 327.
Holly, John, Va. Mag., 1, 385.
Holly, William, F. I. B. W., 2, 554.
Holston, Stephen, D. W., 411; Withers's Chron., 59.
Holt, John, H. B., 1758-61, 26.
Holtzclaw, Joseph, V. C. M., 97; Va. Mag., 7, 306.
Holwell, Walter, D. W., 409.
Homan, Robert, Va. Mag., 2, 153.
Homes, Lewis, D. W., 411.
Homes, Robert, H. S., 7, 184.
Hoof (Huff), Thomas, D. W., 419.
Hooff, Richard, H. S., 7, 201.
Hook, John, Va. Mag., 2, 41.
Hook, William, H. S., 7, 186; Va. Mag., 2, 151; Wash. Mss., 112, 87, 115.
Hooker, John, F. I. B. W., 2, 343; V. C. M., 37.
Hooks, James, H. S., 7, 188
Hooks, William, H. S., 7, 181, 187.
Hooper, James, Va. Mag., 2, 39, 153; Wash. Mss., 112, 114.
Hooper, John, Aug. Rec., 2, 505; Va. Mag., 2, 39; Wash. Mss., 112, 114.
Hooper, William, D. W., 407.
Hope, Thomas, Va. Mag., 1, 390; Wash. Mss., 112, 85.1, 96, 100.
Hopkins, Archibald, H. S., 7, 188.
Hopkins, John (lt.), Aug. Rec., 1, 85; H. S., 7, 188.
Hopkins, John (en.), H. S., 7, 181.
Hopkins, Joseph, V. C. M., 37.
Hopper, Moses, H. B., 1758-61, 24.
Hopper, Rawleigh, H. B., 1758-61, 24.
Hopper, William, H. S., 7, 214; Wash. Mss., 1555.
Horden, John (en.), H. S., 7, 215.
Horn, John, F. I. B. W., 1, 237; V. C. M., 29.

Horn, Joseph, D. W., 402.
Hornback, Joel, Va. Mag., 2, 151; Wash. Mss., 112, 87.
Hornbery, Jacob, H. S., 7, 183.
Horne, Joseph, D. W., 396.
Houghland, Henry, H. B., 1766-69, 88.
Houghland, Richard, H. B., 1766-69, 88.
Hounam, James, Wash. Mss., 1465.
House, Argyle (Argill), H. B., 1752-58, 236, 273; Va. Mag., 1, 280; Wash. Mss., 11, 111.
House, John, H. S., 7, 210.
House, Richard, Wash. Mss., 1476.
Houstoun, John, Aug. Rec., 2, 49.
Howall, Charles, F. I. B. W., 1, 255.
Howard, Abraham, H. S., 7, 203.
Howard, Arthur, Va. Mag., 1, 280; Wash. Mss., 5, 8; Wash. Mss., 11, 111; Wash. Mss., 111, 15.
Howard, Charles, D. W., 411.
Howard, Edward, H. S., 7, 198.
Howard, Eustace, F. I. B. W., 1, 222; V. C. M., 28.
Howard, Henry, D. W., 409.
Howard, Joseph, Wash. Mss., 112, 114; Wash. Mss., 1485.
Howard, Matthew, Va., Mag., 1, 280; Wash. Mss., 11, 111.
Howard, Moses, H. S., 7, 218.
Howard, Shiplet, Va. Mag., 2, 43.
Howard, Stripplehill, Wash. Mss., 1472.
Howard, William, H. S., 7, 226.
Howel, John, Wash. Mss., 112, 90.
Howel, Samuel, Wash. Mss., 112, 90, 95.
Howell, Charles (Prince Edward), Va. Mag., 21, 89.
Howell, Stephen, H. S., 7, 201.
Howell, Thomas, Va. Mag., 2, 153.
Howle, Thomas, H. S., 7, 223.
Hubbard, Edward (capt.), H. B., 1758-61, 175, 206; H. B., 1761-65, 195.
Hubbard, Edward (en.), Va. Mag,, 1, 287.
Huchison, William, D. W., 411.
Hudgens, Drury, F. I. B. W., 2, 407.
Hudnall, John, V. C. M., 97; Va. Mag., 7, 305.
Hudnall, Joseph, V. C. M., 97; Va. Mag., 7, 305.
Hudson, Christopher (capt.), H. B., 1758-61, 164, 206; V. C. M., 15.
Hudson, Christoper, H. B., 1758-61, 143.
Hudson, Ephraim, H. S., 7, 226.
Hudson, James, H. S., 7, 223.

Hudson, John, H. S., 7, 198, 216;
    Wash. Mss., 112, 90.
Hudson, Richard, H. S., 7, 223.
Hudson, Thomas, H. S., 7, 196; Va.
    Mag., 2, 46; Wash. Mss., 112,
    116.
Hudson, William, H. S., 7, 201, 223.
Huff, John, Va. Mag., 2, 38.
Huff, Leonard, D. W., 408.
Huff, Peter, D. W., 408.
Huff, Samuel, D. W., 408.
Huff, Thomas, D. W., 408.
Huffman (Hufman), Nicholas, H. S.,
    7, 181, 183.
Hufman, Honicle, H. S., 7, 187.
Hufman, Philip, H. S., 7, 184.
Hugart, James, H. S., 7, 197.
Hugart, James, Jr., H. S., 7, 198.
Hugget, John, Wash. Mss., 1472.
Huggins, Timothy, Wash. Mss., 1432.
Hugh, James, H. S., 7, 217.
Hughart, Thomas, H. S., 7, 198.
Hughes, Aaron, H. S., 7, 204.
Hughes, Anthony, F. I. B. W., 1, 247.
Hughes, Charles, H. S., 7, 204.
Hughes, Ellis, D. W., 424; V. C. M.,
    89.
Hughes, Henry, Va. Mag., 1, 379.
Hughes, James, H. S., 7, 216; H. S.,
    8, 127.
Hughes, John, F. I. B. W., 1, 138,
    282; J., 192.
Hughes, Joseph, Aug. Rec., 1, 478;
    H. B., 1758-61, 188; J., 139; Wash.
    Mss., 5, 4.
Hughes, Matthias, H. S., 7, 204.
Hughes, Patrick, Va. Mag., 2, 44.
Hughes, Robert, F. I. B. W., 2, 310.
Hughes, Sylvester, F. I. B. W., 1,
    106; V. C. M., 18.
Hughes, Thomas, Va. Mag., 1, 379.
Hughes, William (adj.), Aug. Rec., 2,
    169.
Hughes, William, Aug. Rec., 2, 170;
    F. I. B. W., 1, 114, 137; F. I. B.
    W., 2, 373, 511; H. S., 7, 216; Va.
    Mag., 2, 38.
Hughey, Joseph (James), D. W.,
    412.
Hughs, Henry, Wash. Mss., 112, 88,
    94.
Hughs, John, H. S., 7, 191, 210.
Hughs, Patrick, Wash. Mss., 112, 90.
Hughs, Saunder, Va. Mag., 2, 146.
Hughs, Thomas, Wash. Mss., 112,
    88, 94.
Hughs, William, H. S., 7, 217.
Hughston, James, H. S., 7, 195.
Hulm, Bell, H. S., 7, 202.
Hulm, Thomas, H. S., 7, 202.
Hulman, James, F. I. B. W., 1, 12.

Hume, Francis, Sr. (See Rev. Bounty
    Warrants, 1811, Allison to York-
    shire.)
Humphreys (Humphries, Umphries),
    John, Va. Mag., 1, 381; Wash.
    Mss., 112, 86, 95.
Humphries, Uriah, F. I. B. W., 2, 570.
Hundley, John, D. W., 408.
Hunt, George, Aug. Rec., 2, 49.
Hunt, Godfrey, Wash. Mss., 1478.
Hunt, Thomas, H. S., 7, 205.
Hunt, William (en.), H. S., 7, 223.
Hunt, William, L. to Wash., 1, 300;
    Va. Mag., 2, 150; Wash. Mss.,
    112, 87, 115.
Hunter, John (capt.), H. S., 7, 204.
Hunter, John (comm.), H. B., 1758-
    61, 263.
Hunter, John, H. S., 7, 204.
Hunter, Robert, H. S., 7, 195.
Hunter, Thomas, Va. Mag., 1, 382;
    Wash. Mss., 112, 86, 95.
Hunter, William, Wash. Mss., 1557.
Hurley, Jeremiah, Va. Mag., 2, 45.
Hursh, George, Wash. Mss., 111, 15.
Hurst, George, Va. Mag., 1, 283.
Hurt, James, Jr., H. S., 7, 202.
Hurt, Joel, H. S., 7, 202.
Hurt, William, H. S., 7, 202.
Huse, Joseph, H. S., 7, 223.
Hushman, Holerick, H. S., 7, 187.
Hussey, Isaac, H. S., 7, 218.
Husted, Moses, J., 188.
Huston, Archibald, H. S., 7, 187.
Huston, James (armorer), Aug. Rec.,
    1, 340.
Huston, James, H. S., 7, 196, 216, 217.
Huston, John, Va. Mag., 1, 280; Wash.
    Mss., 11, 111.
Huston, Samuel, H. S., 7, 195.
Hustown, John, Aug. Rec., 2, 49.
Hutcherson, David, F. I. B. W., 2,
    431.
Hutcherson, James, Aug. Rec., 1, 331.
Hutcheson, John, H. S., 7, 191.
Hutcheson, Robert, F. I. B. W., 2,
    483, 554.
Hutcheson (Hutcherson), Thomas,
    F. I. B. W., 1, 253, 295; V. C. M.,
    30.
Hutcheson (Hutcherson, Hutchison),
    William, F. I. B. W., 2, 527; H. S., 7,
    191, 202.
Hutchinson, Jeremiah, H. B., 1752-
    58, 375.
Hutchison, Joseph, Wash. Mss., 1460.
Huts, Jacob, F. I. B. W., 2, 370; Va.
    Mag., 2, 151; Wash. Mss., 112, 87.
Hutson, John, D. W., 411.
Hutson, Thomas, Va. Mag., 1, 388;
    Wash. Mss., 112, 85.1, 96.

Hyde, Isaac, Wash. Mss., 1460.
Hynes, Francis, D. W., 404.
Hyter, James, Wash. Mss., 112, 0.

I.

Ingles, Thomas (lt.), V. C. M., 89.
Ingles, William, J. C., Dec., 1775, 73.
Ingram (Ingeram), James, Va. Mag.,
2, 151; Wash. Mss., 112, 87.
Innes, James, V. H. C., 3, 125.
Ireson (Iresen), James, H. S., 7, 216,
217.
Irvin, Francis, F. I. B. W., 1, 151.
Irvine, David, H. S., 7, 210.
Irvine, John, D. W., 400.
Irvine, William (lt.), H. S., 7, 209.
Irvine, William, H. S., 7, 209.
Irwin, Andrew, J. C., May, 1776, 28.
Irwin, Thomas (maj.), H. B., 1761-
65, 151.
Isbell (Isebell), Benjamin, F. I. B.
W., 1, 187; V. C. M., 25.
Isdale, Samuel, Va. Mag., 1, 280;
Wash. Mss., 11, 111.
Israel, Michael, H. S., 7, 204.
Istobe, William, H. B., 1758-61, 84,
95; Va. Mag., 2, 153.
Isum, William, D. W., 408.

J.

Jack, James, H. S., 7, 216; Hist.
Frederick, 89.
Jackaway, Reeves, Aug. Rec., 1, 479.
Jackios, Samuel, Aug. Rec., 1, 478.
Jackman, Richard, V. C. M., 97; Va.
Mag., 7, 306.
Jackman, Thomas, Jr., V. C. M., 97;
Va. Mag., 7, 306.
Jackson, Benjamin, H. B., 1758-61,
38.
Jackson, Francis, H. B., 1761-65, 254.
Jackson, George, Va. Mag., 2, 45;
Wash. Mss., 112, 90.
Jackson, Henry, H. S., 7, 212.
Jackson, Jacob, H. B., 1766-69, 109.
Jackson, Jesse, H. S., 7, 217.
Jackson, John, H. S., 7, 205.
Jackson, Joseph, Wash. Mss., 5, 4.
Jackson, Mark, H. S., 7, 211.
Jackson, Peter, H. S., 7, 211.
Jackson, Samuel, H. S., 7, 212.
Jackson, William, F. I. B. W., 2, 564;
H. S., 7, 201, 218; Wash. Mss.,
112, 84, 94.
Jackson, Yenty, D. W., 405.
Jacobs, Joseph, Wash. Mss., 1460.
Jacobs, Samuel, J., 164.
Jacobs, William, H. S., 7, 215.
Jacoby, Francis, H. S., 7, 214; Wash.
Mss., 1555.

James, Charles, Aug. Rec., 2, 49; Va.
Mag., 1, 280; Wash. Mss., 11, 111;
Wash. Mss., 111, 15; Wash. Mss.,
112, 0.
James, David, H. S., 7, 215.
James, John, H. B., 1758-61, 24.
Jameson, Alexander, H. S., 7, 203.
Jameson, Andrew, F. I. B. W., 1, 120;
H. S., 7, 197; V. C. M., 19.
Jameson, George, H. S., 7, 197.
Jameson, John, Aug. Rec., 1, 518;
D. W., 403; F. I. B. W., 1, 72;
H. S., 7, 181; V. C. M., 16.
Jameson, Thomas, H. S., 7, 203.
Janet, Richard, F. I. B. W., 2, 559;
V. C. M., 55.
Jaquitt, Hugh, V. C. M., 97; Va. Mag.,
7, 306.
Jarrott, Hezekiah, H. S., 7, 224.
Jefferson, Henry, Va. Mag., 2, 45, 145.
Jefferson, Joseph, H. B., 1752-58, 339,
346.
Jeffries, Alexander, V. C. M., 97; Va.
Mag., 7, 306.
Jeffries, James, V. C. M., 97; Va. Mag.,
7, 306.
Jeffries, William, F. I. B. W., 2, 401.
Jelly, Dudly, Wash. Mss., 112, 87.
Jenkins, Benjamin, Wash. Mss., 112,
115.
Jenkins, Charles, F. I. B. W., 1, 117,
197; V. C. M., 19, 26.
Jenkins, George (drummer), Wash.
Mss., 112, 84.
Jenkins, George, Va. Mag., 1, 385.
Jenkins, James, Va. Mag., 1, 389;
Wash. Mss., 112, 85.1.
Jenkins, Jeremiah, D. W., 411.
Jenkins, John, Aug. Rec., 1, 478; Va.
Mag., 1, 378; Wash. Mss., 112, 94.
Jenkins, Joseph, H. S., 7, 187.
Jenkins, Samuel, H. S., 7, 218.
Jenkins, Thomas, H. S., 7, 218.
Jenkins, William, Aug. Rec., 2, 49,
505; Va. Mag., 2, 41; Wash. Mss.,
111, 15.
Jennings, Daniel, Wash. Mss., 1460.
Jennings, Edmund, D. W., 422.
Jennings, John, H. S., 8, 131.
Jennings, Jonathan, H. S., 7, 205.
Jessee (Jessy), William, Va. Mag.,
1, 389; Wash. Mss., 112, 85.1, 96.
Jewitt, Matt., D. W., 409.
Jinkens, George, Va. Mag., 2, 153.
Jinkins, James, Wash. Mss., 112, 96.
Job, Moses, H. S., 7, 215.
John, Billy, H. B., 1758-61, 86.
Johns, William, D. W., 406.
Johnson, Andrew, Wash. Mss., 1478.
Johnson, Archibald, F. I. B. W., 2,
429.

Keen, Richard, Va. Mag., 2, 39.
Keeneson, Charles, D. W., 410.
Keeny, Abraham, H. S., 7, 191.
Keer, William, D. W., 409.
Kegan, Thomas, Va. Mag., 1, 383;
    Wash. Mss., 112, 89, 95.
Keith, Reuben, H. S., 7, 226.
Kelley, Alexander, D. W., 408.
Kelley, Benjamin, J., 126.
Kelley, Gerrott, D. W., 409.
Kelley, James, Va., Mag., 2, 42.
Kelley, William, V. C. M., 40.
Kelliham (Kellyham), John, Wash.
    Mss., 112, 87; Wash. Mss., 1467.
Kelly, David, H. S., 7, 212.
Kelly, Henry, H. B., 1758-61, 24.
Kelly, John, Va. Mag., 2, 48.
Kelly, Lawrence, Va. Mag., 1, 382;
    Wash. Mss., 112, 95.
Kelly, Michael, H. S., 7, 195.
Kelly, Thomas, F. I. B. W., 1, 80;
    V. C. M., 16.
Kelly, Timothy, H. B., 1773-76, 266.
Kelly, William, F. I. B. W., 2, 374;
    H. B., 1758-61, 24.
Kelsey, John, D. W., 406; Va. Mag.,
    2, 49, 151; Wash. Mss., 112, 87.
Kemp, John, Va. Mag., 1, 379.
Kenaday, James, Aug. Rec., 1, 120;
    H. S., 7, 195.
Kenaday, Joseph, Aug. Rec., 1, 72.
Kenaday, William, H. S., 7, 195.
Kendley, Benjamin (lt.), Aug. Rec.,
    1, 324.
Kenedy, William, D. W., 409.
Kennedy (Kenedy), Anthony, Va.
    Mag., 1, 281; Va. Mag., 2, 42;
    Wash. Mss., 11, 111; Wash. Mss.,
    112, 0, 96.
Kennedy, David (lt.), V. C. M., 30.
Kennedy, David, Aug. Rec., 2, 505;
    F. I. B. W., 1, 249.
Kennedy, Ezekiel, D. W., 406.
Kennedy, Joseph (capt.), H. B., 1752-
    58, 484.
Kennerly, David, Hist. Frederick, 89.
Kennison, Charles, D. W., 424.
Kennison, Edward, D. W., 424.
Kenniss, Andrew, Va. Mag., 2, 148.
Kennot, Zachariah, D. W., 409.
Kent, William, Wash. Mss., 1460.
Kenting, Dennis, Wash. Mss., 111,
    15.
Kenton, Dennis, Va. Mag., 1, 281;
    Wash. Mss., 11, 111.[1]
Kenton, Simon, V. C. M., 89.
Kenton, Anthony, F. I. B. W., 1, 117;
    V. C. M. 19.
Kenty (Canty), Miles, F. I. B. W.,
    1, 198. 266; V. C. M., 26.

Kernal, William, F. I. B. W., 1, 124;
    V. C M. 20.
Kerr, James, D. W., 420; V. C. M., 88.
Kerr, William, H. S., 7, 191.
Kerre, Samuel, H. S., 7, 187.
Kesier, Sandesur, H. S., 7, 209.
Ketcham, John, Va. Mag., 2, 151.
Key, John, Va. Mag., 2, 47.
Kiblar (Kibler), Jacob, Va. Mag.,
    1, 282; Wash. Mss., 5, 2.
Kidd, James, H. S., 7, 226.
Kiggum, Thomas, Wash. Mss., 5, 4.
Killer, Abraham (lt.), H. B., 1766-69,
    71.
Kilpatrick, John, H. S., 7, 197.
Kilson, John, Wash. Mss., 111, 15.
Kinckeid, John (en.), D. W., 396.
Kinder, George, D. W., 399.
Kinder (Kindar), Jacob, D. W., 399,
    404.
Kinder, Peter, D. W., 399.
Kindler, Jacob, H. S., 7, 187.
Kindley, Benjamin, H. S., 7, 186.
King, Edward, Va. Mag., 1, 281;
    Wash. Mss., 5, 8; Wash. Mss., 11,
    111; Wash. Mss., 111, 15; Wash.
    Mss., 112, 0.
King, George, H. S., 7, 187, 195.
King, James, D. W., 411.
King, John (lt.), V. H. C., 4, 401; Va.
    Mag., 1, 287.
King, John, D. W., 399; F. I. B. W.,
    1, 65; H. S., 7, 187, 195; V. C. M.,
    15.
King, William, D. W., 399, 404; F. I.
    B. W., 1, 66, 173; V. C. M., 15;
    Va. Mag., 2, 149.
Kingkeid, David, D. W., 402.
Kingkeid, David, Jr., D. W., 396.
Kingkeid, John, D. W., 402, 404.
Kingston, Francis, Va. Mag., 2, 44.
Kington, Ally, Wash. Mss., 1465.
Kington, Christopher, Wash. Mss.,
    1465.
Kington, Robert, Wash. Mss., 1465.
Kinkaid, George, D. W., 411.
Kinkaid (Kinkade), James, D. W.,
    411; H. S., 7, 203.
Kinkead, John, F. I. B. W., 2, 563.
Kinkead, Thomas, Aug. Rec., 1, 212;
    Aug. Rec., 2, 170; F. I. B. W.,
    1, 77; F. I. B. W., 2, 568; V. C.
    M., 16.
Kinkead (Kinkiad), William, Aug.
    Rec., 1, 211, 212; F. I. B. W., 1,
    113; F. I. B. W., 2, 569.
Kinley (Kinly), Benjamin, H. S., 7,
    179, 181, 183.
Kinsel, Cunrod, H. S., 7, 185.
Kinsey, Benjamin, H. S., 7, 198.
Kinsey, William, H. S., 7, 18

Kinson, George, D. W., 419.
Kinsor, Jacob, D. W., 399.
Kinsor, Michael, D. W., 399.
Kinsor, Walter, D. W., 399.
Kirk, Alexander, Aug. Rec., 1, 209.
Kirk, James, Wash. Mss., 1557.
Kirkland, Isham, Va. Mag., 1, 389;
Wash. Mss., 112, 85.1, 96.
Kirkland, John, Adam Stephen Ps.;
Wash. Mss., 112, 115.
Kirkum, Robert, H. B., 1761-65, 259;
H. S., 7, 128.
Kirtley, Francis (capt.), H. S., 7, 185.
Kishioner, Andrew, D. W., 422.
Kisinger, Matthias, D. W., 409.
Kissinger (Kisinger), Andrew, D.
W., 408.
Kitchen (Citchen, Kitchin), John,
Va. Mag., 1, 386; Wash. Mss.,
112, 82.2, 83.
Kite, Gabriel, H. S., 7, 185.
Kite, George, H. S., 7, 185.
Kite, Jacob, H. S., 7, 185.
Kite, Valentine, H. S., 7, 185.
Kite, William, H. S., 7, 183.
Kitson, John, Va., Mag., 1, 281; Wash.
Mss., 11, 111.
Kitson, Thomas, Va. Mag., 1, 281;
Wash. Mss., 1490.
Knap, Thomas, Wash. Mss., 111, 15.
Knight (Night), Charles, F. I. B. W.,
1, 180; H. S., 7, 225, 226.
Knowland, James, Wash. Mss., 112,
90.
Knowls (Knowles), William, Va.
Mag., 1, 281; Wash. Mss., 5, 8;
Wash. Mss., 11, 111; Wash. Mss.,
112, 0.
Knox, Robert, Aug. Rec., 1, 75.
Kuykendall, Abraham, H. B., 1761-65,
215, 220.
Kuykendall, Elisha, J., 21.
L.
Lacey, Elliott, H. S., 7, 206.
Lacey, John, Va. Mag., 2, 151; Wash.
Mss., 112, 115.
Lackey, John, Wash. Mss., 1460.
Lackie, Adam, H. S., 7, 204.
Lacy, John, Wash. Mss., 112, 87.
Lafaty, John, J., 6.
Laferty, Ralph, H. S., 7, 197.
Lafort, James, Aug. Rec., 2, 49.
Laimer, Levin, Wash. Mss., 112, 86.
Lain, John, Wash. Mss., 112, 90.
Lain, Thomas, Va. Mag., 1, 382; Wash.
Mss., 112, 89.
Laird, David, Aug. Rec., 2, 366, F. I.
B. W., 2, 498.
Lallard, John, Wash. Mss., 1432.
Laman, John, H. S., 7, 216.
Lamb, Archibald, V. C. M., 13.

Lamb, James, Hist. Orange, 60.
Lamb, John, F. I. B. W., 1, 200; Hist.
Orange, 59.
Lamb, Joseph, Wash. Mss., 112, 85.1.
Lamb, Joshua, Va. Mag., 1, 389.
Lamb, Richard, F. I. B. W., 1, 200;
Hist. Orange, 59.
Lamb, Thomas, Va. Mag., 1, 378; Va.
Mag., 2, 37.
Lamb, William, Hist. Orange, 60;
Va. Mag., 1, 389; Wash. Mss.,
112, 85.1, 96.
Lambert, Jonathan, H. D., May, 1777,
16.
Lambert, Joseph, F. I. B. W., 2, 479;
V. C. M., 49.
Lambeth, John, F. I. B. W., 2, 441.
Lammy, Andrew, D. W., 403.
Lampkin (Lambkin), Chattin, V. C.
M., 97; Va. Mag., 7, 305.
Lampkin, James, V. C. M., 97; Va.
Mag., 7, 305.
Lampton, William, F. I. B. W., 1,
152; V. C. M., 128.
Land, Edward, Va. Mag., 1, 379;
Wash. Mss., 112, 88, 94, 114.
Landor, Benjamin, Historic Shep-
herdstown, 25.
Lane, Abraham, Va., Mag., 2, 37.
Lane, Dumas, V. C. M., 31.
Lane, John, Wash. Mss., 112, 95.
Lane, John Burk, H. S., 7, 203.
Lane, Littleberry, F. I. B. W., 2, 573;
V. C. M., 56.
Lane, Thomas, Wash. Mss., 112, 86,
95.
Langdon, Robert, Aug. Rec., 2, 49.
Langdon, Thomas (lt.), H. B., 1761-
65, 119.
Langdon, Thomas, Wash. Mss., 111,
15.
Langworth, Samuel, Va. Mag., 2,
146.
Lanier, Robert, H. S., 7, 212.
Lankford, James, F. I. B. W., 1, 60;
V. C. M., 15.
Lansdown, William, H. B., 1752-58,
249, 273.
Lapesley, William, H. S., 7, 195.
Lapsley, Joseph (capt.), H. B., 1752-
58, 484.
Lapsly, John, D. W., 406.
Lard, David, H. S., 7, 184.
Lare, Edward, Va. Mag., 2, 143.
Lark, Robert, H. S., 7, 224.
Larken, John, D. W., 406.
Larmour, Levin, Va. Mag., 1, 381.
Larrey, Edmund, Aug. Rec., 1, 478.
Larter, John, Wash. Mss., 1460.
Lary, Edward, L. to Wash., 1, 300.
Lashly, John, D. W., 404.

Lasley, Daniel, Va. Mag., 2, 37.
Lattin, Thomas, Va. Mag., 2, 149.
Laughlin, James, D. W., 401.
Lawless, Henry, Withers's Chron., 31.
Lawn, John, H. S., 7, 179.
Lawrence, Edward, H. B., 1758-61, 24.
Lawrence, Henry, D. W., 410.
Lawrence, James, H. S., 7, 186.
Lawrence, John, J., 31.
Lawrence, Peter, H. B., 1758-61, 24.
Lawrence, Thomas, H. S., 7, 183, 184.
Lawson, John, F. I. B. W., 2, 309; H. S., 7, 204, 205.
Layland, John, Wash. Mss., 112, 82.2, 97.
Layne, William, H. S., 7, 205.
Lea, John, F. I. B. W., 2, 395; V. C. M., 41.
Leak (Leake), John, Va. Mag., 1, 383; Wash. Mss., 112, 89, 95.
Leake, Robert (comm.), Aug. Rec., 1, 339.
Leather, William, F. I. B. W., 2, 504; V. C. M., 51.
Leatherin, James, Wash. Mss., 112, 0.
Ledbetter, William, H. S., 7, 212.
Ledbetter, William, Jr., H. S., 7, 212.
Lee, Charles (lt.), F. I. B. W., 2, 384.
Lee, Clement, H. S., 7, 220.
Lee, James, H. S., 7, 199.
Lee, John, Va. Mag., 1, 283; Wash. Mss., 111, 13; Wash. Mss., 112, 116; Wash. Mss., 1490.
Lee, Mark, J., 14.
Lee, Richard, J., 30.
Lee, Sefniah, D. W., 405.
Lee, Zacarias, D. W., 405.
Leechenan, Leonard, H. B., 1758-61, 147, 204.
Leeper, Going (Gaun), H. S., 7, 187, 195.
Leftwich, Thomas, H. S., 7, 225.
Leftwich, William, H. S., 7, 225.
Leftwick, Augustine, H. S., 7, 206.
Legat, Alexander, H. S., 7, 197.
Legat, James, H. S., 7, 216.
Le Grand, Alexander (Prince Edward), Va. Mag., 21, 88.
Le Grand, Alexander, F. I. B. W., 1, 103; V. C. M., 18.
Leland (Leeland), John, Va. Mag., 1, 387; Va. Mag., 2, 145; Wash. Mss., 1542.
Lemaster, Richard, D. W., 411.
Lemay, John, F. I. B. W., 1, 185; V. C. M., 25.
Lemen, Thomas (lt.), V. C. M., 41.
Lemen, Thomas, F. I. B. W., 2, 392.
Lemmon, John, F. I. B. W., 1, 131.
Lemmons, John, Aug. Rec., 2, 229.

Lemon, ——, V. H. C., 4, 400.
Lemon, Alexander, F. I. B. W., 2, 355.
Lemon, John, Historic Shepherdstown, 26.
Lendar, Lawrence, H. S., 7, 216.
Lenham, Henry, Wash. Mss., 112, 9b.
Lenore, Clement, Wash. Mss., 112, 115.
Leonard, Adam, Va. Mag., 1, 281; Wash. Mss., 11, 111.
Leonard, Henry, Va. Mag., 1, 282; Va. Mag., 1, 283; Wash Mss., 5, 2; Wash. Mss., 111, 13.
Leonard, John, H. S., 7, 183.
Lesly, John, D. W., 400.
Letcher, John, F. I. B. W., 1, 125.
Letort, James, Va. Mag., 1, 281; Wash. Mss., 11, 111.
Lett, James, H. S., 7, 224.
Lett, John, H. S., 7, 225.
Levil, George, H. S., 7, 224.
Levingston, Matthew, Wash. Mss., 111, 15.
Lewelling, Freeman (Prince Edward), Va. Mag., 21, 89.
Lewelling, Freeman, F. I. B. W., 1, 255.
Lewis, Andrew (brig. gen.), V. H. C., 3, 113.
Lewis, Andrew (col.), H. S., 8, 127.
Lewis, Andrew (capt.), Aug. Rec., 1, 517; Va. Mag., 1, 279.
Lewis, Charles (col.), V. C. M., 88.
Lewis, Charles (capt.), H. B., 1761-65, 332; V. C. M., 18; V. H. C., 4, 401.
Lewis, Charles, Aug. Rec., 1, 210; F. I. B. W., 1, 101; F. I. B. W., 2, 398; H. B., 1766-69, 63; Wash. Mss., 1485.
Lewis, David (maj.), H. B., 1761-65, 264.
Lewis, David (capt.), Aug. Rec., 1, 68, 80.
Lewis, George, H. S., 7, 179.
Lewis, Henry, Va. Mag., 1, 386; Wash. Mss., 112, 83; Wash. Mss., 1465.
Lewis, Jacob, Va. Mag., 1, 387; Va. Mag., 2, 145; Wash. Mss., 112, 82.2, 94; Wash. Mss., 1432.
Lewis, John (capt.), V. C. M., 89.
Lewis, John, Aug. Rec., 1, 335; D. W., 401; H. B., 1766-69, 63; H. S., 7, 219.
Lewis, Johnson, Wash. Mss., 1465.
Lewis, Joshua (capt.), V. H. C., 4, 622; Wash. Mss., 5.
Lewis, Nathan, V. H. C., 4, 399.

Lewis, Nathaniel, Va. Mag., 1, 281; Wash. Mss., 11, 111.
Lewis, Samuel, D. W., 424; V. C. M., 89.
Lewis, Thomas, D. W., 424; F. I. B. W. 2, 329; V. C. M., 89.
Lewis, Warner (capt.), V. C. M., 107.
Lewis, William (lt.), H. S., 7, 195.
Lewis, Zachary (lt.), F. I. B. W., 1, 293.
Lewis, Zebulon, H. S., 7, 211.
Librough, Henry, D. W., 398.
Lightfoot, Francis, F. I. B. W., 2, 479; V. C. M., 49.
Lile, James, L. to Wash., 1, 300.
Lilvy, John, Va. Mag., 2, 149.
Lindsey, Isaac, H. S., 7, 215, 216.
Lindsey, James, H. S., 7, 216.
Lindsey, John, H. S., 7, 220.
Lindsey, (Linsey), Matthew, H. S., 7, 196.
Lindsey (Linsey), Thomas, H. S., 7, 215, 216.
Lingo, John, Wash. Mss., 112, 90; Wash. Mss., 112, 95.
Link, Barton, H. S., 8, 131.
Link, John, H. S., 8, 131.
Links, Jacob, Wash. Mss., 112, 87.
Linn (Lin), Adam, D. W., 409; Wash. Mss., 1557.
Linn, William (capt.), J. C., Dec., 1775, 93.
Linn, William, D. W., 421.
Linsey, Edward, H. S., 7, 215.
Linsey, Francis, H. S., 7, 223.
Linsie, Daniel Crawley, Va. Mag., 2, 150.
Liptrot (Lipbiot), James, Va. Mag., 1, 389; Wash. Mss., 112, 85.1, 100.
Littel, Charles, Wash. Mss., 1557.
Little, Adam, H. S., 7, 184, 185.
Little, Andrew, H. S., 7, 179, 185, 187.
Little, John, Va. Mag., 2, 45.
Little, Thomas, Va. Mag., 2, 44.
Littlepage, James (en.), Aug. Rec., 1, 320, 321.
Littlepage, John Dickinson, F. I. B. W., 2, 338; V. C. M., 37.
Littleton, Charles, H. S., 7, 215, 216.
Littleton, Solomon, H. S., 7, 216.
Litton, Burton, D. W., 396.
Litton, Solomon, D. W., 402.
Litz, William, D. W., 400.
Lively, Mark, H. S., 7, 203.
Livingston, James (maj.), Adam Stephen Ps.; L. to Wash., 2, 93.
Livingston, James (adj.), Va. Mag., 1, 287.
Livingston, John, H. D., 1776, 4, 6.
Livingston, Matthew, Wash. Mss., 111, 13.

Lloyd, Thomas (surg.), F. I. B. W., 1, 4; V. C. M., 9.
Loakey, John, Va. Mag., 1, 390; Wash. Mss., 112, 85.1, 96, 100.
Locard, William, H. S., 7, 215.
Lock, Joseph, J., 127.
Lockart, Andrew, Va. Mag., 2, 143.
Lockart, Charles, H. S., 8, 129.
Lockart, James (capt. Augusta m.), Wash. Mss., 5, 15.1.
Lockart, James (capt.), L. to Wasn., 1, 305.
Lockart (Lockhart), James, F. I. B. W., 2, 547; H. S., 7, 181, 191.
Lockart (Lockard), Thomas, Va. Mag., 1, 283; Wash. Mss., 111, 15.
Lockett, James, H. S., 7, 201.
Lockhart (Lockard), Archibald, F. I. B. W., 2, 491; Va. Mag., 2, 147.
Lockhart, Jacob, D. W., 410.
Lockhart, Qeavy, D. W., 410.
Lodwick, Edward, Wash. Mss., 112, 82.2.
Loffman, John, Va. Mag., 2, 44.
Loflan, Morgan, Va. Mag., 2, 40.
Loflin, Daniel, Wash. Mss., 1460.
Logan (Login), Colloe (Coley, Cully), Va. Mag., 2, 44; Wash. Mss., 112, 90, 95.
Logan, David, Jr., H. S., 7, 223.
Logan, Hugh, D. W., 406.
Logan, James, D. W., 406; H. S., 7, 195.
Loggins, James, F. I. B. W., 1, 144; V. C. M., 21.
Logan, John, H. S., 8, 131.
Lohone, Ben, V. C. M., 16.
Lomax, H. (lt.), V. H. C., 4, 401.
Lomax, John, L. to Wash., 1, 385; Wash. Mss., 1557.
Lomax, John Edward (lt.), Va. Mag., 1, 287.
Lome, Dumas, F. I. B. W., 1, 262.
London, John, H. S., 7, 206.
Londren, William, Va. Mag., 1, 388.
Long, Ambrose, Va. Mag., 2, 147.
Long, Daniel, H. S., 7, 185.
Long, Henry, H. S., 7, 186, 191.
Long, John, H. S., 7, 181, 191.
Long, Joseph (en.), D. W., 424.
Long, Reuben, H. S., 7, 214.
Long, William (comm.), Aug. Rec., 1, 183.
Long, William, F. I. B. W., 1, 9; H. S., 7, 190.
Longdon, Thomas, H. B., 1752-58, 441, 449; Wash. Mss., 11, 111.
Longdon, Thomas, Sr., Va. Mag., 1, 281.
Longes, Daley, F. I. B. W., 1, 161.

27

Longest, Richard, F. I. B. W., 1, 166.
Longest, Timothy, F. I. B. W., 1, 155.
Longworth, Samuel, L. to Wash., 1, 299.
Lonsdale, William, J. C., May, 1776, 13.
Looney, Joseph, H. S., 7, 204.
Looney, Peter, F. I. B. W., 2, 524; H. S., 7, 191; V. C. M., 53.
Loson, David, H. S., 7, 205.
Loson, John, H. S., 7, 205.
Lovatt, John, Wash. Mss., 112, 87.
Love, Ephraim (capt.), H. P., 1752-58, 484; H. S., 7, 187.
Love, Ephraim, Aug. Rec., 1, 80.
Love, Joseph, D. W., 408.
Love, Philip (capt.), D. W., 407.
Love, Philip (en.), Aug. Rec., 1, 346.
Lovell, Richard, H. B., 1761-65, 70.
Lovet (Lovit), John, Va. Mag., 2, 151; Wash. Mss., 112, 115.
Lovett, Thomas, F. I. B. W., 1, 91; V. C. M., 17.
Loving, John, H. S., 7, 202.
Lovingston, Matthew, Va. Mag., 1, 283.
Low, Beverly, Va. Mag., 1, 384.
Low, John, Aug. Rec., 1, 499; H. S., 7, 197; Wash. Mss., 112, 0.
Low, Littleberry, Hist. Orange, 60.
Lowden, John, Wash. Mss., 111, 15.
Lowdren, William, Wash. Mss., 112, 116.
Lowe, James, Wash. Mss., 112, 115.
Lowe, John, Va. Mag., 1, 282; Wash. Mss., 5, 2; Wash. Mss., 111, 13, 15.
Lowery, James, Aug. Rec., 1, 478.
Lowery (Lowrey, Lowry), William, Aug. Rec., 2, 49; Va. Mag., 1, 281; Va. Mag., 2, 145; Wash. Mss., 11, 111; Wash. Mss., 112, 0; Wash. Mss., 1470.
Lowrey (Lowry), Patrick, Aug. Rec., 1, 72; H. S., 7, 195, 196.
Lowry, Evans, Va. Mag., 2, 49.
Lowry (Lowery), James, H. B., 1758-61, 188; Wash. Mss., 5, 4.
Lowry, John (lt.), V. H. C., 4, 401; Va. Mag., 1, 287.
Lowry (Lowrey), John, H. S., 7, 195, 196; Va. Mag., 2, 151; Wash. Mss., 112, 87.
Lowther, William (capt.), H. D., May, 1777, 14.
Lucaner, William, Va. Mag., 1, 383.
Lucas, Barton (en.), H. B., 1761-65, 120.
Lucas, Charles, Jr., D. W., 398.

Lucas, Edward, H. S., 7, 216; Wash. Mss., 1490.
Lucas (Lucus, Lukis), John, Aug. Rec., 1, 341, 490; D. W., 398; H. S., 7, 223; Hist. Orange, 59.
Lucas (Lucus) William, D. W., 398; J., 180.
Luce, Edward, F. I. B. W., 2, 354.
Lucks, William, H. S., 7, 205.
Lucraner, William, Wash. Mss., 112, 95.
Ludlow, James, Aug. Rec., 2, 49; Va. Mag., 1, 281; Wash. Mss., 11, 111; Wash. Mss., 111, 15.
Ludwick, Edward, V. C. M., 128; Va. Mag., 1, 385; Wash. Mss., 112 83.1.
Luisey, Thomas, H. S., 7, 215.
Lundeman, Abraham, H. B., 1761-65, 115.
Luney, Mical, D. W., 411.
Luney, Peter, H. B., 1752-58, 501, 502.
Lusk, Robert, Aug. Rec., 1, 333, 340; H. S., 7, 195, 198.
Lutrel, Samuel, H. B., 1758-61, 24.
Lyle, Daniel, H. S., 7, 196.
Lyle, David, F. I. B. W., 1, 65; V. C. M., 15.
Lyle, James, Va. Mag., 2, 143; Wash. Mss., 112, 90, 95.
Lyle, John, D. W., 424; H. D., May, 1777, 44.
Lyle, John, Jr., H. S., 7, 195.
Lyle, Samuel, H. S., 7, 196.
Lyn, James, D. W., 411.
Lynch, Charles (capt.), H. B., 1766-69, 71.
Lynch, Head, H. S., 7, 206.
Lynch (Linch), James, H. S., 7, 212; Va. Mag., 2, 45.
Lynch (Linch), Matthew, Va. Mag., 1, 379; Va. Mag., 2, 37; Wash. Mss., 112, 88.
Lynch, Patrick, J., 33.
Lynn, ———, H. B., 1742-49, 101.
Lynn, Michael, H. B., 1761-65, 13, 22.
Lynn, William, H. B., 1773-76, 218, 225.
Lyon, James (en.), H. S., 8, 130.
Lyon, Joseph, H. S., 7, 216.
Lyons, Williams, D. W., 406.

M.

McAbey, Lacey, Wash. Mss., 112, 95.
McAlhaney, John, H. S., 7, 191.
McAllister (McCalister, McCallister), James, Aug. Rec., 2, 505; D. W. 406; F. I. B. W., 2, 466.
McAnally, Charles, H. S., 7, 196.
McAnally, John, H. S., 7, 204.

McAnulty, William, Aug. Rec., 1, 478.
McBride, Daniel, H. S., 7, 191.
McBride, James, Aug. Rec. 1, 332, 340; D. W., 409; H. B., 1773-76, 181; Va. Mag., 1, 283; Wash. Mss., 5, 2; Wash. Mss., 111, 13.
McBride, Joseph, D. W., 406.
McCain, George, Wash. Mss., 111, 15.
McCandless, John, D. W., 410.
McCann, Moses, V. C. M., 39.
McCannon, Michael, H. B., 1752-58, 236, 245, 273; Va. Mag., 1, 281; Wash. Mss., 111, 13, 15.
McCarmick, George, F. I. B. W., 1, 297.
McCarmick, William, F. I. B. W., 1, 296.
McCarney, Robert, H. S., 7, 179.
McCarty, Daniel, F. I. B. W., 1, 294; Wash. Mss., 112, 0; Wash. Mss., 1557.
McCarty, Dennis (en.), L. to Wasn., 1, 298.
McCarty, Dennis, Wash. Mss., 5.
McCarty, James, D. W., 402.
McCarty, Nathaniel, J., 203.
McCaslen, William, D. W., 411.
McCauley, Neil, F. I. B. W., 1, 240.
McCauley, Thomas, F. I. B. W., 2, 476.
McCay, John, H. S., 7, 188.
McClanahan, Absalom, D. W., 409.
McClanahan, Alexander, H. B., 1761-65, 332; H. S., 7, 195; J. C., Dec., 1775, 101; V. C. M., 89.
McClanahan, Elijah, H. B., 1766-69, 32.
McClanahan, John, D. W., 409.
McClanahan (McClenahan), Robert (capt.), V. C. M., 88, 89.
McClanahan, Thomas (capt.), H. S., 7, 229.
McClanahan, Thomas, H. B., 1758-61, 21; V. C. M., 97; Va. Mag., 7, 305.
McClane, Francis, Wash. Mss., 1460.
McClaren (McClaran), Daniel, Va. Mag., 1, 281; Wash. Mss., 111, 13, 15.
McClayland, Daniel, Hist. Orange, 59.
McClelan, Abraham, H. S., 7, 208.
McClellan, Joseph, H. S., 8, 129.
McClenachan, —------ (en.), Aug. Rec., 1, 346.
McClenachan, Alexander (capt.), Aug. Rec., 1, 210.
McClenachan, John, Aug. Rec., 1, 210.

McClenachan, Robert, Aug. Rec., 1, 210.
McClong, James, H. S., 7, 195.
McClong, John, H. S., 7, 195.
McCloskey, Patrick, H. S., 7, 196.
McCloud, Alexander, H. B., 1742-49, 165, 175.
McCloud, Mordecai, Va. Mag., 2, 49, 151; Wash. Mss., 112, 87.
McCloud, William, Va. Mag., 1, 379; Wash. Mss., 112, 88, 94, 115.
McClung, James, H. S., 7, 196.
McClung (McClunge), Joseph, F. I. B. W., 2, 473; H. S., 7, 198; V. C. M., 49.
McClunge, Thomas, H. S., 7, 198.
McClure, Arthur, H. S., 7, 195.
McClure (McClurr), Halbert, H. B. 1766-69, 159; H. S., 7, 191.
McClure, Herbert, H. B., 1758-61, 192.
McClure, James, H. S., 7, 181, 184, 187.
McClure, John, D. W., 406; H. S., 7, 181.
McClure, Thomas, D. W., 406.
McColister, William, D. W., 409.
McCollom, Hendrey, H. S., 7, 198.
McCollom, Henry, H. S., 7, 195.
McCollums, William, J., 80.
McComb, Thomas, H. S., 7, 185.
McCommac, James, Va. Mag., 1, 281; Wash. Mss., 111, 13.
McConnal, John, H. S., 7, 223.
McCorkle, William, D. W., 406.
McCormack, Joshua, Aug. Rec., 1, 344; H. S., 7, 199.
McCormack, Thomas, H. S., 7, 225.
McCormack, William, H. B. 1761-65, 334.
McCormick, Adam, H. S., 7, 183; Wash. Mss., 112, 87.
McCormick, Daniel, Aug. Rec., 1, 340.
McCormick, Francis, H. S., 7, 215.
McCormick, Maxwell, Aug. Rec., 3, 342.
McCorne, Thomas, H. S., 7, 187.
McCorney, Robert, H. S., 7, 188.
McCoun, Moses, F. I. B. W., 2, 366.
McCoun, Robert, H. B., 1761-65, 81, 84.
McCoy, Elijah, Va. Mag., 1, 380.
McCoy, Elisha, Wash. Mss., 112, 88, 94.
McCoy, Finley, F. I. B. W., 2, 387.
McCoy, Hugh, Aug. Rec., 2, 51; Va. Mag., 1, 281.
McCoy, James, H. B., 1758-61, 188.
McCoy, John, F. I. B. W., 1, 174; H. S., 7, 181, 198; Wash. Mss., 1479.

McCoy, Robert, H. S., 7, 179; **Wash. Mss.**, 112, 0.
McCoy, William (lt.), D. W., 410.
McCoy, William, H. S., 7, 218.
McCrackin, Cyrus, J., 28.
McCray, Robert, Wash. Mss., 1557.
McCrimar, Francis, H. S., 7, 216.
McCroskey, David, H. S., 7, 196.
McCulley, John, H. S., 7, 198.
McCullock, John (capt.), H. B., 1766-69, 71.
McCullock, Samuel, V. C. M., 90.
McCullom, Henry, H. S., 7, 196.
McCully, John, L. to Wash., 2, 210; Wash. Mss., 111, 13, 15; Wash. Mss., 112, 89.
McCulroy, Robert, Va. Mag., 1, 281; Wash. Mss., 111, 13.
McCulty, John, L. to Wash., 1, 299.
McCune, William, D. W., 424.
McCutcheon, Samuel, Aug. Rec., 1, 213.
McCutcheon, William, D. W., 424.
McCutchin, James, F. I. B. W., 1, 65; V. C. M., 15.
McCutchison, James, H. S., 7, 197.
McCutchison, Samuel, H. S., 7, 197.
McCutchison, William, H. S., 7, 197.
McCutty, John, Va. Mag., 1, 281.
McDade, Patrick, H. S., 7, 205.
McDaniel, James, H. B., 1758-61, 7.
McDaniel, Joseph, H. S., 7, 207.
McDaniel, Tarrance (Terence), H. S., 7, 224; Va. Mag., 2, 49.
McDanold, John, Wash. Mss., 1542.
McDavid, Patrick, H. S., 7, 206.
McDearmonroe, Bryant (Prince Edward), Va. Mag., 21, 89.
McDoel, Samuel, Va. Mag., 1, 387.
McDonald (McDonnald), Alexander (lt.), F. I. B. W., 2, 498; V. C. M., 35.
McDonald, Angus, Aug. Rec., 2, 49; L. to Wash., 1, 299; Va. Mag., 1, 281; Va. Mag., 2, 147; Wash. Mss., 5, 8; Wash. Mss., 111, 13, 15; Wash. Mss., 112, 0.
McDonald, Daniel, D. W., 407.
McDonald, Edward, H. S., 7, 192.
McDonald, Isaac, F. I. B. W., 2, 438.
McDonald, James, D. W., 407.
McDonald, Jerra., Wash. Mss., 112, 87.
McDonald (McDonnald), John, F. I. B. W., 1, 121; Va. Mag., 2, 143; Wash. Mss., 1478.
McDonald, Patrick, Va. Mag., 2, 42; Wash. Mss., 112, 95.
McDonald, Robert, Va. Mag., 2, 44.
McDonald, Terrence, Va. Mag., 2, 151.

McDonald, Travance, Wash. Mss., 111, 15.
_McDonald, William, H. S., 8, 129.
McDonnald, Alexander, F. I. B. W., 2, 311.
McDonnald, Allan, Wash. Mss., 1557.
McDonnald, Bryan, H. S., 7, 199.
McDowell, Archibald, D. W., 410.
McDowell, James (capt.), H. B., 1766-69, 159.
McDowell, James (lt.), H. S., 7, 195.
McDowell, John (capt.), Withers's Chron., 52.
McDowell, Joseph (lt.), H. S., 7, 216.
McDowell, Samuel (capt.), J. C., Dec., 1775, 95.
McDowell (McDuel, McDuell), Samuel, Aug. Rec., 1, 85; H. S., 7, 196; Va. Mag., 2, 145; Wash. Mss., 112, 82.
McEdent, James, Wash. Mss., 112, 88.
McElhaney, Francis (q. m.), D. W., 407.
McElhenny (McClehaney), James, Aug. Rec., 1, 340; D. W., 403.
McElvan, Alexander, H. S., 7, 198.
McEntire, John, Va. Mag., 1, 383; Wash. Mss., 112, 89, 95.
McEntyre, Daniel, Va. Mag., 2, 143.
McFaddin, Pharrel, F. I. B. W., 1, 74; V. C. M., 16.
McFall, James, H. S., 7, 210.
McFane (McFain), Daniel, Wash. Mss., 112, 88, 144.
McFaun, Daniel, Wash. Mss., 112, 94.
McFarland, Alexander, Aug. Rec., 1, 254.
McFarland, William, D. W., 396.
McFarlin, John, Wash. Mss., 112, 96, 100.
McFarlin, William, H. D., 1776, 46; H. S., 7, 181.
McFarling (McFarlinn), John, Va. Mag., 1, 389; Wash. Mss., 112, 85.1.
McFerrin, James, H. S., 7, 199.
McFerrin, John, H. S., 7, 199.
McFerrin, Samuel, Aug. Rec., 1, 344; H. S., 7, 199.
McFerrin, Thomas, H. S., 7, 199.
McFoll, Daniel, H. S., 7, 210.
McGarey, Edward, H. S., 7, 187.
McGarey, Hugh, H. S., 7, 188.
McGavet, David, F. I. B. W., 2, 516.
McGeary (McGarey), Robert, H. S., 7, 181, 188.
McGee, John, D. W., 406.

McNeale, Archelus, H. S., 7, 206.
McNeel, John, D. W., 424.
McNeil, Archibald, Wash. Mss., 1460.
McNeil, James, Wasn. Mss., 1311.
McNeill (McNeil, McNiell), Daniel, D. W., 407, 421; H. B., 1758-61, 142, 143.
McNeill, Hugh, F. I. B. W., 2, 484, 558.
McNeill, John (lt. col.), H. B., 1766-69, 87.
McNeill, John (maj.), Aug. Rec. 3, 88.
McNeill (McNeil), John (capt.), H. B., 1761-65, 263; V. C. M., 36.
McNeill, John (lt.), V. H. C., 4, 219.
McNeill, Thomas, H. B., 1766-69, 293.
McNelly, Alexander, J., 129.
McNelly, John (armorer), H. B., 1761-65, 240.
McNely, Dennis, H. S., 7, 198.
McNess, John, H. S., 7, 223.
McNiel, Peter, D. W., 406.
McNiell, Daniel (lt.), D. W., 407.
McNight, Daniel, H. S., 7, 179.
McNitt, James, D. W., 409.
McNutt, Alexander, D. W., 422.
McNutt, John, Withers's Chron., 81.
Macomb, George, Va. Mag., 1, 281.
McPherson, William, Va. Mag., 2, 47.
McPike (McPyke), Patrick, Va. Mag., 1, 383; Wash. Mss., 111, 13; Wash. Mss., 112, 86, 89, 95.
McQueen, Charles, H. S., 7, 213; Wash. Mss., 1555.
McQuell, Samuel, Wash. Mss., 112, 83.1.
McRoberts, John, Aug. Rec., 1, 344.
McRonalds (McRunnals), James, H. S., 7, 204, 208.
McSwine, George, Va. Mag., 1, 281.
McTwain, George, Wash. Mss., 112, 11.
McWhorter, Robert, H. S., 7, 204.
McWilliams, Br'dt., Va. Mag., 1, 389.
McWilliams, Brood, Wash. Mss., 112, 85.1.
McWilliams, John, Wash. Mss., 112, 116.
Maddox, David, H. S., 7, 224.
Madison, —— (en.), Aug. Rec., 2, 511.
Madison, Humphrey (en.), V C. M., 15.
Madison, Humphrey, F. I. B. W., 1, 63.
Madison, John (capt.), F. I. B. W., 2, 425; V. C. M., 44.
Madison, John, F. I. B W., 1, 57.
Madison, William, F. I. B. W., 1, 290.

Magavock, James (lt.), H. B., 1752-58, 484.
Magavock, James, H. S., 7, 195.
Magee, William, Aug. Rec., 2, 168.
Magennett, David, Va. Mag., 2, 145.
Magery, Robert, H. S., 7, 185.
Magill, James, Hist. Frederick, 89.
Magill, John, H. S., 7, 217.
Magin, Charles, J., 88.
Maginis, Francis, H. S., 7, 216.
Maid, John, Aug. Rec., 2, 49; Va. Mag., 1, 283; Wash. Mss., 111, 13.
Major, John, Va. Mag., 1, 386; Wash. Mss., 112, 84; Wash. Mss., 1557.
Major, Nicholas, Wash. Mss., 5, 8; Wash. Mss., 111, 13, 15; Wash. Mss., 112, 0.
Major, Richard, Va. Mag., 1, 281.
Makin, Nicholas, J., 86.
Malcomb, George, Aug. Rec., 2, 49; H. S., 7, 184; Wash. Mss., 111, 13.
Malcomb (Malcom), John, H. S., 7, 181, 184.
Mallett, Stephen, F. I. B. W., 2, 326; V. C. M., 36.
Mallow (Malow), Michael, H. S., 7, 179, 184, 185, 187.
Malone, James, Va. Mag., 1, 378; Wash. Mss., 112, 88.
Malotte, Daniel, Va. Mag., 1, 281; Wash. Mss., 111, 13.
Malow, George, H. S., 7, 185.
Man, Abel, H. S., 7, 201.
Man, Charles, H. S., 7, 185, 201.
Man, George, H. S., 7, 186.
Man, Jacob, H. S., 7, 186.
Man, John, H. B., 1766-69, 63.
Man, Thomas, Aug. Rec., 1, 338.
Man, William (scout), H. B., 1761-65, 253, 259.
Man, William, Aug. Rec., 1, 338; D. W., 409.
Manadue, Henry, D. W., 401.
Mander, William, Va. Mag., 1, 387; Wash. Mss., 112, 86, 89, 95.
Manger, Henry Du Val (surg. mate), H. B., 1761-65, 278, 289.
Manin, Peter, H. S., 7, 219.
Mank, Daniel, H. S., 7, 215.
Mank, Henry, H. S., 7, 215.
Mank, Rendy, H. S., 7, 215.
Mank, Richard, H. S., 7, 215.
Manley (Manly) William, H. S., 7, 205, 208, 209.
Mann, Samuel, H. S., 7, 201.
Mann, William, F. I. B. W., 1, 63; V. C. M., 15.
Mannen, Edward, Va. Mag., 2, 148.
Mannin, John, H. S., 7, 224.
Mannin, Thomas, H. S., 7, 211.

Manns (Mans), John, Va. Mag., 1, 387; Wash. Mss., 112, 82.
Mans, Martin, Wash. Mss., 112, 100.
Mansfield, Richard, Wash. Mss., 112, 89.
Manuel, ——, H. B., 1742-49, 94.
Maples, Richard, H. S., 7, 210.
Mar, William, H. S., 7, 192.
Marchel, George, H. S., 7, 192.
Marcum, George, Wash. Mss., 5, 8.
Markes, John, D. W., 407.
Markham, John, H. B., 1758-61, 27; H. S., 7, 230.
Marr, John, F. I. B. W., 2, 445.
Marr, Nathan, Va. Mag., 2, 153.
Marsh, James, Va. Mag., 1, 388; Wash. Mss., 112, 85.1, 116.
Marshall, Thomas, Wash. Mss., 112, 95.
Marshall, William, Va. Mag., 2, 145.
Martain, John, H. S., 7, 209.
Martain, Patrick (capt.), Aug. Rec., 1, 518.
Martain, Richard, Va. Mag., 1, 381.
Martain, William, Aug. Rec., 1, 518.
Martin, Abraham, H. S., 7, 211, 224.
Martin, Brice, D. W., 422.
Martin, Charles, H. S., 7, 217; V. C. M., 97; Va. Mag., 7, 306.
Martin, Christy, D. W., 398.
Martin, David (en.), H. S., 7, 203.
Martin, Dudley, H. B., 1773-76, 242.
Martin, Edward, H. S., 7, 215.
Martin, George, Jr., D. W., 398.
Martin, Henry, V. C. M., 97; Va. Mag., 7, 305.
Martin, James, Aug. Rec., 1, 320; H. S., 7, 204, 224; Wash. Mss., 112, 95.
Martin, Jesse, F. I. B. W., 2, 443; H. S., 7, 217.
Martin, John (maj.), H. S., 7, 231.
Martin, John, H. S., 7, 204; Va. Mag., 1, 281; Wash. Mss., 111, 1?, 15.
Martin, Joseph, H. B., 1752-58, 374; H. S., 7, 218.
Martin, Patrick (capt.), L. to Wash., 1, 305.
Martin, Philip, D. W., 398.
Martin, Richard, F. I. B. W., 1, 190; Wash. Mss., 112, 86, 95.
Martin, Robert, H. S., 7, 205, 206, 224.
Martin, Thomas (lt.), H. B., 1758-61, 81.
Martin, Thomas Bryan, V. H. C., 4, 179.
Martin, William, D. W., 420; H. S., 7, 203, 211; V. C. M., 88.
Marston, John, Wash. Mss., 111, 15.
Masc, Richard, H. S., 7, 198.

Mash, James, Wash. Mss., 112, 96; Wash. Mss., 1543.
Mashaw, Abraham, Va. Mag., 1, 283; Wash. Mss., 111, 13.
Mason, Abel, Va. Mag., 2, 146.
Mason, George, Wash. Mss., 1460.
Mason, Robert, Aug. Rec., 2, 506.
Mason, Samuel, H. S., 7, 215.
Mason, Thomas (drummer), F. I. B. W., 2, 459; V. C. M., 47.
Mason, Thomas, J., 84.
Mason, William, Va. Mag., 2, 46.
Massey, John, H. S., 7, 186.
Massey, William, H. S., 7, 218.
Masterson, Edward, H. B., 1752-58, 374.
Mastin, Thomas, F. I. B. W., 1, 26; V. C. M., 12.
Maston, John, Va. Mag., 1, 281; Wash. Mss., 111, 13.
Mathers, William, Aug. Rec., 1, 317.
Matson, Ralph, J., 81.
Mathew, William, H. S., 7, 215.
Matthews, Arthur, H. S., 7, 226.
Matthews, Barry, Va. Mag., 2, 37.
Matthews, George (capt.), J. C., Dec., 1775, 101; V. C. M., 89.
Matthews, George (comm.), J. C., Dec., 1775, 73.
Matthews, George, Aug. Rec., 1, 184; H. S., 7, 195.
Matthews, Jacob, H. S., 7, 225.
Matthews, John (en.), H. S., 7, 195.
Matthews (Mathews), John, H. B., 1752-58, 498, 500; H. S., 7, 195; L. to Wash., 1, 299; Va. Mag., 2, 147.
Matthews, John Twitty, H. S., 7, 226.
Matthews, Joshua, H. S., 7, 195.
Matthews, Laurence, H. S., 7, 226.
Matthews, Richard, F. I. B. W., 1, 203; H. S., 7, 195.
Matthews, Sampson (comm.), J. C., Dec., 1775, 73.
Matthews, Thomas, F. I. B. W., 2, 327; J., 189, 195.
Matthews, William, H. S., 7, 195, 198.
Mattox (Mattocks), John, H. S., 7, 206, 209.
Mauford (Moffet), Robert, D. W., 404.
Maupin, Daniel, H. S., 7, 203.
Maupin, John, H. S., 7, 203.
Maupin, William, H. S., 7, 203.
Maury, Abraham (col.), H. S., 7, 219.
Maury, Daniel, Wash. Mss., 1536.
Maxedent, James, Va. Mag., 1, 380.
Maxey, John, F. I. B. W., 2, 469; V. C. M., 48.

Maxey, William, V. C. M., 9.
Maxfield, Thomas, J., 171.
Maxfield, Willoby, Wash. Mss., 112, 87.
Maxon (Maxom), Henry, Va. Mag., 1, 388; Wash. Mss., 112, 116.
Maxwell, Basilael, D. W., 412.
Maxwell, David, D. W., 400.
Maxwell, John (capt.), Aug. Rec., 1, 317; H. B., 1752-58, 484; H. S., 7, 194, 199.
Maxwell, John, D. W., 399.
Maxwell, Thomas, D. W., 404.
Maxwell, William, F. I. B. W., 2, 414.
May, James, F. I. B. W., 1, 249.
May, Jesse, F. I. B. W., 2, 399; V. C. M., 42; Va. Mag., 1, 381; Wash. Mss., 111, 13, 15; Wash. Mss., 112, 95.
May, John, Va. Mag., 1, 281; Wash. Mss., 111, 13, 15; Wash. Mss., 1476.
May, Martin, Va. Mag., 1, 388; Wash. Mss., 5, 4; Wash. Mss., 112, 85.1, 96, 116.
Maynard, William, Va. Mag., 2, 143; Wash. Mss., 112, 90, 95.
Mays (Mayes), John, F. I. B. W., 2, 434; H. S., 7, 196.
Mays (Mayse, Maze), Joseph, Aug. Rec., 1, 230, 253; D. W., 422.
Mead, Abiel (Abel), F. I. B. W., 2, 381; H. S., 7, 209; V. C. M., 40.
Mead, John, H. S., 7, 209.
Mead, Nicholas, D. W., 409.
Mead, Thomas, D. W., 399.
Mead, William (capt.), L. to Wash., 2, 308.
Meade, William (lt.), H. S., 7, 207.
Meader, Israel, D. W., 405.
Meadows, Benjamin, H. S., 7, 201.
Meads, Thomas, D. W., 404.
Meaks, Joshua, H. S., 7, 218.
Meamack, James, H. S., 7, 215.
Mears, John, Va. Mag., 1, 281; Wash. Mss., 111, 13, 15; Wash. Mss., 112, 0.
Mecrary, Thomas, D. W., 411.
Medley, John, H. S., 7, 191.
Meek, William, D. W., 399.
Megary, Edward, H. S., 7, 181.
Megary, Robert, H. S., 7, 181
Meggs, James, Va. Mag. 1. 283; Wash. Mss., 111, 13, 15; Wash. Mss., 112, 0.
Meggs, John, Va. Mag., 2, 43; Wash. Mss., 1472.
Melcum, John, H. S., 7, 180.
Melcum, Joseph, H. S., 7, 180.
Melton, James, F. I. B. W., 1, 258.
Melton, William, F. I. B. W., 1, 258.

Mennis, Robert, V. C. M., 50.
Menzie, Peter, H. B., 1758-61, 138, 140.
Menzies, Robert, Aug. Rec., 2, 366.
Mercer, George (capt.), F. I. B. W., 1, 285; L. to Wash., 2, 173; V. H. C., 3, 114; Wash. Mss., 5.
Mercer, George, Va. Mag., 1, 279.
Mercer, George Fenton, F. I. B. W., 1, 285.
Mercer, Hugh, L. to Wash., 3, 90.
Mercer, James (capt.), F. I. B. W., 1, 289.
Mercer, John (capt.), V. H. C., 4, 400; Wash. Mss., 5.
Mercer, John (en.), Va. Mag., 1, 279; Wash. Mss., 5, 8.
Mercer, John Fenton (lt.), V. H. C., 3, 110.
Mercer, Richard, J., 27.
Merchant, Philip, H. S., 7, 218.
Meredith, Samuel (capt.), V. C. M., 50.
Meredith, Samuel, F. I. B. W., 2, 494; H. B., 1761-65, 259; H. S., 8, 128.
Mergee, Edward, H. S., 7, 216.
Mergee, Jacob, H. S., 7, 216.
Meriwether, Nicholas, H. S., 7, 222.
Messersmith, Barnet, D. W., 399.
Messersmith, John, D. W., 399.
Meteer, James, H. S., 7, 181.
Micalister, William, D. W., 411.
Middleton, Holland, Wash. Mss., 1460.
Middleton, Thomas, Wash. Mss., 1460.
Miland, James, Wash. Mss., 112, 94.
Mildebarler, Nicholas, H. S., 7, 186.
Miles, James, Va. Mag., 1, 385; Wash. Mss., 112, 82.
Milican, John, D. W., 406.
Millar, James, F. I. B. W., 2, 523.
Miller, Adam, H. S., 7, 186, 187.
Miller, David, H. S., 7, 199.
Miller, George (scout), H. B., 1766-69, 294.
Miller, Jacob, H. S., 7, 186.
Miller, James, D. W., 405.
Miller, John, F. I. B. W., 1, 71; H. S., 7, 185, 215; V. C. M., 15, 97; Va. Mag., 1, 305; Wash. Mss., 111, 15; Wash. Mss., 1483.
Miller, Patrick, Aug. Rec., 1, 212; F. I. B. W., 2, 562.
Miller, Peter, H. S., 7, 186.
Miller, Richard, Wash. Mss., 1432.
Miller, Robert, D. W., 400; F. I. B. W., 1, 26; V. C. M., 12.
Miller, Samuel, F. I. B. W., 2, 478.
Miller, Thomas, F. I. B. W., 2, 491.

Moorhead, Gasper, Va. Mag., 1, 282; Wash. Mss., 5, 2; Wash. Mss., 111, 13.

Moran (Moorin, Moren), Dominick, Va. Mag., 1, 281; Va. Mag., 2, 49, 151; Wash. Mss., 111, 13; Wash. Mss., 112, 87.

Morde-Gosling, ——, L. to Wash., 1, 300.

More, Samuel, H. S., 7, 218.

Morean, Gasper, Va. Mag., 1, 283; Wash. Mss., 111, 13.

Moreland, Francis, L. to Wash., 1, 300; Va. Mag., 2, 47.

Moreton, James (capt.), H. B., 1758-61, 81.

Morgain, John, Wash. Mss., 1555.

Morgan, Charles, J., 26.

Morgan, Daniel (capt.), D. W., 421; H. D., 1776, 48.

Morgan, Daniel, Va. Mag., 2, 152.

Morgan (Morgin), David, Va. Mag., 1, 379; Wash. Mss., 112, 88, 94.

Morgan, Edward, H. S., 8, 131.

Morgan, Evan, H. S., 7, 205, 207.

Morgan, Gilbert, Wash. Mss., 112, 0.

Morgan, Haynes, F. I. B. W., 2, 433; V. C. M., 45.

Morgan, James, V. C. M., 97; Va. Mag., 7, 306.

Morgan (Morgin), John, H. B., 1752-58, 462; H. S., 7, 205, 207, 209, 214; V. C. M., 97; Va. Mag., 2, 147; Va. Mag., 7, 305.

Morgan, Nicholas, Va. Mag., 1, 281; Wash. Mss., 111, 13.

Morgan, Richard (capt.), Historic Shepherdstown, 25.

Morgan, Richard, Va. Mag., 1, 387; Wash. Mss., 112, 82.2, 83; Wash. Mss., 1472.

Morgan, Simon, V. C. M., 97; Va. Mag., 7, 305.

Morgan, Thomas, H. S., 7, 205, 218.

Morgan, William, H. S., 7, 205, 206, 209; Historic Shepherdstown, 25.

Morgan, William, Jr., H. S., 7, 207.

Morrell, James, L. to Wash., 1, 300.

Morris, Darby, Wash. Mss., 1485.

Morris, Jacob, F. I. B. W., 1, 298; Va. Mag., 1, 380; Wash. Mss., 112, 114.

Morris, James, H. S., 7, 208, 215, 216.

Morris, Jesse, Va. Mag., 1, 281; Wash. Mss., 11, 111; Wash. Mss., 112, 0.

Morris, John, Adam Stephen Ps.; Aug. Rec, 2, 68; Wash. Mss., 1460.

Morris, Joseph, Va. Mag., 2, 147.

Morris, Richard, Aug. Rec., 2, 49; Va. Mag., 1, 281; Wash. Mss., 111, 13, 15.

Morris, Thomas, F. I. B. W., 1, 255; Hist. Orange, 60; Va. Mag., 2, 143.

Morris, William (lt.), V. C. M., 11.

Morris, William, D. W., 419, 421; F. I, B. W., 1, 24.

Morrison, James, H. S., 7, 204.

Morrison, John, Wash. Mss., 112, 0.

Morrison, Michael, H. S., 7, 204.

Morriss, Jacob, Wash. Mss., 112, 88.

Morriss, William, V. C. M., 97.

Morrow, James, D. W., 411.

Morrow, James, Jr., D. W., 411.

Morse, David, H. S., 7, 208.

Morse, Thomas, Aug. Rec., 2, 171.

Morton, George, Va. Mag., 1, 379; Wash. Mss., 112, 88.

Morton, John (lt.), (Prince Edward), Va. Mag., 21, 88.

Morton, John (lt.), F. I. B. W., 1, 104.

Morton, Joseph, H. S., 7, 220.

Morton, Samuel, H. S., 7, 224.

Morton, Thomas (lt.), (Prince Edward), Va. Mag., 21, 88.

Morton, Thomas (lt.), F. I. B. W., 1, 104.

Morton, William, F. I. B. W., 1, 126.

Mosby, Poindexter (capt.). H. S., 7, 213.

Moseley, Sampson, H. S., 7, 212.

Mosely (Moseley, Mosley), Jacob, Va. Mag., 1, 380; Wash. Mss., 112, 88, 94.

Mosely, Robert, J., 29.

Mosely, Thomas, H. S., 7, 221.

Moses, George, H. S., 7, 183.

Moses, Peter, H. S., 7, 183.

Moss, —— (capt.), H. S., 8, 132.

Moss, David, H. S., 7, 212.

Moss, Francis (lt.), H. B., 1742-49, 37.

Moss, James, F. I. B. W., 1, 284; V. C. M., 33.

Moss, John (capt.), H. B., 1761-65, 248, 253.

Moss, John, H. S., 7, 222.

Moss, John, Jr., H. S., 7, 222.

Moss, Thomas (drummer), Wash. Mss., 111, 110.

Moss, Thomas, Aug. Rec., 2, 49; Va. Mag., 1, 281, 385; Va. Mag., 2, 144; Wash. Mss., 111, 13, 15; Wash. Mss., 1432.

Mothershead, George, F. I. B. W., 2, 548.

Mourning, Thomas, F. I. B. W., 1, 221.

Mouse, George, H. S., 7, 184.

Moxom, Henry, H. B., 1761-65, 7, 10; Wash. Mss., 112, 85.1, 100.
Moyers, Jacob, H. S., 7, 186.
Muckleroy, Robert, Va. Mag., 2, 143; Wash. Mss., 112, 90.
Mulholland, John, Va. Mag., 1, 281; Wash. Mss., 111, 13.
Mullen, Peter, Va. Mag., 2, 39; Wash. Mss., 112, 114.
Mullin (Mullen), Thomas, D. W., 396; F. I. B. W., 2, 585.
Mullins, Matthew, H. S., 7, 203.
Mullnar, Tolley, F. I. B. W., 1, 12.
Mumford, Robert (capt.), V. C. M., 36.
Munday, Christopher, H. S., 7, 206.
Munday, Isaac, H. S., 7, 224.
Munday (Monday), James, Va. Mag., 1, 379; Wash. Mss., 112, 88, 94.
Munday, John, F. I. B. W., 1, 145.
Munday, Reuben, F. I. B. W., 1, 133.
Mungle, Daniel, D. W., 412.
Mungle (Mongle), Frederick, D. W., 412.
Munjoy, Thomas, Va. Mag., 2, 149.
Munk, John, H. B., 1752-58, 462.
Murfee, William, H. S., 7, 220.
Murphy, James, H. S., 7, 208.
Murphy (Murphey), John, Va. Mag., 1, 386; Wash. Mss., 112, 82.2.
Murphy (Murphey), Laurence, H. S., 7, 198.
Murphy, Luke, H. S., 7, 208.
Murphy, Richard, H. S., 7, 215.
Murphy (Murphey), Robert, Aug. Rec., 2, 171; Va. Mag., 1, 281, 283; Wash. Mss., 111, 13; Wash. Mss., 112, 86, 89, 95.
Murphy, Samuel, D. W., 421.
Murphy, Thomas, F. I. B. W., 1, 294.
Murray, Daniel (Prince Edward), Va. Mag., 21, 89.
Murray, Duncan, Va. Mag., 2, 147.
Murray, Henry, H. S., 7, 195.
Murray (Murry), John (capt.), D. W., 406; H. D., May, 1777, 44; V. C. M., 88, 89.
Murray, John (en.), Aug. Rec., 1, 211; V. C. M., 17.
Murray, John, D. W., 406; F. I. B. W., 1, 97; H. B., 1758-61, 27; H. B., 1766-69, 63.
Murray, Richard, Va. Mag., 1, 282, 283; Va. Mag., 2, 49; Wash. Mss., 5, 2; Wash. Mss., 111, 13.
Murrell, William, F. I. B. W., 2, 584.
Murry, Thomas, H. S., 7, 206.
Murty, Joseph, H. S., 7, 209.
Muse, George (lt. col.), H. S., 7, 213; Hist. Frederick. 89; V. H. C., 3, 107; Va. Mag., 1, 279.

Muse, George, Aug. Rec., 2, 49; F. I. B. W., 1, 116; H. B., 1742-49, 265.
Musgrove, William, H. B., 1752-58, 374.
Mushaw, Abraham, Wash. Mss., 111, 15.
Myas, William, Wash. Mss., 1460.
Myer, Jacob, Va. Mag., 1, 281; Wash. Mss., 111, 13.
Myler, James, Wash. Mss., 112, 83.1.
Mynor, Richard, J., 128.
Myres, William, D. W., 421; V. C. M., 88.

N.

Nail, Dennis, D. W., 408.
Nail, Thomas, D. W., 406.
Nalle, Martain (lt.), D. W., 405.
Nalle, Martin, F. I. B. W., 2, 382; V. C. M., 40,
Nalle, William (capt.), D. W., 405; Hist. Rockingham, 63.
Nalle, William, Wash. Mss., 1555.
Nalle, William, Jr., H. S., 7, 214.
Nance, Robert, H. S., 7, 212.
Nance, Thomas, H. S., 7, 212.
Napp (Nap, Nappe), Thomas, Aug. Rec., 2, 167, 505; Va. Mag., 1, 281; Va. Mag., 2, 146; Wash. Mss., 111, 13.
Nash, John, F. I. B. W., 1, 6; V. C. M., 9; Va. Mag., 2, 150; Wash. Mss., 112, 115.
Nash, John, Jr. (capt.), H. B., 1752-58, 484; H. S., 7, 229.
Nash, Marvell, F. I. B. W., 2, 533.
Nash, Robert, Va. Mag., 2, 146; Wash. Mss., 1534.
Naughty, John, L. to Wash., 1, 300; Va. Mag., 2, 151; Wash. Mss., 112, 87, 115.
Naull, William, Aug. Rec., 1, 184.
Nave, Conrad, D. W., 412.
Neal, Benjamin, H. B., 1758-61, 24.
Neal (Neall), James, Aug. Rec., 2, 168; Va. Mag., 2, 49, 151; Wash. Mss., 112, 87.
Neale, William, D. W., 396.
Nealy, Matthew, Va. Mag., 2, 147.
Neaville, John, D. W., 421.
Neaville, Joseph, D. W., 421.
Nedly, Matthew, Wash. Mss., 1432.
Neely, Andrew, Aug. Rec., 1, 344.
Neely, James (cadet), D. W., 407.
Neely, William, D. W., 406.
Neile, Henry, Va. Mag., 1, 281; Wash. Mss., 111, 13.
Neill, Charles, Aug. Rec., 2, 506.
Neill, Thomas, Aug. Rec., 1, 478.
Neilly, John, Aug. Rec., 1, 344.
Neilson, John, H. S., 7, 208.
Nelson, John, D. W., 406.

Neveston, Matthews, Wash. Mss., 112, 0.
Nevil, Gabriel, Va. Mag., 2, 149.
Nevil, Henry, Va. Mag., 2, 147.
Nevill (Nevil), James (capt.), H. B., 1758-61, 28; H. S., 7, 202.
Nevison, Matthew, Va. Mag., 1, 281; Wash. Mss., 111, 13.
Newberry (Newbery), Samuel, F. I. B. W., 1, 27; H. S., 8, 129; V. C. M., 12.
Newberry, Thomas, J., 3.
Newburn, Thomas, Wash. Mss., 1472.
Newell, James, D. W., 419.
Newell, Richard, Wash. Mss., 1460.
Newell (Newel, Newil), William, Va. Mag., 1, 387; Va. Mag., 2, 145; Wash. Mss., 112, 82.2, 83.1, 97; Wash. Mss., 1460.
Newkirk, Elias, J., 52.
Newland, Alsam, D. W., 412.
Newland, Isaac, D. W., 412.
Newland, James, Wash. Mss., 112, 88.
Newland, John, D. W., 403.
Newman, Daniel, H. S., 7, 220.
Newman, Joseph, F. 1. B. W., 2, 409.
Newman, Nimrod (fifer), V. C. M., 40.
Newman, Nimrod, F. I. B. W., 2, 379.
Newman, Walter, D. W., 424.
Newport, Richard, Aug. Rec., 1, 341, 490.
Newton, John (capt.), H. S., 7, 231.
Niblet, Joel, Wash. Mss., 1311.
Nicholls, Edward, Va. Mag., 1, 387; Wash. Mss., 112, 82.2.
Nicholson, Thomas, Va. Mag., 1, 281; Wash. Mss., 111, 13, 15.
Nickels, Isaac, D. W., 408.
Nickols, Edward, Wash. Mss., 112, 83.
Nisbett, James, Wash. Mss., 1557.
Nix, William, H. S., 7, 209.
Nixon, Henry, F. I. B. W., 2, 397.
Nixon, John, F. I. B. W., 2, 571.
Noble, Ross, H. B., 1761-65, 278; H. B., 1766-69, 60.
Noland, James, F. I. B. W., 2, 509.
Noland, Samuel, Aug. Rec., 2, 505.
Nonery, Griffith, Va. Mag., 2, 145.
Norman, Isaac, H. B., 1758-61, 103.
Norrell, Francis, H. S., 7, 225.
Norrell, James, H. S., 7, 224.
Norris, John, F. I. B. W., 2, 521; V. C. M., 52; Wash. Mss., 1465.
Norris, William (en.), V. C. M., 97; Va. Mag., 7, 305.
Norris (Norriss), William, H. B., 1752-58, 374; Va. Mag., 7, 305.
North, William, F. I. B. W., 2, 362.
Northcut, William, V. C. M., 39.

Norton, Thomas (lt.), Withers's Chron., 81.
Norton, Thomas, H. S., 7, 220.
Norwood, Benjamin, Aug. Rec., 1, 478.
Norwood, Samuel (capt.), H. S., 7, 191.
Norwood, Samuel, Aug. Rec., 1, 73.
Nosler, Poston, H. S., 7, 187.
Nott, Walter, Va. Mag., 2, 144.
Nourse, James, F. I. B. W., 2, 385.
Norvell, James, Va. Mag., 2, 47.
Norvell, John, D. W., 399.
Nowling, Bryan, H. S., 8, 131.
Nugent, John, Va. Mag., 2, 146.
Nugent, William, Va. Mag., 2, 40.
Nuland, John, D. W., 400.
Nuland, Thomas, Va. Mag., 1, 380.
Null, Jacob, D. W., 405.
Null, John, D. W., 405.
Null, Nicholas, H. S., 7, 186.

O.

Oaks, John, Wash. Mss., 112, 90, 95.
Obrian, James, Wash. Mss., 111, 15.
Oburk, Michael, Wash. Mss., 111, 15.
O'Conner, William, Va. Mag., 2, 48; Wash. Mss., 1465.
O'Daniel, William, H. S., 7, 218.
Odell, Jeremiah (capt.), H. B., 1766-69, 71.
Odle, Jeremiah, H. S., 7, 215.
Odle, Jonathan, H. S., 7, 215.
Ogden, Thomas, Va. Mag., 1, 281; Wash. Mss., 111, 13.
Ogilvie, John, Va. Mag., 1, 281; Wash. Mss., 111, 13; Wash. Mss., 112, 0.
Ogle, William, J., 87.
Ogleby, John, H. B., 1752-58, 256, 273.
Oglesby, Robert, H. S., 7, 206.
Oglesby, Thomas, H. S., 7, 208.
Oglesby, William, F. I. B. W., 1, 270.
Ogullion, Barnett, D. W., 412.
Ogullion, Hugh, D. W., 412.
O'Haara, Charles, D. W., 410.
O'Haara, Robert, D. W., 410.
O'Haara, William, D. W., 410.
Ohair, Edward, H. S., 7, 208.
Oldham, Jesse, Va. Mag., 2, 153.
Oliver, Benjamin, F. I. B. W., 1, 222; V. C. M., 28.
Oliver, James, V. C. M., 97; Va. Mag., 7, 306.
Olverson, Joseph, D. W., 396.
Oneal, John, F. I. B. W., 216; J., 85.
O'Neal, Ludowick, F. I. B. W., 1, 152; V. C. M., 129.
O'Neil (Oneal), Michael, Wash. Mss., 112, 90, 95.

Orchard, James, H. S., 7, 210.
Orchard, Anthony, H. B., 1758-61, 24.
Organ, John, Va. Mag., 2, 148.
Orme (Orm), Henry, H. B., 1761-65, 7, 10; Va. Mag., 2, 149.
Ormsbey, Daniel, D. W., 407.
Ormsby, John, F. I. B. W., 2, 420.
Orr, John, H. S., 7, 224.
Orrack, John, H. S., 7, 210.
Osborn, Daniel, Historic Shepherdstown, 26.
Osborn, Thomas, H. B., 1752-58, 374.
Osborne, Charles, V. C. M., 107.
Osbourn, John, F. I. B. W., 2, 326; V. C. M., 36.
Ourry, —— (capt.), H. B., 1761-65, 297.
Overstreet, Thomas, H. S., 7, 208, 209.
Overstreet, William, D. W., 409.
Overton, James (en.), H. S., 7, 221.
Overton, Samuel (capt.) (Prince Edward), Va. Mag., 21, 88.
Overton, Samuel (capt.), V. H. C., 4, 157.
Overton, Samuel, H. B., 1752-58, 372.
Owen (Owin), James, F. I. B. W., 2, 326; V. C. M., 36.
Owen, Robert, D. W., 407.
Owen, Thomas, D. W., 409.
Owens, Peter, Wash. Mss., 112, 96.
Owens, Thomas, H. S., 7, 210.
Owler, Henry, D. W., 405.
Owler, John, D. W., 405.
Owsley, John, H. S., 7, 222.
Owsley, Nudegate, Wash. Mss., 1460.
Owsley, William, H. B., 1752-58, 374.
Ozban, John, H. S., 7, 186.

P.

Pabley (Pably), John, H. S., 7, 214; Wash. Mss., 1555.
Packer, Augustine, J. C., May, 1776, 48.
Packett (Packet), William Stewart (Stuart), F. I. B. W., 2, 400; L. to Wash., 1, 299; Va. Mag., 2, 146.
Packwood, Richard, D. W., 408.
Page, Alexander, F. I. B, W., 2, 542.
Page, Bryant, Va. Mag., 1, 281; Wash. Mss., 111, 13.
Page, John, H. S., 8, 131.
Page, Thomas, Wash. Mss., 111, 15.
Pain, Joseph, D. W., 407.
Painter, Edward, Wash. Mss., 5, 4.
Palmore, George, Va. Mag., 2, 44.
Pannell (Pannill), Samuel, H. S., 7, 214; Wash. Mss., 1555.
Pannell, Thomas, H. B., 1758-61, 26.
Parchment, Peter, D. W., 421.

Pardoe, John, Va., Mag., 2, 46.
Parham, William, H. S., 7, 211, 226.
Paris (Pearis), Richard (capt.), H. B., 1761-65, 140.
Paris, Richard, H. B., 1752-58, 379.
Parish, David, H. S., 7, 225.
Parish, James, F. I. B. W., 2, 386.
Parish, John (lt.), H. S., 7, 211.
Parish, Joseph, F. I. B. W., 1, 148; H. S., 7, 212.
Parke, John, H. S., 7, 216.
Parker, Nathaniel, H. S., 7, 213.
Parker, Richard, H. S., 7, 214.
Parker, Thomas, H. B., 1758-61, 36.
Parkes, John, Wash. Mss., 5, 4.
Parkinson, James, Wash. Mss., 112, 95.
Parks, Richard, H. S., 7, 214; Wash. Mss., 1555.
Parks, William, Va. Mag., 2, 47.
Parmer, Jonathan, Aug. Rec., 2, 506.
Parrish, Moses, F. I. B. W., 1, 273.
Parrott, Benjamin, H. S., 7, 202.
Parrott (Parrot), Daniel, H. B., 1758-61, 188; Wash. Mss., 5, 4.
Parsinger, Abraham, V. C. M., 17.
Parsinger, Jacob, F. I. B. W., 1, 83.
Parsinger, Philip, V. C. M., 17.
Parsley, Augustine, Va. Mag., 2, 145.
Parsons, David, H. B., 1752-58, 462.
Parsons, James, D. W., 421; H. D., 1776, 44.
Parsons, William, H. S., 7, 211, 225.
Parsons, Willis, Wash. Mss., 1478.
Pate, Anthony, H. S., 7, 205, 210.
Pate, Jacob, H. S., 7, 205, 206, 210.
Pate, Jeremiah, H. S., 7, 205, 206.
Pate, John, H. S., 7, 205, 206, 210.
Pate, Matthew, H. S., 7, 205, 210.
Pate, Thomas, H. S., 7, 225; Va. Mag., 1, 389; Wash. Mss., 112, 85.1, 112.
Paton, William, Wash. Mss., 112, 90.
Patrick, Charles, H. S., 7, 191.
Patrick, John, H. S., 7, 190.
Patten, John, D. W., 411.
Patterson, James, H. S., 7, 187, 190, 195, 208.
Patterson, Nathaniel, H. S., 7, 204, 208.
Patterson, Robert, H. S., 7, 181, 187, 195.
Patterson, Samuel, H. S., 7, 187, 188.
Patterson (Paterson, Patteson), Thomas, F. I. B. W., 1, 19; H. S., 7, 185, 187.
Patterson, William, J., 110; Va. Mag., 1, 380; Va. Mag., 2, 46; Wash. Mss., 112, 88, 94.
Patton, James, Va. Mag., 2, 37.
Patton (Patten), Matthew, H. S., 7, 180, 187.

Paty, Jesse, H. S., 7, 209.
Paugh, Nicholas, J., 174.
Paul, Aaron, Va. Mag., 2, 41.
Paul, Audley (capt.), Withers's Chron., 79, 81.
Paul, Audley (lt.), H. S., 7, 129.
Paul, Audley (en.), H. S., 7, 196.
Paul, Hugh, Aug. Rec., 2, 49; Va. Mag., 1, 281; Wash. Mss., 5, 8; Wash. Mss., 112, 0; Wash. Mss., 1311.
Paul, Thaddius (Thedius), Wash. Mss., 112, 82.2.
Pauley, John, D. W., 410.
Paulin, Henry, H. S., 7, 202.
Paulley, James, D. W., 410.
Paulling, Henry (capt.), D. W., 411.
Paxton, Samuel, D. W., 400, 403.
Paxton, Thomas, H. S., 7, 196.
Payne, John (lt.), V. C. M., 25.
Payne, John, F. I. B. W., 1, 182.
Payne, William, Wash. Mss., 1557.
Payton, John, H. B., 1758-61, 26; H. S., 7, 213.
Peachey, William (col.), H. B., 1758-61, 174; H. B., 1761-65, 82.
Peachey, William (capt.), L. to Wash., 2, 181; Wash. Mss., 5.
Peachey, William (p. m.), F. I. B. W., 1, 23.
Peachey, William, F. I. B. W., 1, 281.
Peake, William, Jr., H. B., 1752-58, 374.
Pearce, Thomas, Va. Mag., 1, 281; Wash. Mss., 111, 15.
Pearcy (Pearcey), Charles, F. I. B. W., 2, 577; Hist. Orange, 60.
Pearls, Richard (capt.), V. H. C., 3, 266.
Pearls, Robert (capt.), Aug. Rec., 1, 485.
Pearpoint, Larkin, H. S., 7, 181, 184.
Pearsefull, John, J., 93.
Pearson, Simon, Wash. Mss., 1460.
Pearson, Thomas, Va. Mag., 1, 283; Wash. Mss., 111, 13.
Peary, John, H. S., 7, 181.
Peary (Pearee), Thomas, D. W., 406; Wash. Mss., 111, 13.
Peasly, Augustine, Wash. Mss., 1538.
Peat, Thomas, Wash. Mss., 112, 100.
Pedder, John, Va. Mag., 2, 144; Wash. Mss., 112, 95.
Peebles, Robert, H. S., 7, 211.
Peed (Pead), Philip, Va. Mag., 1, 390; Wash. Mss., 112, 85.1, 96, 100.
Pell, Richard, H. S., 7, 218.
Pence, Jacob (en.), D. W., 405.

Pence, Jacob, Aug. Rec., 2, 366; F. I. B. W., 2, 496; H. S., 7, 185; V. C. M., 50.
Pendegrass (Pendergrass), John, Va. Mag., 1, 386; Wash. Mss., 112, 82.2.
Pendleton, James, V. C. M., 97; Va. Mag., 7, 306.
Peninger (Peniger), Henry, H. S., 7, 181, 187.
Penison, William M., V. C. M., 97; Va. Mag., 7, 305.
Penix, Edward (Prince Edward), Va. Mag., 21, 89.
Penix, John, F. I. B. W., 1, 38.
Penmore, John, Va. Mag., 2, 39; Wash. Mss., 112, 94, 114.
Penn, John, Wash. Mss., 1460.
Pepper, Robert, H. S., 7, 207.
Pepper, Samuel, H. S., 7, 207.
Perce, Thomas, D. W., 407.
Perdue, John, Wash. Mss., 112, 90, 95.
Perdue, Joseph, Wash. Mss., 112, 85.1.
Peregin, Molastin, D. W., 409.
Peregoy, Edward, H. S., 7, 219, 220.
Perkins, George, Va. Mag., 2, 43; Wash. Mss., 1472.
Perkins, Valentine, Va. Mag., 2, 37.
Perkinson, James, Wash. Mss., 112, 86.
Perkison, James, Wash. Mss., 112, 89.
Perkisson, Thomas, Va. Mag., 1, 383.
Perkley, Jacob, Va. Mag., 1, 282; Wash. Mss., 5, 2; Wash. Mss., 111, 13.
Perrin, John, F. I. B. W., 1, 190; H. S., 7, 224.
Perritt (Perrit), Edward, Va. Mag., 1, 386; Wash. Mss., 112, 83.
Perry (Perrey), Alexander, Va. Mag., 1, 281; Wash. Mss., 111, 13, 15; Wash. Mss., 112, 0.
Perry, Franklin, H. S., 7, 218.
Perry, Holaway, H. S., 7, 216.
Perry (Perrie), John, Aug. Rec., 1, 518; Va. Mag., 2, 40.
Perry, Joseph, Va. Mag., 2, 148.
Perryman, David, H. S., 7, 224.
Persinger, Jacob, D. W., 422.
Person, William, H. S., 7, 201.
Pert, Griffin (en.), L. to Wash., 1, 298, 385.
Petanger, Peter, H. S., 7, 215.
Peter, John, Wash. Mss., 112, 114.
Peter, John, Jr., H. B., 1758-61, 209, 211.
Peterfish, Gunrod, H. S., 7, 186.
Peters, Edmund, F. I. B. W., 2, 361; V. C. M., 39.
Peterson, Edwin (lt.), H. S., 7, 199.

Posey, Francis, F. I. B. W., 2, 532.
Posey, John (capt.), L. to Wash., 3, 341.
Posey, John, Wash. Mss., 112, 90, 95.
Posey, Richard, L. to Wash., 1, 300; Va. Mag., 2, 45.
Posey, Thomas (comm. gen.), V. C. M., 90.
Potter, John, H. B., 1752-58, 273; Va. Mag., 1, 281; Wash. Mss., 5, 8; Wash. Mss., 111, 13, 15.
Potter, Thomas, D. W., 403.
Pottlet, Nathan, H. S., 7, 208.
Poulson, William (capt.), V. H. C., 3, 114.
Poulter, William, F. I. B. W., 1, 279; V. C. M., 32.
Pouston, Richard, F. I. B. W., 2, 416.
Powell, Ambrose (capt.), F. I. B. W., 2, 386.
Powell, Ambrose (aid), F. I. B. W., 2, 452.
Powell, Ambrose (staff-off.), Hist. Orange, 60.
Powell, Benjamin, Hist. Orange, 59.
Powell, George, Va. Mag., 1, 386.
Powell, Jacob, Va. Mag., 2, 38.
Powell, John, F. I. B. W., 2, 580; H. S., 7, 203, 213.
Powell, Joseph, Va. Mag., 1, 281; Wash. Mss., 5, 8; Wash. Mss., 111, 13.
Powell, Joshua (capt.), H. B., 1761-65, 181.
Powell, Joshua (en.), H. B., 1770-72, 50, 84.
Powell, Richard, H. S., 7, 203.
Powell, Simon, H. B., 1761-65, 332, 339; Hist. Orange, 60.
Powell, Thomas, H. S., 7, 186; 203; Hist. Orange, 59.
Power, James, Va. Mag., 2, 149.
Powers, John, Va. Mag., 1, 281.
Powers, Richard, Va. Mag., 2, 143; Wash. Mss., 112, 90, 95.
Prater, Jonathan, H. S., 7, 210.
Prater, Nehemiah, H. S., 7, 220.
Prather, Thomas (en.), H. S., 7, 205.
Prather, Thomas, H. S., 7, 207.
Prator, Ningum, H. S., 7, 220.
Pratt, John, H. S., 7, 208.
Pratt, Martial (Marshall), Va. Mag., 1, 281; Va. Mag., 2, 151; Wash. Mss., 112, 87; Wash. Mss., 1311.
Pratt, Nathaniel, Va., Mag., 2, 49.
Prentis, John (maj.), H. S., 7, 231.
Presnal, James, H. S., 7, 210.
Preston, David, H. S., 7, 207.
Preston, Moses, H. S., 7, 206.
Preston, Philip, H. S., 7, 207.

Preston, William (cnty-lt., Fincastle), D. W., 430.
Preston, William (col.), J. C., May, 1776, 21.
Preston, William (maj.), H. S., 8, 127.
Preston, William (capt.) (Botetourt), Withers's Chron., 81.
Preston, William (capt.), Aug. Rec., 1, 212; H. B., 1752-58, 459, 477; H. S., 7, 189; V. C. M., 10; V. H. C., 4, 153; Withers's Chron., 81.
Preston, William, F. I. B. W., 1, 11.
Prewitt, Henry, H. S., 7, 223.
Price, Daniel, H. S., 7, 186.
Price, James, D. W., 396, 402.
Price, John, Va. Mag., 2, 40.
Price, Joseph, Va. Mag., 2, 47, 148.
Price, Joseph Shores, V. C. M., 39.
Price, Leonard (adj.), H. B., 1761-65, 57.
Price, Leonard (en.), Va. Mag., 1, 287.
Price, Rees (Reece), D. W., 412, 419.
Price, Richard, D. W., 402.
Price, Thomas, D. W., 396, 401; F. I. B. W., 2, 313; H. S., 7, 216; J. C., May, 1776, 33.
Prichard, Thomas, H. S., 7, 183.
Pricket (Pucket), Drury, D. W., 396.
Pricket, Jacob, H. S., 7, 215, 216.
Priest, David, D. W., 401.
Priest, John, H. B., 1758-61, 24.
Priest, Samuel, D. W., 401.
Priest, Thomas, H. B., 1766-69, 212, 214.
Priest, William, D. W., 401, 404.
Pright, John, D. W., 405.
Prince, —— (capt.), V. H. C., 4, 598, 605.
Prince, William, D. W., 419.
Pringle, Samuel (scout), H. B., 1766-69, 294.
Pruit, Thadeus, Va. Mag., 1, 386.
Prior (Pryor), John, D. W., 424.
Prior, Richard, H. S., 7, 204.
Prisnall, Daniel, H. S., 7, 201.
Pritchard, Isaac, J., 113.
Pritchard, Richard, H. S., 7, 210, 211; Va. Mag., 1, 283; Wash. Mss., 111, 13.
Pritchard, Thomas, J., 72, 199; Va. Mag., 2, 45.
Pritchet, Andrew, H. B., 1742-49, 237.
Pritchet, Thomas, Wash. Mss., 1460.
Pritnar, Rudolph, Wash. Mss., 111, 15.
Proctor (Procter), George, Va. Mag., 1, 378; Wash. Mss., 112, 88; Wash. Mss., 1483.

Props, Adam, H. S., 7, 180.
Props, Michael, H. S., 7, 180.
Provo, William, V. C. M., 55.
Pruett, Thodesis, Wash. Mss., 112, 83.
Prunk, Henry, H. S., 7, 206.
Pryar, Richard, H. S., 7, 196.
Pryor, Nicholas, H. S., 7, 203.
Pryor, William, H. S., 7, 203.
Puckett, Drury, F. I. B. W., 1, 129.
Puckett, Jeremiah, Aug. Rec., 1, 344.
Pullen, William, Va. Mag., 1, 281; Wash. Mss., 111, 13, 15.
Pullin (Pullen), Lofftus, Aug. Rec., 1, 212; F. I. B. W., 2, 564.
Pulling (Pullin), Robert, Va. Mag., 2, 48; Wash. Mss., 1478.
Purcell, Edward, Va. Mag., 1, 385; Wash. Mss., 112, 82, 83.1.
Purdue, Joseph, Va. Mag., 1, 389.
Purzins, William, H. S., 7, 195.
Putt, John, H. S., 7, 191, 196.
Puttect, James, H. S., 7, 208.
Puttect, William, H. S., 7, 208.
Pyburn, John, H. S., 7, 205.

Q.

Quarles, John (capt.), H. B., 1761-65, 274; H. S., 7, 209.
Quchan, Paul, Wash. Mss., 5, 4; Wash. Mss., 1543.
Quhan, Paul, Wash. Mss., 112, 116.
Quinn, Thomas, Va. Mag., 1, 378; Wash. Mss., 112, 88, 94.
Quisenberry (Quesenbury, Quisanbury), Humphrey, Va. Mag., 2, 42, 151; Wash. Mss., 112, 87; Wash. Mss., 1477.
Quisenberry (Quisanbury), Nicholas, Va. Mag., 2, 43; Wash. Mss., 1476.

R.

Raby, Moses, Va. Mag., 1, 383; Wash. Mss., 112, 86, 95.
Radford, Thomas, Wash. Mss., 112, 86.
Rafferty (Raffaty), Thomas, Wash. Mss., 112, 86, 95.
Ragsdale, John, H. S., 7, 223.
Ragsdale, Peter, H. S., 7, 206, 209.
Ragsdale, Richard, H. S., 7, 206, 226.
Ragsdale (Ragsdel), William, F. I. B. W., 2, 406; H. S., 7, 209; Va. Mag., 1, 379; Wash. Mss., 112, 88, 94.
Rainger (Raingers), Garret, Va. Mag., 1, 390; Va., Mag., 2, 49; Wash. Mss., 112, 85.1, 96.
Rains, Robert, D. W., 405.
Ralston, William, H. S., 7, 185.

Rameshall, John, Wash. Mss., 112, 87.
Ramsay (Ramsey), Augustine, F. I. B. W., 1, 235; V. C. M., 29.
Ramsay, James, H. S., 7, 180.
Ramsey, Bartholomew, H. S., 7, 203.
Ramsey, Charles, H. S., 8, 129.
Ramsey, Dennis, Wash. Mss., 1557.
Ramsey (Ramsay), John, Aug. Rec., 2, 49; H. B., 1761-65, 179, 185; H. S., 7, 212; Va. Mag., 1, 281; Wash. Mss., 111, 13; Wash. Mss., 112, 0.
Ramsey, Josiah, H. S., 7, 210.
Ramsey, Richard, H. S., 7, 212.
Ramson, George, Wash. Mss., 1460.
Randal (Randel), James, H. S., 7, 203; Wash. Mss., 112, 95.
Randolph, Henry, H. S., 7, 203.
Randolph, Peyton, Campbell's Hist. of Virginia, 486.
Randolph, William, H. S., 7, 212.
Randols, Francis, H. S., 7, 196.
Rankins, Alexander, Wash. Mss, 5, 4.
Ransdale, William, V. C. M., 97; Va. Mag., 7, 305.
Rap, Frederick, D. W., 400.
Ratan, John (scout), H. B., 1766-69, 294.
Ratchford, Hugh, Va. Mag., 1, 282, 283; Wash. Mss., 5, 2; Wash. Mss., 111, 13.
Ratcliff (Ratcliffe), James, F. I. B. W., 1, 153; Va. Mag., 2, 44.
Ratcliff, Silas, H. S., 7, 220.
Ratcliff, William, H. S., 7, 220.
Ratliff, James, F. I. B. W., 1, 113, 165; V. C. M., 19.
Ratliff, Matthew, D. W., 411.
Raun, Bat., Aug. Rec., 1, 478.
Rauthwell, Clebourn, F. I. B. W., 1, 176.
Ravenscroft, (Ravenscraft, Ravenscrop), Thomas, D. W., 421; H. S., 7, 212; Wash. Mss., 112, 115.
Rawlins, Anthony, H. S., 7, 206.
Rawlins, Peter, H. S., 7, 206.
Rawls, David, Va. Mag., 2, 42.
Rawls, James, Va. Mag., 2, 47.
Ray, John, H. B., 1761-65, 240; H. S., 7, 212; H. S., 8, 131; Wash. Mss., 1536.
Ray, Joseph (en.), Aug. Rec., 1, 530.
Ray, Joseph, Aug. Rec., 1, 209; F. I. B. W., 1, 265; H. S., 7, 206; H. S., 8, 129; V. C. M., 31.
Ray, Thomas, H. S., 7, 213, 218; Wash. Mss., 1555.
Ray, William, D. W., 411; H. S., 7, 201.

Rayburn, Robert, F. I. B. W., 2, 300.
Razor, Michael, D. W., 404.
Reaburn, Henry, Aug. Rec., 1, 73.
Reaburne, John, F. I. B. W., 2, 450;
   V. C. M., 46.
Read, Clement (cnty-lt.), V. H. C.,
   4, 156.
Read, Hankerson (Hankinson), H.
   B., 1766-69, 88; H. S., 7, 214.
Read, John, D. W., 409.
Read, William, J., 147.
Reade, Edward, Wash. Mss., 1460.
Reade, Thomas, H. S., 7, 206.
Reafner, Garrett, H. B., 1766-69, 294.
Reagh, Archibald, D. W., 400.
Reagh, John, D. W., 400.
Reah, William, H. S., 7, 196.
Reams, Frederick, H. S., 7, 201.
Reary, James, D. W., 405.
Reasoner, Michael, F. I. B. W., 2,
   328.
Reburn, Adam, H. S., 7, 187.
Reburn, John, D. W., 408; H. S., 7,
   187.
Redford, Richard, Wash. Mss., 1460.
Rediford, Benjamin, D. W., 404.
Redman (Redmain), Christopher, Va.
   Mag., 2, 145; Wash. Mss., 112,
   83.
Redmayne, Charles, Va. Mag., 1, 387.
Redmond, Christopher, Wash.
   Mss., 112, 82.2.
Reed, Alexander, D. W., 424; V. C.
   M., 89.
Reed, Eldad, H. S., 7, 191.
Reed, George, Aug. Rec., 1, 478.
Reed, Joseph, Wash. Mss., 1460.
Reed, William, H. S., 7, 195.
Reede, Edward, Wash. Mss., 1460.
Reely, Bernard, Wash. Mss., 112, 95.
Reese, Azaria, D. W., 421.
Reese, Henry, Va. Mag., 2, 45.
Reeves, John, Aug. Rec., 1, 478; F. I.
   B. W., 1, 277; V. C. M., 32.
Regan, John, H. S., 7, 216.
Regan, Michael, H. B., 1752-58, 374.
Regsbee, Larance, Wash. Mss., 112,
   82.
Reid, Andrew, D. W., 422.
Reid, Thomas, D. W., 411.
Reiger John, H. S., 7, 185.
Reiley, Barney, Wash. Mss., 112, 86.
Reiley, Michael, Va. Mag., 1, 281;
   Wash. Mss., 111, 13.
Reily, John, Wash. Mss., 112, 86, 95;
   Wash. Mss., 1460.
Reily, Nathan, Wash. Mss., 1460.
Reily, Peter, Wash. Mss., 1460.
Reity, Francis, H. S., 7, 199.
Remeshall (Remishal), John, Va.
   Mag., 2, 152; Wash. Mss., 112,
   115.

Rem (Reme), Daniel, H. S., 7, 183,
   185.
Remold, Benjamin, F. I. B. W., 1,
   163.
Rennick, Robert (lt.), H. S., 7, 199.
Rennold, Benjamin, V. C. M., 23.
Rentfroe, James, H. S., 7, 208.
Rentfroe, Joseph, H. S., 7, 207, 208.
Rentfroe, Stephen, H. S., 7, 208.
Reyley, John, F. I. B. W., 2, 473.
Reynold, John, Aug. Rec., 2, 505.
Reynolds, John, V. C. M., 14; Va.
   Mag., 2, 152; Wash. Mss., 112,
   87, 116.
Reynolds, Richard, F. I. B. W., 1,
   175; V. C. M., 129.
Reynolds, Thomas, Va. Mag., 2, 152;
   Wash. Mss., 112, 87.
Reynolds, William, F. I. B. W., 1,
   301.
Rheah, Archibald, H. S., 7, 196.
Rheah, Robert, H. S., 7, 196.
Rhoads, Thomas, Aug. Rec., 1, 333.
Rhodes, Clifton, H. S., 7, 222.
Rice, Edward, H. S., 7, 218.
Rice, George (capt.), Hist. Fred-
   erick, 89.
Rice, George, Aug. Rec., 2, 505; F. I.
   B. W., 2, 509; H. S., 7, 215.
Rice, James, H. S., 7, 202.
Rice, John, H. S., 7, 220.
Rice, Michael, F. I. B. W., 1, 175;
   Hist. Orange, 60.
Rice, Richard, Va. Mag., 2, 44.
Richards, Jacob, H. S., 7, 187.
Richards, James, V. C. M., 128.
Richards, John, H. S., 7, 187.
Richardson, Daniel, H. S., 7, 206,
   207.
Richardson, Ezekiel (drum. maj.),
   V. C. M., 128.
Richardson, Ezekiel, Va. Mag., 1,
   282; Va. Mag., 2, 43; Wash. Mss.,
   111, 13.
Richardson, George, J., 143.
Richardson, Holt (lt.), Aug. Rec., 1,
   321, 322.
Richardson, James, Va. Mag., 2, 49;
   Wash. Mss., 112, 87; Wash. Mss.,
   1470.
Richardson, John, H. S., 7, 205.
Richardson, Jonathan, H. S., 7, 205.
Richardson, Joseph, H. S., 7, 207.
Richardson, Joshua, H. S., 7, 205.
Richardson, Nathan, H. S., 7, 208.
Richardson, Thomas, Wash. Mss.,
   112, 95.
Richardson, Turner, F. I. B. W., 2,
   382; V. C. M., 41.
Richbell, Richard, H. B., 1752-58,
   273.

Rodgers, James, D. W., 400.
Rodgers, John, Va. Mag., 1, 281.
Rodgers, Thomas, D. W., 400.
Roe, Buddy, Wash. Mss., 1476.
Roe, James, F. I. B. W., 1, 3, 74;
V. C. M., 9; Va. Mag., 1, 378;
Wash. Mss., 112, 88.
Roe, John, Wash. Mss., 111, 13.
Rogers, Andrew, H. S., 7, 223.
Rogers, Benjamin, Va. Mag., 1, 382;
Wash. Mss., 112, 86, 89, 114.
Rogers, Chesly, D. W., 405.
Rogers (Rodgers), David, D. W., 421.
Rogers, Francis, Va. Mag., 1, 383;
Wash. Mss., 5, 8; Wash. Mss.,
111, 13; Wash. Mss., 112, 89, 95.
Rogers, George, H. S., 7, 195.
Rogers, James, D. W., 401, 403.
Rogers, John, Va. Mag., 1, 282.
Rogers, Jonathan, J., 69.
Rogers, Joseph, Wash. Mss., 112, 86.
Rogers, Peter (lt.), H. S., 8, 130, 131.
Rogers, Richard, L. to Wash., 1, 273.
Rogers, Thomas, D. W., 404.
Rogers, William, F. I. B. W., 1, 155;
Hist. Orange, 59; Va. Mag., 1,
385; Wash. Mss., 112, 82; Wash.
Mss., 1311.
Rolestone, Matthew, H. S., 7, 179.
Rolestone, William, H. S., 7, 179, 181,
188.
Rollens, Richard, D. W., 411.
Rollin, James, H. D., May, 1777, 44.
Rollin, Matthew, H. S., 7, 199.
Rollins, Mark, H. S., 7, 212.
Rollins, Vincent, V. C. M., 55.
Rolman (Roleman), Jacob, H. S., 7,
184, 188.
Rolston, Samuel, H. S., 7, 199.
Rose, William, H. S., 7, 211.
Rosebury, William, H. S., 8, 131.
Ross, Andrew, Va. Mag., 2, 148.
Ross, Edward, D. W., 411.
Ross, James, H. S., 7, 223.
Ross, Philip (lt.), F. I. B. W., 2, 398;
V. C. M., 42.
Ross, Philip, H. B., 1766-69, 88.
Ross, Robert, Aug. Rec., 1, 213; F. I.
B. W., 2, 520; V. C. M., 52.
Ross, Taff, J., 108.
Ross, Taverner, J., 109.
Ross, William, F. I. B. W., 1, 173;
H. S., 7, 188, 222; V. C. M., 128;
Va. Mag., 2, 143, 152; Wash.
Mss., 112, 87.
Rosser, David, H. S., 7, 204, 208.
Rosser, John, F. I. B. W., 2, 396; Va.
Mag., 2, 48; Wash. Mss., 1465.
Rounday (Roundy), David, Va. Mag.,
1, 386; Wash. Mss., 112, 83.

Rountree (Roundtree), William, Va.
Mag., 2, 43; Wash. Mss., 1472.
Rouse, John, F. I. B. W., 2, 358; V.
C. M., 38; Va. Mag., 2, 152.
Routhwell, Clabourn, V. C. M., 24.
Row, Benjamin, F. I. B. W., 2, 563.
Row, John, Wash. Mss., 112, 0.
Rowan, Charles, Wash. Mss., 5, 4.
Rowbottom (Robotom Robottom,
Roebottom), Matthew, F. I. B.
W., 2, 393; V. C. M., 41; Va. Mag.,
1, 388; Wash. Mss., 112, 85.1, 96,
116.
Rowe, James, Va. Mag., 1, 281; Wash.
Mss., 111, 13.
Rowe, John, Va. Mag., 1, 281.
Rowe, Thomas, Va. Mag., 2, 38.
Rowell, Jacob, Va. Mag., 2, 152;
Wash, Mss., 112, 87.
Rowell, James, Wash. Mss., 1542.
Rowland, Augustine, H. S., 7, 223.
Rowland, George, H. S., 7, 191.
Rowley, William (capt.), H. S., 7,
221.
Rowt, Andrew, Va. Mag., 1, 390.
Roy, James, Wash. Mss., 5.
Roy, Peter, F. I. B. W., 2, 361; V. C.
M., 39.
Royalty, Daniel, Va. Mag., 1, 381;
Wash. Mss., 112, 86.
Royley, Pharaoh, H. S., 7, 207.
Rucker, George, D. W., 405.
Rucker, Peter, H. S., 7, 214; Wash.
Mss., 1555.
Rucker, William, Wash. Mss., 1555.
Rudd, John, F. I. B. W., 2, 403.
Ruddall, Archibald (lt.), H. S., 7,
215.
Ruddle (Riddle), George, D. W., 412.
Rue, Abraham, D. W., 405.
Rue, Isaac, J., 218.
Rumley, Doctor, Wash. Mss., 1557.
Runkle, Jacob, H. S., 7, 186.
Runnals, Stephen, H. S., 7, 206.
Rupert, Frederick, Va. Mag., 1, 281;
Wash. Mss., 111, 13, 15.
Rush, Charles, H. S., 7, 185.
Rush, Jacob, F. I. B. W., 2, 357.
Rush, Michael, Aug. Rec., 1, 183.
Rushea, George, F. I. B. W., 2, 379;
V. C. M., 40.
Rusk, James, H. S., 7, 197.
Russel, James, F. I. B. W., 1, 145.
Russel, Samuel, H. S., 7, 212.
Russell, George, Wash. Mss., 1460.
Russell, John, V. C. M., 97; Va. Mag.,
7, 306.
Russell, William (lt. col.), Withers's
Chron., 66.
Russell, William (capt.), J. C., May,
1776, 28; V. C. M., 89.

Russell, William, F. I. B. W., 2, 453; H. S., 7, 226; V. C. M., 97; Va. Mag., 7, 306.
Rutherford (Rotherford), Adam, Va. Mag., 1, 389; Wash. Mss., 112, 85.1, 96, 100.
Rutherford, Ben., D. W., 400.
Rutherford, Robert (capt.), Adam Stephen Ps.; L. to Wash., 2, 317, 318; V. C. M., 38.
Rutledge, George, H. B., 1761-65, 325, 328.
Ryaltree, Daniel, Wash. Mss., 112, 95.
Ryan (Rian), Daniel, Wash. Mss., 112, 82.2, 83; Wash. Mss., 1465.
Ryan, Francis, Wash. Mss., 112, 114; Wash. Mss., 1485.
Ryan, James, F. I. B. W., 2, 444; Va. Mag., 1, 387; Wash. Mss., 112, 82.2, 83.
Ryler, James, Wash. Mss., 112, 94.
Ryley, Barnaby, Va. Mag., 1, 283; Wash. Mss., 111, 13.
Ryley, Barney, F. I. B. W., 2, 493; V. C. M., 50.
Ryley, John, Va. Mag., 2, 143.
Ryley, Pharaoh, H. S., 7, 205.
Ryon, James, Va. Mag., 2, 145.
Ryon, Joseph, H. S., 7, 205.

S.

Sabbey (Saffey) Josea, Wash. Mss., 5, 4.
Saddler, William, Wash. Mss., 1557.
Sage, Henry, H. S., 7, 226.
Saint Laurence, Patrick, D. W., 412.
Sale, John, Va., Mag., 2, 143; Wash. Mss., 112, 90.
Salady, John Malchi, J., 154.
Sallard, ——, V. H. C., 4, 400.
Sallard, John (lt.), Aug. Rec., 1, 487.
Sallard, John, F. I. B. W., 1, 236.
Salley, John, H. S., 7, 198.
Salling, George Adam, H. S., 7, 203.
Sallis, Nicholas, Aug. Rec., 1, 211; F. I. B. W., 1, 96; V. C. M., 17.
Sallord, John (lt.), Aug. Rec., 3, 409.
Salmon, Archibald, Va. Mag., 2, 147.
Salmon, George, Wash. Mss., 112, 82; Wash. Mss., 1311.
Salmon, John, H. S., 8, 131.
Sample, Moses, H. S., 7, 186.
Samples, Samuel, D. W., 412.
Sampson, John, F. I. B. W., 1, 163.
Samuel (Samuell), James, Aug. Rec., 2, 49; F. I. B. W., 1, 180; V. C. M., 25; Va. Mag., 1, 282; Wash. Mss., 111, 13.
Sanday, Garrard, Wash. Mss., 1432.
Sanders, George, H. B., 1752-58, 374; Va. Mag., 2, 153.

Sanders, James, D. W., 421; V. C. M., 88.
Sanders, John, F. I. B. W., 1, 174.
Sanders, Robert, F. I. B. W., 1, 171; H. S., 7, 223.
Sanders, Thomas, F. I. B. W., 1, 283; V. C. M., 32.
Sandsbury, Gabriel, Wash. Mss., 1460.
Sandy (Sanday), William, Va. Mag., 2, 49; Wash. Mss., 1432.
Sanford, William, Wash. Mss., 1557.
Sansome, Richard, F. I. B. W., 1, 143; V. C. M., 21.
Satterwhite, James, F. I. B. W., 1, 151.
Satterwhite, William, H. S., 7, 220.
Saulsbury, William, D. W., 424.
Saunders, Francis, Va. Mag., 2,. 40; Wash. Mss., 1467.
Saunders, John, Va. Mag., 2, 40, 41.
Saunders, Robert, V. C. M., 129.
Saunders, Samuel, Va. Mag., 2, 46.
Saunders, Thomas (drummer), F. I. B. W., 1, 12.
Saunders, Thomas, H. S., 7, 218.
Savage, John (capt.), Aug. Rec., 2, 50.
Savage, John, Aug. Rec., 2, 49, 169; D. W., 408; F. I. B. W., 1, 55; V. H. C., 3, 115; Va. Mag., 1, 279.
Savage, Patrick, H. S., 7, 196.
Savage, Samuel, D. W., 407.
Sawyer (Sawer), Joseph, Va. Mag., 1, 387; Va. Mag., 2, 145; Wash. Mss., 112, 84.
Sawyers, James, Aug. Rec., 1, 210.
Sayer, Alexander, F. I. B. W., 2, 379; V. C. M., 40.
Sayer, David, H. S., 7, 196.
Sayer alias Garrett, Joseph, Wash. Mss., 1478.
Sayers, Alexander (capt) (Augusta), H. S., 7, 179.
Sayers, Alexander (capt.), Aug. Rec., 1, 329.
Sayers, Alexander, H. B., 1758-61, 149, 204; H. S., 8, 129.
Sayers, David, F. I. B. W., 2, 426; H. S., 7, 197.
Sayers, John, D. W., 412.
Sayers, Sampson, H. S., 7, 191.
Sayers, William (en.), F. I. B. W., 2, 462; V. C. M., 48.
Scails, William, D. W., 405.
Scarbara, James, D. W., 409.
Scarlock, Hemcrest, H. S., 7, 219.
Scattergood, William, Va. Mag., 2, 49.
Scholar, Aleck, H. B., 1758-61, 86.
Scoggins, Micaiah, H. S., 7, 225.
Scople (Scoppel), Willis, Va. Mag., 1, 386; Wash. Mss., 112, 82.2.

Scot, John, Wash. Mss., 112, 87.
Scot, William, Wash. Mss., 1489.
Scotborn, William (capt.), Aug. Rec., 1, 184.
Scott, Alexander, J., 105.
Scott, Archelaus, D. W., 396.
Scott, Archibald, D. W., 402.
Seott, Charles (en.), Aug. Rec., 2, 170.
Scott, Charles, F. I. B. W., 1, 243; Va. Mag., 1, 378; Wash. Mss., 112, 88, 114.
Scott, Clemmit, Wash. Mss., 5, 4.
Scott, Daniel (capt.), D. W., 425.
Scott, David, H. S., 7, 181.
Scott, Francis, F. I. B. W., 1, 111.
Scott, James (drummer), H. S., 7, 211.
Scott, James, D. W., 396, 402; Wash. Mss., 1479.
Scott, John, Va. Mag., 2, 48, 150.
Scott, Joseph, Va. Mag., 1, 282; Wash. Mss., 111, 13.
Scott, Robert (capt. Augusta m.), Wash. Mss., 5, 15.1.
Scott, Robert (capt.), L. to Wash., 1, 305.
Scott, Robert, H. S., 7, 213.
Scott, Roger, Wash. Mss., 112, 115.
Scott, Thomas, F. I. B. W., 1, 100; J., 158; V. C. M., 18; Va. Mag., 1, 282; Wash. Mss., 111, 13.
Scott, William, D. W., 407; F. I. B. W., 2, 474.
Scruggs, Gross, H. S., 7, 205.
Scrugs, Henry, H. S., 8, 131.
Scully, Christopher, Va. Mag., 2, 148.
Scully (Sculley), Michael, Va. Mag., 1, 282, 382; Wash. Mss., 112, 0, 86.
Scutt, William, H. B., 1752-58, 374.
Seal, Thomas, L. to Wash., 1, 300; Va. Mag., 2, 47.
Seales, William, H. S., 7, 220.
Sealey, Jeremiah, Aug. Rec., 1, 73.
Seaman, Jeremiah, F. I. B. W., 2, 354.
Seaman, Jonathan, V. C. M., 38.
Seaman, Robert, Va. Mag., 2, 149.
Seaton, George, Va., Mag., 2, 148.
Sedbery, John, D. W., 406.
See, James, Aug. Rec., 1, 73.
Seed, Edward, Wash. Mss., 1460.
Seed, Francis, D. W., 409.
Seirl, Thomas, H. S., 7, 196.
Selby, James, D. W., 405.
Selden, Richard (maj.), Wash. Mss., 1470.
Self, Francis, F. I. B. W., 1, 185; Va. Mag., 1, 282; Wash. Mss., 5, 8; Wash. Mss., 112, 0.
Self, Jeremiah, F. I. B. W., 1, 141; Wash. Mss., 112, 90, 95.

Sellars, ——, Wash. Mss., 112, 0.
Seller, John, H. S., 7, 185.
Sellers, Thomas, Va. Mag., 1, 282; Wash. Mss., 5, 2; Wash. Mss., 111, 13.
Selser, Henry, H. S., 7, 215.
Semple, Samuel, H. S., 7, 179.
Serle, John, Wash. Mss., 112, 95.
Sevier, Valentine, Hist. Rockingham, 63.
Seward, William, Jr. (capt.), H. S., 7, 230.
Sexton, Samuel, H. S., 7, 212.
Sexton, Thomas, H. S., 7, 206.
Shackleford (Shackelford), Henry, F. I. B. W., 2, 573; Hist. Orange, 60; V. C. M., 56.
Shaddin, Matthew, H. S., 7, 199.
Shadow, Ludwick, Aug. Rec., 1, 213; F. I. B. W., 2, 519; V. C. M., 52.
Shampe, Mathias, Wash. Mss., 5, 8; Wash. Mss., 111, 13.
Shampe, Matthew, Va. Mag., 1, 282.
Shanklin, Edward, H. S., 7, 181.
Shanklin, John, H. S., 7, 180, 188.
Shanklin, Richard, H. S., 7, 187.
Shannon (Shanon, Shennon), William, H. S., 7, 186, 188; Va. Mag., 2, 42.
Sharp, Abraham, D. W., 409.
Sharp, Edward, D. W., 403.
Sharp, Jacob, F. I. B. W., 1, 268; V. C. M., 31.
Sharp, John, D. W., 404.
Sharp, Thomas, Wash. Mss., 112, 0.
Shaver, Paul, H. S., 7, 184.
Shaw, Abram, Aug., Rec., 1, 478; Va. Mag., 2, 150; Wash. Mss., 112, 87.
Shaw (Span), Henry, D. W., 412.
Shaw, James, F. I. B. W., 2, 475.
Shaw, Jarvis, Wash. Mss., 1460.
Shaw, Samuel, Aug. Rec., 1, 478.
Shaw, William, H. B., 1758-61, 66, 68; H. B., 1761-65, 179, 185; H. S., 7, 184, 187; L. to Wash., 1, 299.
Sheddin, Matthew, H. S., 7, 199.
Sheffleit, Thomas, Wash. Mss., 112, 86.
Sheilds, George, Wash. Mss., 112, 88.
Shelby, Evan (capt.), D. W., 412; J. C., May, 1776, 28.
Shelby, Isaac, V. C. M., 89.
Shelby, James, D. W., 412.
Shelby, William (capt.), D. W., 424; V. C. M., 89.
Shell, Arnold, D. W., 399.
Shelp, John, D. W., 421; V. C. M., 88.
Shelton, Ralph, H. S., 7, 201.
Shelton, Thomas, Wash. Mss., 1460.
Shepard, Jacob, H. S., 8, 131.
Sheperson, William, Va. Mag., 2, 152.

Shepherd, William, H. B., 1773-76, 192, 205; J., 186.
Shepherdson, William, Wash. Mss., 112, 87.
Shepperson, John, F. I. B. W., 1, 262; V. C. M., 31.
Shepperson, William, F. I. B. W., 2, 380; V. C. M., 40; Wash. Mss., 112, 115.
Sherington, Robert, V. C. M., 55.
Sherly, Jervice, F. I. B. W., 2, 418; V. C. M., 44.
Sherly, Walter, F. I. B. W., 2, 357.
Sherman, John, Va. Mag., 2, 37.
Sherrill, Joshua, H. S., 7, 213.
Sherrin, William, H. B., 1758-61, 38.
Sherrod, Henry Francis, Va. Mag., 2, 39.
Sherwin, Samuel, L. to Wash., 1, 273.
Shever, Paul, H. S., 7, 181.
Shidmore, James, H. S., 7, 188.
Shidmore, John, H. S., 7, 188.
Shidmore, Joseph, H. S., 7, 181.
Shield, Robert (capt.), H. S., 7, 231.
Shields, George, Va. Mag., 1, 378.
Shields, John, Aug. Rec., 1, 213; F. I. B. W., 1, 40; H. S., 7, 181; V. C. M., 13.
Shields, William, Aug. Rec., 1, 213; F. I. B. W., 1, 41.
Shifflet, Thomas, Va. Mag., 1, 381; Wash. Mss., 112, 95.
Shill, John, H. S., 7, 180.
Shillinger, George, H. S., 7, 186.
Shingleton, John, H. S., 7, 213.
Shipley, Edward, H. S., 7, 224.
Shipley, Robert, H. S., 7, 206.
Shipley, Robert, Jr., H. S., 7, 206.
Shipman, Isaiah, H. S., 7, 184.
Shipman, Josiah, H. S., 7, 181.
Shirley, James, F. I. B. W., 2, 356.
Shirley, Jarvis, H. S., 7, 216.
Shirley, Walter, H. S., 7, 215.
Shoatt, Emanuel, D. W., 412.
Shoehan, Daniel, Jr., H. B., 1766-69, 294.
Shoemaker, Daniel, H. B., 1752-58, 374.
Shoemaker, George, H. S., 7, 218.
Shoemaker, Simon, H. B., 1752-58, 374; H. S., 7, 218.
Shoemaker, William, H. S., 7, 203.
Shore, John, H. S., 7, 218.
Short, Thomas, Wash. Mss., 112, 96.
Short, William, Va. Mag., 1, 386; Wash. Mss., 112, 84.
Shortridge, George, H. B., 1752-58, 375.
Shortridge, William, H. S., 7, 213.
Shover, Philip, J., 169.
Shumake, Joshua, H. B., 1758-61, 24.

Siglar, Christian, Wash. Mss., 1555.
Sigrif, Hugh, Wash. Mss., 112, 88.
Sillivant, John, H. S., 7, 220.
Simkins, Daniel, D. W., 406.
Simkins, James, D. W., 406.
Simmerman, George, D. W., 411.
Simmons, Charles, H. S., 7, 208.
Simmons (Simmon, Simonds), Dempsey, Va. Mag., 1, 282; Wash. Mss., 5, 8; Wash. Mss., 111, 13, 15.
Simmons (Simmonds, Simonds), Joel, Va. Mag., 1, 379; Wash. Mss., 112, 88, 94.
Simmons (Simons), John, Va. Mag., 2, 37; Wash. Mss., 112, 88.
Simmons (Simonds), Thomas, Adam Stephen Ps.; Wash. Mss., 112, 87, 90, 115.
Simmons (Simon, Simonds, Simons), William, H. S., 7, 205, 206, 219; Wash. Mss., 5, 8; Wash. Mss., 111, 13, 15; Wash. Mss., 112, 95; Wash. Mss., 1472.
Simms, William, Wash. Mss., 112, 90.
Simpson, Benjamin, H. S., 7, 212.
Simpson, Daniel, F. I. B. W., 1, 149; V. C. M., 128.
Simpson, Gilbert, H. B., 1752-58, 374; Wash. Mss., 1460.
Simpson, Gilbert, Jr., H. B., 1752-58, 374, 375.
Simpson, James, H. S., 7, 191.
Simpson, John, D. W., 406.
Simpson, Samuel, V. C. M., 97; Va. Mag., 7, 305.
Simpson, Solomon, F. I. B. W., 2, 503; Va. Mag., 1, 387; Wash. Mss., 112, 82.
Simpson, Thomas, Va. Mag., 1, 388; Wash. Mss., 112, 85.1, 96, 116.
Simpson, William, D. W., 406; F. I. B. W., 2, 504; Va. Mag., 1, 382; Wash. Mss., 112, 86.
Sims, Drury, H. S., 7, 212.
Sims, George, F. I. B. W., 1, 119; V. C. M., 19.
Sims, William, Hist. Orange, 60.
Simson, James D. W., 407.
Sinclair (Cinclair, Sinclare), John, H. B., 1752-58, 374; Va. Mag., 1, 378; Wash. Mss., 112, 88.
Sinclair, Peter, H. S., 7, 212.
Singer, William, Wash. Mss., 1534.
Sinkfield, Robert, Aug. Rec., 1, 478.
Sinkes (Sinks), Jacob (Scout), H. B., 1766-69, 294; Va. Mag., 2, 152.
Sitolentown, Andrew, H. S., 7, 198.
Sitton, Christopher, H. S., 7, 205.
Siver, Francis, H. S., 7, 205.
Sivers, Nicholas, H. S., 7, 184, 185.
Skean, Jonathan, J. C., May, 1776, 57.

Skelton, John, Wash. Mss., 5, 4.
Skelton, William, H. S., 7, 224.
Skidmore, I. (capt.), V. C. M., 89.
Skidmore, John, V. C. M., 88.
Skillem, William (en.), V. C. M., 52.
Skillem, William, F. I. B. W., 2, 520.
Skinner, Dudley, Va. Mag., 1, 282; Wash. Mss., 111, 13.
Skully, Michael, Wash. Mss., 112, 95.
Slaughter, George (capt.), J. C., May, 1776, 20.
Slaughter, George, D. W., 424; H. B., 1766-69, 153, 241.
Slaughter, Robert (col.), H. S., 7, 214.
Slaughter, Thomas, H. S., 7, 213; Va. Mag., 1, 282; Wash. Mss., 111, 13.
Slaughter, William (lt.), H. S., 7, 213, 214.
Slayton, Daniel, H. S., 7, 224.
Slinker, Charles, H. S., 8, 129.
Slodser, Lodowick, H. S., 7, 199.
Small, Matthew, F. I. B. W., 2, 531.
Smedley (Smedly), John, Wash. Mss., 1432.
Smith, Abraham (maj.), H. B., 1761-65, 324, 328; H. B., 1766-69, 87.
Smith, Abraham (capt.) (Augusta), H. S., 7, 179.
Smith, Abraham, H. S., 7, 206.
Smith, Adam, H. B., 1758-61, 26.
Smith, Benjamin, Va. Mag., 1, 282; Wash. Mss., 5, 2; Wash. Mss., 111, 13.
Smith, Bruten, D. W., 405.
Smith, Charles (lt.), H. B., 1761-65, 179, 185.
Smith, Charles, Aug. Rec., 1, 212; F. I. B. W., 2, 530; H. S., 7, 201; Va. Mag., 1, 282; Va. Mag., 2, 44; Wash. Mss., 1311.
Smith, Christian, Wash. Mss., 1472.
Smith, Conrad, D. W., 424.
Smith, Daniel (capt.), D. W., 396, 401; V. C. M., 89.
Smith, Daniel (lt.), H. S., 7, 187; J. C., May, 1776, 63.
Smith, David, H. B., 1752-58, 374; H. S., 7, 181, 188.
Smith, Edward, D. W., 410.
Smith, Ericus, D. W., 401.
Smith, Francis (lt.), Aug. Rec., 1, 344; F. I. B. W., 2, 456.
Smith, Francis, H. S., 7, 201; Va. Mag., 2, 146.
Smith, Gasper, H. S., 7, 183, 185.
Smith, George, H. S., 7, 206, 209.
Smith, Henry, H. S., 7, 180, 184.
Smith, James, H. B., 1742-49, 304; Va. Mag., 1, 282: Va. Mag, 2, 41.
Smith, Joel, H. S., 7, 212.

Smith, John (col.), Aug. Rec., 1, 341, 490.
Smith, John (maj.), H. S., 7, 191; V. H. C., 4, 153.
Smith, John (capt.), Aug. Rec., 2, 366; F. I. B. W., 1, 247; H. B., 1752-58, 499, 500, 505; H. B., 1758-61, 20, 26; Withers's Chron., 81.
Smith, John (Prince Edward), Va. Mag., 21, 89.
Smith, John, Va. Mag., 1, 282, 383; Wash. Mss., 112, 86, 89, 95.
Smith, Jonathan (lt) (Prince Edward), Va. Mag., 21, 89.
Smith, Jonathan, F. I. B, W., 1, 299.
Smith, Joseph, V. C., M., 97; Va. Mag., 7, 305.
Smith, Joshua, H. S., 8, 131.
Smith, Josiah (maj.), Wash. Mss., 1479.
Smith, Laurence, H. S., 7, 204.
Smith, Levi, Va. Mag., 1, 383; Wash. Mss., 112, 86, 89, 95.
Smith, Matthew, Wash. Mss., 112, 90.
Smith, Mecagh, D. W., 405.
Smith, Moses, D. W., 405.
Smith, Nicholas, F. I. B. W., 1, 12.
Smith, Patrick, Va. Mag., 1, 283; Wash. Mss., 111, 13; Wash. Mss., 1465.
Smith, Richard, Va. Mag., 1, 282; Va. Mag., 2, 152; Wash. Mss., 112, 87.
Smith, Simon, Wash. Mss., 112, 90, 95.
Smith, Stephen, F. I. B. W., 1, 229.
Smith, Thomas, Aug. Rec., 1, 212; H. S., 7, 197, 224; Va. Mag., 1, 380, 387; Va. Mag., 2, 145; Va. Mag., 7, 305; Wash. Mss., 112, 88, 94.
Smith, William, D. W., 405; Hist. Orange, 60; Va. Mag., 1, 386; Va. Mag., 2, 37; Wash. Mss., 112, 86, 89, 89.
Smith, William, Jr., Va., Mag., 7, 306.
Smith, Zachariah, Va. Mag., 1, 282.
Smither, William, F. I. B. W., 1, 167, 204.
Smithers, Gabriel, D. W., 409.
Smolenski, Christopher, Wash. Mss., 112, 95.
Smuling, Christopher, Wash. Mss., 112, 90.
Snipes, Thomas, Va. Mag., 2, 148.
Snodgrass, James, H. S., 7, 199.
Snodgrass, John, H. S., 7, 196.
Snow, Henry, H. S., 7, 225.
Snow, John, H. S., 7, 206.
Soanes, Charles, Va. Mag., 1, 283; Wash. Mss., 111, 13.
Socketts, Philip, Va Mag., 2, 45.

Stephenson, Hugh (capt.), D. W., 421.

Stephenson, Hugh, F. I. B. W., 2, 500; H. S., 7, 216.

Stephenson, James, H. S., 7, 183, 187.

Stephenson, John, F. I. B. W., 2, 497; H. S., 7, 181, 187, 215, 216; Wash. Mss., 1460.

Stephenson, Matthew, J., 160.

Stephenson, Nathaniel, Va. Mag., 2, 44.

Stephenson, Robert, D. W., 400.

Stephenson, Thomas, H. S., 7, 187.

Stephenson, William, H. S., 7, 216.

Steuart, Alexander, H. S., 7, 191.

Steuart, Andrew, Wash. Mss., 1557.

Steuart, David (col.), H. S., 7, 195.

Steuart, John, Wash. Mss., 5, 8.

Steuart, Robert, H. S., 7, 197.

Stevens, Joseph, F. I. B. W., 1, 277.

Stevenson, Adam, H. S., 7, 187.

Stevenson, Hugh, H. B., 1766-69, 88.

Stevenson, James, H. S., 7, 187, 188, 195, 197.

Stevenson, John, Aug. Rec., 2, 366; H. S., 7, 179, 187, 188.

Stevenson, Nathaniel, Wash. Mss., 1477.

Stevenson, Robert, H. S., 7, 197.

Steward, John, D. W., 424; H. D., Oct., 1777, 53, 124.

Stewart, Alexander, F. I. B. W., 2, 586; J. C., May, 1776, 14; Va. Mag., 1, 282, 388; Wash. Mss., 111, 13; Wash. Mss., 112, 0, 116.

Stewart, Asael, Va. Mag., 2, 46.

Stewart, David (cnty-lt. & comm.), V. H. C., 4, 100.

Stewart, David (col.), L. to Wash., 1, 305.

Stewart, David, F. I. B. W., 1, 218.

Stewart, James, H. S., 7, 195; H. S., 8, 129.

Stewart, John (capt.), V. C. M., 89.

Stewart, John, D. W., 412; H. B., 1752-58, 371; Va. Mag., 1, 282; Wash. Mss., 111, 13; Wash. Mss., 112, 0.

Stewart, Peter, Wash. Mss., 1432.

Stewart, Robert (eapt.), Wash. Mss., 5.

Stewart, Robert, H. S., 7, 216; Va. Mag., 1, 282, 385; Wash. Mss., 111, 13; Wash. Mss., 112, 82.2.

Stewart, Walter (capt.), H. B., 1758-61, 101, 107.

Stewart, Walter (lt.), V. H. C., 3, 320.

Stewart, Walter (adj.), H. D., 1776, 12, 14.

Stewart, Walter, D. W., 422.

Stewart, William, D. W., 411; F. I. B. W., 2, 421.

Stiff, Abraham, H. S., 7, 218.

Still, John, H. S., 7, 184.

Stills, Anthony, Wash. Mss., 112, 85.1.

Stilt, John, H. S., 7, 185.

Stilts (Stillts), Anthony, Va. Mag., 1, 390; Va. Mag., 2, 41; Wash. Mss., 112, 96, 100.

Stinnett, Benjamin, H. S., 7, 203.

Stinnett, Benjamin, Jr., H. S., 7, 203.

Stobo, Robert (capt.), H. B., 1758-61, 150; V. H. C., 3, 113.

Stobo, Robert, Va. Mag., 1, 279.

Stockstill, William, Va. Mag., 2, 45.

Stockton, Samuel, H. S., 7, 203.

Stockton, William, H. S., 7, 203.

Stockwell, William, J., 144.

Stoder, Christopher, H. S., 7, 199.

Stokes, Henry, H. S., 7, 224.

Stokes, William (lt.), H. S., 7, 224.

Stone, Hugh, Va. Mag., 1, 282; Wash. Mss., 111, 13; Wash. Mss., 112, 0.

Stone, William, H. S., 7, 209.

Stonsafer, Henry, H. S., 7, 213.

Story, James, H. S., 7, 214; Wash. Mss., 1555.

Stoten, Timothy, H. S., 7, 191.

Stoxdale, William, L. to Wash., 2, 163.

Stradler, Stephen, H. S., 7, 215.

Strange, Alexander, H. S., 7, 223.

Stribling, Samuel, Va. Mag., 2, 147.

Strong, Sherwood, V. C. M., 52.

Strother, Anthony, H. S., 7, 213.

Strother, Francis, H. S., 7, 213.

Strother, French, H. S., 7, 214; Wash. Mss., 1555.

Stroud, William, Va. Mag., 1, 283; Wash. Mss., 111, 15.

Stuart, Alexander, Wash. Mss., 112, 85.1, 96.

Stuart, Archibald, Aug. Rec., 1, 72.

Stuart, David (col., Augusta m.), Wash. Mss., 5, 15.1.

Stuart, David, Aug. Rec., 1, 518.

Stuart, James, D. W., 408; H. S., 7, 198; Wash. Mss., 1557.

Stuart, John (capt.), D. W., 410.

Stuart, John, D. W., 419; H. S., 7, 198.

Stuart, Richard, J., 153.

Stuart, Robert, Aug. Rec., 1, 215.

Stuart, William, Aug. Rec., 1, 213.

Stubblefield, George, F. I. B. W., 1, 65a; V. C. M., 15.

Stubbs, Butler (lt.), F. I. B. W., 1, 20; V. C. M., 11.

Stubbs, Samuel, H. S., 7, 215.

Stull, Martin, D. W., 421; V. C. M., 88.
Sturd, James, H. S., 7, 220.
Sturd, John, H. S., 7, 220.
Sucker, William, Wash. Mss., 1460.
Sucrainer, William, Wash. Mss., 112, 89.
Sulivan, Samuel, D. W., 410.
Sullivan, Cornelius, H. S., 7, 188.
Sullivan, Daniel, Va. Mag., 1, 388.
Sullivan (Sullivann), Dennis, Wash. Mss., 112, 85.1, 96, 116.
Sullivan, James, D. W., 421.
Sullivant, Cornelius, H. S., 7, 181.
Sully, Michael, Aug. Rec., 2, 49.
Sultif, John, Wash. Mss., 112, 87.
Sumer, William, Wash. Mss., 112, 90.
Summer, Jethro (lt.), H. B., 1761-65, 268.
Summers, Francis, H. S., 7, 217.
Summers, John, F. I. B. W., 1, 242.
Summers, William, Va. Mag., 2, 44; Wash. Mss., 112, 95.
Sumner, Jethro (lt.), L. to Wash, 1, 298.
Sumter, Thomas, Aug. Rec., 1, 331.
Supple (Suple, Suppell), Maurice (Morris), Va. Mag., 1, 388; Wash. Mss., 112, 85.1, 96, 100, 116.
Suter, Charles, F. I. B. W., 2, 370.
Suthard, Stephen, H. S., 7, 215, 216.
Sutherland, Alexander, H. S., 7, 197.
Satliff, John, Va. Mag., 2, 152.
Suttle, Isaac, H. B., 1758-61, 24.
Sutton, Edward, F. I. B. W., 1, 133; V. C. M., 21, 128.
Swain, William, Va. Mag., 2, 148.
Swallow, William, Va. Mag., 1, 282; Wash. Mss., 111, 13.
Swearengen, Thomas, F. I. B. W., 2, 395.
Sweene, William, H. B., 1761-65, 118, 135.
Sweeney, Terrence, Aug. Rec., 1, 478.
Sweeny (Sweeney, Sweny), Aaron, Va. Mag., 1, 379; Wash. Mss., 112, 88, 114.
Sweet, Benjamin, H. S., 7, 216.
Sweet, Timothy, Adam, Stephen Ps.
Swimmer, John Lee, Wash. Mss., 111, 15.
Swinburn (Swinbourn), John, Va. Mag., 1, 383; Wash. Mss., 5, 4; Wash. Mss., 112, 86, 89, 95.
Swiney, George, Va. Mag., 1, 283; Wash. Mss., 111, 13.
Swiney, Terrence, Va., Mag., 1, 282, 383; Wash. Mss., 112, 89, 95.
Swoop, John, D. W., 408.
Syme, John, V. C. M., 107.

Symmons, William, Va. Mag., 1, 282.

T.

Taite, William (maj.), H. S., 7, 228.
Talbot, Charles (lt.), H. S., 7, 206.
Talbot, Charles, H. S., 7, 205.
Talbot, James, H. S., 7, 206.
Talbot, John, H. S., 7, 204, 206, 220.
Talbot, Matthew (col.), L. to Wash., 2, 312.
Talbot, Matthew (capt.), H. S, 7, 205.
Talbot Matthew, H. S., 7, 206, 207.
Talbot, William, H. B., 1761-65, 68, 71; Va. Mag., 2, 46.
Talbot, Haly, F. I. B. W., 2, 405.
Talbott, Matthew (capt., Bedford m.), V. H. C., 4, 109.
Talley, Henry, Jr., H. S., 7, 226.
Tanner, Branch (lt.), H. S., 7, 201; V. H. C., 4, 157.
Tapman, Joseph, Va. Mag., 1, 383; Wash. Mss., 112, 86.
Tapman, Joshua, Wash. Mss., 112, 95.
Tarress, William, Va. Mag., 2, 43.
Tate, David, Va. Mag., 1, 382; Wash. Mss., 112, 86, 89, 95.
Tate, Magnus (en.), H. S., 7, 216.
Tate, Nathan, H. S., 7, 206, 209.
Tate, Samuel, Va. Mag., 2, 153.
Tate, T. (lt.), D. W., 424.
Tate, William, D. W., 424; H. S., 7, 206, 209.
Tate, Zenus, H. S., 7, 222.
Tatham, John, F. I. B. W., 2, 525.
Tatum, Edward, H. S., 7, 212.
Tatum, Nathaniel, H. S., 7, 211.
Taucett, Joseph, H. S., 7, 216.
Tawnahall, Mindan, J., 104.
Tayler, Henry, Wash. Mss., 1460.
Tayler, Christian, Va. Mag., 1, 282; Wash. Mss., 5, 2; Wash. Mss., 111, 13.
Taylor, Daniel, D. W., 410.
Taylor (Tayler), George, Va. Mag., 1, 282; Wash. Mss., 5, 8; Wash. Mss., 111, 13.
Taylor, George, Jr., F. I. B. W., 1, 58.
Taylor, Isaac, D. W., 408.
Taylor, James, F. I. B. W., 1, 254; F. I. B. W., 2, 405; H. S., 7, 225; J., 106.
Taylor, Jeremiah, Va. Mag., 1, 385; Wash. Mss., 112, 82.
Taylor, Jerry, Va. Mag., 2, 41.
Taylor, John, F. I. B. W., 2, 449; H. S., 7, 216; Va. Mag., 2, 144.
Taylor, Joseph, H. B., 1758-61, 24; V. C. M., 97; Va. Mag., 7, 305.

Taylor, Law, V. C. M., 97; Va. Mag., 7, 305.
Taylor, Peter, V. C. M., 97; Va. Mag., 7, 306.
Taylor, Richard, H. S., 7, 205.
Taylor, Samuel, F. I. B. W., 2, 302; V. C. M., 35.
Taylor, Sieltor, D. W., 407.
Taylor, William, D. W., 406; H. S., 7, 196.
Taylor, Zachariah, Wash. Mss., 112, 87.
Teager, John, Wash. Mss., 112, 86, 95.
Teasy, William, D. W., 407.
Tebbs, William (capt.), H. S., 7, 229.
Tedman, Thomas, Va. Mag., 1, 282; Wash. Mss., 111, 13.
Tegan, John, Va. Mag., 1, 383.
Tegar, John, Wash. Mss., 112, 89.
Teibolt, Michael, H. S., 8, 127.
Tell, Robert, Va. Mag., 2, 40.
Temple, Benjamin, F. I. B. W., 1, 22, 245.
Tencher, William, H. S., 7, 195.
Tendall, Nehemiah, Wash. Mss., 111, 13.
Tenny, William, F. I. B. W., 2, 454.
Tent, Joseph, Va. Mag., 1, 48.
Terngate, Thomas, Wash. Mss., 1476.
Terrell, John, J., 20.
Terrence (Torrence), Andrew, D. W., 412.
Terrent, Henry, Wash. Mss., 112, 116.
Terry, Joseph (capt.), H. B., 1770-72, 50.
Terry, Joseph, F. I. B. W., 2, 453.
Terry, Joseph, Jr., H. B., 1761-65, 211, 221.
Terry, Nathaniel (capt.), H. B., 1766-69, 213.
Terry, Nathaniel, H. S., 7, 220.
Thatcher, Stephen, H. S., 8, 132.
Thirman, Thomas, H. S., 7, 210.
Thomas, Abraham, J., 102.
Thomas, Cornelius (lt.), H. S., 7, 203.
Thomas, Edward, D. W., 411.
Thomas, Francis, Va. Mag., 2, 43; Wash. Mss., 1536.
Thomas, George, H. S., 7, 207.
Thomas, Isaac, H. S., 7, 216.
Thomas, James, H. S., 7, 217; Va. Mag., 1, 282, 388; Wash. Mss., 111, 13; Wash. Mss., 112, 85.1, 96, 114, 116.
Thomas, James Bowman, Wash. Mss., 1490.
Thomas, John, H. B., 1758-61, 24; H. B., 1766-69, 212, 241, 257; H. S., 7, 205, 222; Va. Mag., 1, 283; Va. Mag., 2, 39; Wash. Mss., 5, 2; Wash. Mss., 111, 13.

Thomas, Michael, H. B., 1758-61, 26.
Thomas, Robert, H. S., 7, 222.
Thomas, Samuel, Aug. Rec., 2, 506; F. I. B. W., 2, 392; V. C. M., 41; Va. Mag., 2, 148.
Thomas, William, Va. Mag., 2, 143.
Thompson (Thomson), Abraham, H. S., 7, 199, 209; H. S., 8, 129.
Thompson (Thomson), Adam, Aug. Rec., 1, 518; H. S., 7, 226.
Thompson, Alexander (lt.), H. S., 7, 196.
Thompson, Alexander, H. S., 7, 190.
Thompson, Anthony, F. I. B. W., 1, 261.
Thompson, Archibald, H. S., 7, 220; V. C. M., 11.
Thompson, Collin, Wash. Mss., 5, 4.
Thompson, David, F. I. B. W., 2, 389; Hist. Orange, 59.
Thompson, Edward, Va. Mag., 1, 387; Va. Mag., 2, 145; Wash. Mss., 112, 82.2.
Thompson, Henry, Va. Mag., 1, 384; Wash. Mss., 112, 95.
Thompson, James, F. I. B. W., 2, 410; Va. Mag., 1, 380; Wash. Mss., 112, 94.
Thompson, John, H. S., 7, 195, 208, 223; Va. Mag, 1, 282; Va. Mag., 2, 40; Wash. Mss., 5, 8; Wash. Mss., 111, 13, 15.
Thompson, Moses, H. S., 7, 191.
Thompson, Nathaniel (lt.), L. to Wash., 2, 266.
Thompson, Richard, D. W., 402.
Thompson, Robert, D. W., 424; H. S., 7, 191, 196.
Thompson, Thomas, Va. Mag., 2, 38.
Thompson, William (capt.), F. I. B. W., 1, 25.
Thompson, William (en.), D. W., 399.
Thompson, William, Aug. Rec., 1, 68; D. W., 403, 411; F. I. B. W., 2, 413; Va. Mag., 2, 48; Wash. Mss., 1538; Wash. Mss., 1557.
Thomson, Herman, H. S., 7, 201.
Thomson, James, H. S., 7, 187, 188; Wash. Mss., 112, 114.
Thomson, John, H. S., 7, 191.
Thomson, Nathaniel (en.), Va. Mag., 1, 287.
Thomson, Robert, H. S., 7, 190.
Thomson, William, F. I. B. W., 2, 315.
Thorn, Edmund, Va. Mag., 2, 144.
Thorn, Robert, Va. Mag., 1, 380; Wash. Mss., 112, 88.
Thornhill, William, H. S., 7, 214; Wash. Mss., 1555.

Trotter, Richard, Aug. Rec., 2, 50;
D. W., 424; L. to Wash., 1, 300;
Va. Mag., 1, 283; Va. Mag., 2,
150; Wash. Mss., 112, 115.
Troutback, John, Wash. Mss., 5, 4.
Troy, Simon, Va. Mag., 2, 49; Wash.
Mss., 112, 87.
Truly (Truley), Peter, Va. Mag., 1,
379; Wash. Mss., 112, 88, 116.
Truman, Joseph (Prince Edward),
Va. Mag., 21, 89.
Truman, Joseph, F. I. B. W., 1, 103.
Trusler, Peter, H. S., 7, 186.
Truston, John, Va. Mag., 1, 282;
Wash. Mss., 111, 13.
Tucker, William, D. W., 412.
Tuder, Thomas, Va. Mag., 2, 46.
Tuley, Christian, H. S., 7, 198.
Tully (Tulley), Peter, H. B., 1758-
61, 31; Va. Mag., 2, 146.
Tuly, Charles (en.), H. S., 7, 203.
Tummens, Edward, H. S., 7, 215.
Tunley, John, F. I. B. W., 2, 506.
Tunstall (Tunstal), Robert, Aug.
Rec., 2, 49; Va. Mag., 1, 282;
Wash. Mss., 111, 15.
Turley, Sampson (lt.), H. B., 1752-
58, 375.
Turley, Sampson, Wash. Mss., 1557.
Turnbull, Alexander, Va. Mag., 2, 45.
Turner, Anthony, H. S., 7, 216.
Turner, Benjamin, F. I. B. W., 1,
178; V. C. M., 129.
Turner, Charles, F. I. B. W., 1, 213.
Turner, Edward (surg.), Wash. Mss.,
111, 15.
Turner, Fielding (capt.), H. B., 1758-
61, 195.
Turner, George, F. I. B. W., 1, 204.
Turner, James, F. I. B. W., 2, 407;
Va. Mag., 1, 380; Wash. Mss.,
112, 88, 94, 114; Wash. Mss.,
1485.
Turner, John Baker, F. I. B. W., 1,
278.
Turner, Richard, H. S., 8, 131.
Turner, Simeon, Historic Shepherds-
town, 26.
Turner, Thomas, Va. Mag., 2, 153.
Turner, William, F. I. B. W., 1, 178;
Va. Mag., 1, 283; Wash. Mss.,
111, 15.
Turk, James, H. S., 7, 190.
Turnley, John, V. C. M., 51.
Turnstile, Robert, Va. Mag., 2, 38.
Tutt, William, H. S., 7, 213.
Tuttle, John, Wash. Mss., 1460.
Twedey (Tweedy), William, H. S.,
7, 208, 209.
Twentyman, John, H. B., 1752-58,
402.

Twiddy, William, H. S., 7, 205.
Twiner, William, H. B., 1752-58, 262.
Twopence, James, F. I. B. W., 1, 156.
Tyan, William, Va. Mag., 1, 283;
Wash. Mss., 111, 13.
Tybus, James, Va. Mag., 1, 282.
Tygert, John, F. I. B. W., 2, 364; V.
C. M., 39.
Tyrell, George, Va. Mag., 1, 282.
Tyrell, James, Wash. Mss., 111, 13;
Wash. Mss., 112, 0.
Tytus, James, Wash. Mss., 111, 13.

U.

Umble, Gunrod, H. S., 7, 186.
Umble, Martin, H. S., 7, 187.
Umble, Ury, H. S., 7, 187.
Umphries, John, Wash. Mss., 112, 89.
Underwood, George, F. I. B. W., 1,
218.
Underwood, Thomas, Va. Mag., 1,
380; Wash. Mss., 112, 88, 94.
Underwood, William, H. S., 7, 214;
V. C. M., 97; Va. Mag., 1, 282; Va.
Mag., 7, 305; Wash. Mss., 111,
13; Wash. Mss., 1555.
Upchurch, Michael, H. S., 7, 212.
Upchurch, William, H. S., 7, 212.
Upshaw, Forest (capt.), H. S., 7, 214.

V.

Vachob, John, F. I. B. W., 1, 7; V.
C. M., 9.
Vahab, John, Aug. Rec., 1, 213.
Vails, John, D. W., 400.
Vallendigham, George (lt.), H. D.,
1776, 92.
Vallendigham (Vallendingham),
George, D. W., 421; H. S., 7, 218.
Van Bibber, Isaac, D. W., 424.
Van Bibber, Jesse, D. W., 424.
Van Bibber, John, D. W., 424; V. C.
M., 89.
Van Bibber, Peter, D. W., 424; V. C.
M., 89.
Van Braam, Jacob (capt.), V. H. C.,
3, 51.
Vanbraam, Jacob, Va. Mag., 1, 279.
Vanbuskirk, Michael, F. I. B. W., 2,
522.
Vance, Andrew, H. S., 7, 216.
Vance, John, Aug. Rec., 1, 518; H.
S., 7, 191, 215, 216, 217.
Vance, Patrick, H. S., 7, 209.
Vance, Samuel, H. S., 7, 216; H. S.,
8, 129.
Vance, Thomas, H. S., 7, 198.
Vance, William, D. W., 412.
Vanhook, Samuel, D. W., 396.
Vanimon, Peter, H. S., 7, 184.
Vanmeter, Henry, H. S., 7, 216.

Vanmeter, Jacob, Historic Shepherdstown, 25.
Vanmeter, Joseph, H. S., 7, 216.
Vardeman, John, H. S., 7, 206.
Vass, Reuben, F. I. B. W., 1, 192; Va. Mag., 2, 144; Wash. Mss., 111, 110; Wash. Mss., 1432.
Vaughan (Vaughn), Andrew, L. to Wash., 1, 300; Va. Mag., 2, 41; Wash. Mss., 112, 96.
Vaughan, George, F. I. B. W., 1, 51; V. C. M., 14.
Vaughan (Vaughn), Gist, L. to Wash. 1, 300; Va. Mag., 2, 45.
Vaughan, James, H. S., 7, 226.
Vaughan, Richard, Wash. Mss., 112, 90.
Vaughan, William (capt.), H. S., 7, 221.
Vaughn, Abraham, H. S., 7, 224.
Vauhob, Joseph, H. S., 7, 192.
Vaun, John, D. W., 411.
Vaut, Andrew, D. W., 400.
Vaut, Christly, D. W., 400.
Vaut, George, D. W., 400, 404.
Vawn, Andrew, J., 133.
Vawter, William, Hist. Orange, 59.
Veal, William, Wash. Mss., 1460.
Venable (Vennable), James, Va. Mag., 1, 389; Wash. Mss., 112, 85.1, 100.
Venable, William, D. W., 421; V. C. M., 88.
Veneman, Peter, H. S., 7, 180.
Vernon, James, H. S., 7, 223.
Vernon, Richard (comm.), V. C. M., 14.
Vernon, Richard, F. I. B. W., 1, 59.
Vernor, John, H. S., 7, 224.
Vert, George, J., 152.
Virgin, John, J., 103.

W.

Wabreaner, Jones, H. S., 7, 199.
Waddy, Charles, Va. Mag., 1, 282; Wash. Mss., 111, 13.
Waddy, Samuel (capt.), H. S., 7, 222.
Wade, Henry, H. S., 7, 223.
Wade, John, H. S., 7, 219, 220; Wash. Mss., 112, 116.
Wade, Joseph, J., 94, 98.
Wade, Robert (capt.), H. B., 1758-61, 31, 35; H. S., 8, 130.
Wade, Robert, Jr. (capt.), H. S., 7, 219.
Wagener, Edmund, Aug. Rec., 2, 49; Va. Mag., 1, 283; Wash. Mss., 111, 13.
Waggener, Peter, Wash. Mss., 1557.

Waggener, Thomas (capt.), L. to Wash., 1, 188; V. H. C., 3, 114.
Waggener, Thomas, Va. Mag., 1, 279.
Wagner, Edmund, F. I. B. W., 1, 15; V. C. M., 11.
Waggoner, Andrew, D. W., 424.
Waggoner, Henry, D. W., 399.
Waggoner, Henry, Jr., D. W., 399.
Wagoner, Lodowick, H. S., 7, 187.
Waid, John, Va. Mag., 1, 388; Wash. Mss., 112, 96.
Wainwright, George, Wash. Mss., 1483.
Wakefield, Charles, H. S., 7, 203.
Wakefield, Henry, H. S., 7, 204.
Wakefield, William, H. S., 7, 204.
Waker, Michael, Va. Mag., 1, 282; Wash. Mss., 111, 13.
Walden, Edward, Wash. Mss., 1471.
Walden, James, F. I. B. W., 1, 194; V. C. M., 26.
Walden, John, Wash. Mss., 1460.
Walden, Samuel, Va. Mag., 2, 48; Wash. Mss., 1471.
Walding, John, J., 96.
Walker, Adam, D. W., 399.
Walker, Alexander, H. S., 7, 196.
Walker, Asaph, F. I. B. W., 2, 363; V. C. M., 39.
Walker, Charles, Hist. Orange, 59.
Walker, Francis, L. to Wash., 1, 300; Va. Mag., 2, 47.
Walker, James (capt.), H. B., 1758-61, 234, 237.
Walker, James (lt.), Aug. Rec., 1, 338, 452; H. B., 1761-65, 184.
Walker, James, D. W., 406.
Walker, John (surg.) (comm. gen.), H. B., 1758-61, 275.
Walker, John, H. S., 7, 181.
Walker, Moses, J., 200.
Walker, Thomas (comm. gen.), F. I. B. W., 1, 43.
Walker, Thomas (comm.), V. H. C., 4, 558.
Walker, Thomas, H. S., 8, 128; Hist. Orange, 59.
Walker, William, H. S., 7, 199, 210.
Wall, Charles, H. S., 7, 211.
Wall, Daniel, H. S., 7, 211.
Wall, John, Wash. Mss., 112, 90.
Wall, Robert, H. S., 7, 211.
Wall, William, H. S., 7, 213.
Wallace, Adam (en.), D. W., 406.
Wallace, Andrew, D. W., 406.
Wallace, David, D. W., 406.
Wallace, John, H. S., 7, 203.
Wallace, Oliver, Wash. Mss., 1471.
Wallace, Robert, D. W., 406.
Wallace, Samuel (lt.), D. W., 406.

Wallace, William, Va. Mag., 2, 152; Wash., Mss., 112, 87, 115.
Waller, John, Wash. Mss., 1470.
Walls (Watts), Charles, F. I. B. W., 2, 576.
Walls, John, Wash. Mss., 112, 95.
Walter, Michael, D. W., 400.
Walters, John, Wash. Mss., 112, 86, 95.
Walters, Robert, Va. Mag., 1, 388; Wash. Mss., 5, 4; Wash. Mss., 112, 85.1, 96, 116.
Walton, George, Jr., H. S., 7, 212.
Walton, Thomas, H. S., 7, 212.
Wambler, George, D. W., 400.
Wambler, Michael, D. W., 400.
Ward, Barnard, Va. Mag., 1, 380; Wash. Mss., 112, 88, 94, 114.
Ward, Charles (capt.), V. C. M., 88.
Ward, Charles, H. B., 1758-61, 24.
Ward, David (en.). D. W., 396, 403, 404.
Ward, Edward (en.), V. H. C., 3, 151.
Ward, Elisha, Va. Mag., 1, 283; Wash. Mss., 111, 13.
Ward, James (capt.), V. C. M., 89.
Ward, James, F. I. B. W., 1, 233; H. B., 1766-69, 63; H. S., 7, 196; V. C. M., 29.
Ward, James, Jr., H. S., 7, 196.
Ward, John, H. S., 7, 210, 223; Wash. Mss., 112, 85.1.
Ward, Joseph, H. S., 7, 196.
Ward, Nolley, Wash. Mss., 1460.
Ward, Pledge, Va. Mag., 1, 283; Wash. Mss., 111, 13.
Ward, Richard, H. S., 7, 224.
Ward, Wells, H. S., 7, 220.
Ward, William (lt.), V. C. M., 51.
Ward, William, D. W., 399; F. I. B. W., 2, 505; H. S., 7, 196, 197.
Warden, William, Va. Mag., 2, 47.
Wardlaw, James, H. S., 7, 195.
Ware, Daniel, Aug. Rec., 1, 184.
Ware, Francis, Aug. Rec., 2, 50.
Warner, Daniel (scout). H. D., May, 1777, 14, 20.
Warner, James, Va. Mag., 1, 378.
Warner, John, Hist. Orange, 60.
Warner, Whitnell, L. to Wash., 1, 300; Wash. Mss., 112, 88, 114.
Warren, John, H. S., 7, 226.
Warren, William, Wash. Mss., 1465.
Warton, Anthony, Va. Mag., 1, 386.
Warwick, Jacob, D. W., 422.
Wash, John, H. B., 1761-65, 278, 284.
Washbun, James, D. W., 405.
Washburn, Charles (en.), H. D., May, 1777, 14, 20.
Washburn, Steven, D. W., 405.

Washington, George (col.), Va. Mag., 1, 279.
Washington, Lun-d, Wash. Mss., 1557.
Waters, John, Va. Mag., 1, 383; Wash. Mss., 112, 89, 114.
Waters, Phil., Wash. Mss., 111, 13.
Waters, Philemon, L. to Wash., 1, 299; Va. Mag., 2, 40.
Waters, Philip, Va. Mag., 1, 282.
Waters, William, Va. Mag., 2, 47.
Watkins, Henry (en), H. S., 7, 229.
Watkins, Philip, Aug. Rec., 1, 344; F. I. B. W., 2, 367; V. C. M., 39.
Watkins, Robert, D. W., 411; H. D., 1776, 56, 68.
Watson, John, Wash. Mss., 1460.
Watson, Jonathan, D. W., 406.
Watson, Mathew, H. S., 7, 224.
Watson, William, F. I. B. W., 1, 64; Hist. Orange, 60.
Wattbroke, Joseph, H. S., 7, 217.
Watts, Arthur, Va. Mag., 1, 282; Wash. Mss., 111, 13.
Watts, David, Hist. Orange, 60.
Watts, Edward, H. S., 7, 179, 210.
Watts, George, H. S., 7, 183, 188, 210.
Watts, John, H.`S., 7, 207, 210.
Watts, Samuel, F. I. B. W., 2, 467.
Watts, Thomas, Va. Mag., 1, 378; Va. Mag., 2, 37; Wash. Mss., 112, 88.
Watts, William, F. I. B. W., 2, 327; V. C. M., 36.
Waugh, ——, D. W., 409.
Waugh, Alexander, Jr., F. I. B. W., 2, 512; H. B., 1761-65, 13, 14.
Wausley, William, F. I. B. W., 1, 217.
Weatherborn, John, Wash. Mss., 5, 4.
Weatherhead, Joseph, Wash. Mss., 1555.
Weathers, William, Wash. Mss., 5, 4.
Weaver, Christly, D. W., 399.
Weaver, Michael, D. W., 399.
Webb, Julius, F. I. B. W., 2, 485, 557; V. C. M., 50.
Webb, Martin, F. I. B. W., 1, 75; V. C. M., 16.
Webster, John, Wash. Mss., 5, 4.
Webster, Joseph, F. I. B. W., 1, 45; V. C. M., 13.
Webster, Peter, H. S., 7, 201.
Wech, James, Va. Mag., 1, 282.
Weeden, George (en.), Va. Mag., 1, 287.
Weedon, George (capt.), F. I. B. W., 1, 267.
Weill, Frederick, H B., 1758-61, 38.
Weir, Edward, H. S., 7, 203.

Welch, Daniel, Va. Mag., 1, 282; Wash. Mss., 111, 13; Wash. Mss., 112, 0.
Welch, James, D. W., 424; V. C. M., 90; Wash. Mss., 111, 13.
Welch, John, Aug. Rec., 1, 234; D. W., 409; H. B., 1770-72, 18, 31; Wash. Mss., 112, 90, 95.
Welch, Joshua, H. B., 1752-58, 462.
Welch, Thomas, D. W., 407.
Welch, Thomas, Jr., D. W., 407.
Wells, James, F. I. B. W., 2, 410.
Wells, Joseph, Wash. Mss., 112, 96.
Wells, Samuel, D. W., 421.
Welsh, Christopher, D. W., 408.
Welsh, John, Aug. Rec., 1, 213.
Welsh, Richard, D. W., 405.
West, Abram, H. S., 7, 201.
West, Christopher, H. B., 1758-61, 141.
West, John (lt.), V. H. C., 3, 115.
West, John, Va. Mag., 1, 279.
West, William, Wash. Mss.. 1460.
Westfall, William (scout), H. B., 1766-69, 294.
Wetherall, Joseph, Wash. Mss., 112, 87.
Wetzel, John, D. W., 421.
Wetzel, Martin, D. W., 421
Wharton, Anthony, Wash Mss., 112, 83.
Wharton, Joseph, H. B., 1758-61, 38.
Wharton, Joshua (en.), H. S., 7, 224.
Whayne, Humphrey, F. I. B. W., 2, 432.
Whayne, William, F. I. B W., 2, 432.
Wheedon, Nathan, F. I. B. W., 2, 517.
Wheeler, Benjamin, V. C M., 26.
Wheeler, Charles (maj), J. C., Dec., 1775, 93,
Wheeler, John, F. I. B. W., 2, 332; H. B., 1742-49, 99, 104.
Wheeler, William, F. I. B. W., 2, 333.
Wheeley, Benjamin, F. I. B. W., 1, 193.
Wheelon, Nathan, V. C. M., 52.
Wheelor, John, V. C. M., 37.
Wheelor, William, V. C. M., 37.
Whipple, John, L. to Wash., 1, 248; V. H. C., 4, 400; Va. Mag., 2, 37.
Whitaker, John, Wash. Mss., 1536.
Whitby, Moses, D. W., 406.
White, Augustine, V. C. M., 14.
White, Chapman, F. I. B. W., 1, 135.
White, Cornous, H. S., 7, 186.
White, David, Aug., Rec., 1, 183; D. W., 422.
White, Elisha (lt.), F. I. B. W., 2, 432.
White, George, F. I. B. W., 1, 168.
White, Isaac, H. S., 7, 216.

White, James, H. S., 7, 203.
White, John, Va. Mag., 2, 149; Wash. Mss., 112, 0.
White, Joseph, Adam Stephen Ps.; D. W., 409.
White, Samuel, Jr., F. I. B. W., 1, 172.
White, Solomon, D. W., 408.
White, Thomas, L. to Wash., 1, 300; Va. Mag., 1, 378; Va. Mag., 2, 45; Wash. Mss., 112, 88.
White, William, D. W., 422; H. S., 7, 216, 226; V. C. M., 97; Va. Mag., 1, 388; Va. Mag., 7, 306; Wash. Mss., 112, 85.1, 96, 116.
Whitecotton, George, Va. Mag., 2, 48.
Whitehead, Edward, Va. Mag., 1, 282; Va. Mag., 2, 146; Wash. Mss., 5, 4, 8; Wash. Mss., 112, 0.
Whitehead, Matthew, Va. Mag., 1, 386; Wash. Mss., 112, 82.2.
Whitelock, Michael, J., 101.
Whiteside, Edward, Wash. Mss., 111, 13.
Whiteside, Moses, H. S., 7, 195.
Whiteside, William, H. S, 7, 203.
Whitesides, Roger, Wash. Mss., 1479.
Whitesite, William, H. S., 7, 206.
Whitley, Jonathan, H. S., 7, 195.
Whitlock, Achilles, F. I. B. W., 2, 579.
Whitman, John, Va. Mag., 1, 282; Wash. Mss., 111, 13.
Whittaker (Wittaker), Abraham, Va. Mag., 2, 45.
Whitten, Thomas, D. W., 404.
Whitten, Thomas, Jr., D. W., 404.
Whitter, Abraham, H. S., 8, 131.
Whitticor, Joseph, D. W., 411.
Whitton, Jeremiah, D. W., 404.
Whitworth, William, H. S., 7, 201.
Wiece, Jacob, H. S., 7, 184.
Wiece, Joseph, H. S., 7, 184.
Wiers, William, Wash. Mss., 112, 96.
Wilber, David, Wash. Mss., 112, 89.
Wilber (Wilfer, Wilper, Wilpert), John David, Aug. Rec., 1, 318; Va. Mag., 1, 282; Wash. Mss., 5, 2; Wash. Mss., 111, 13.
Wilchire, Richard, Wash. Mss., 112, 90.
Wildgoose, Thomas, Wash. Mss., 1535.
Wildridge, John, Va. Mag., 1, 384.
Wiley, Allen, H. S., 7, 214; Wash. Mss., 1555.
Wiley, James, D. W., 421; V. C. M., 88.
Wiley, John, F. I. B. W., 2, 352, 528.
Wiley, Peter, F. I. B. W., 2, 408, 528.
Wilkerson, David, Va. Mag., 1, 283.

Wilkerson, Edward, F. I. B. W., 2, 550.
Wilkerson, George, Wash. Mss., 1476.
Wilkerson, John, Wash. Mss., 1476.
Wilkinson, David, Wash. Mss., 111, 13.
Wilkinson, James, F. I. B. W., 2, 518.
Wilks, Francis, H. S., 7, 222.
Willard, Daniel, Wash. Mss., 112, 95.
Willet, Benjamin, Va. Mag., 2, 40.
Willey, John, H. S., 7, 191.
Willey, Robert, H. S., 7, 191, 195.
Williams, ——, H. B., 1742-49, 94.
Williams, Aaron, H. S., 7, 223.
Williams, Alden, D. W., 396.
Williams, Benjamin, H. S., 7, 218.
Williams, Charles, Wash. Mss., 112, 87.
Williams, Daniel, Wash. Mss., 1535.
Williams, David, D. W., 420; H. B., 1758-61, 97; H. S., 7, 216; V. C. M., 88.
Williams, Edgcomb G., V. C. M., 15.
Williams, George, Va. Mag., 1, 387; Wash. Mss., 112, 82.2.
Williams, Henry, H. B. 1742-49, 44; Va. Mag., 1, 388; Wash. Mss., 112, 85.1, 96, 116.
Williams, Isaac, D. W., 425.
Williams, Jacob, Hist. Orange, 59.
Williams, James, Aug. Rec., 1, 478; Va. Mag., 1, 382, 384; Va. Mag., 2, 148; Wash. Mss., 112, 95.
Williams, Jarrett, D. W., 412.
Williams, John (lt.), V. H. C., 4, 401; Va. Mag., 1, 287.
Williams, John, D. W., 399, 403, 405, 411, 412; F. I. B. W., 2, 369; H. S., 7, 193, 198, 220, 224; Hist. Orange, 59; J., 92; Va. Mag., 1, 387, 388; Va. Mag., 2, 2, 49, 145; Wash. Mss., 5, 4: Wash. Mss., 112, 82.2, 96, 114, 116; Wash. Mss., 1478; Wash. Mss., 1538.
Williams, Joseph, Va. Mag., 2, 148.
Williams, Joshua, H. B., 1752-58, 417; Wash. Mss., 112, 114.
Williams, Mark, D. W., 412.
Williams, Peregrine, Va. Mag., 1, 282; Wash. Mss., 111, 13.
Williams, Peter, Va. Mag., 2, 46.
Williams, Petey, Wash. Mss., 112, 0.
Williams, Rembrance, H. S., 7, 216.
Williams, Robert, D. W., 411.
Williams, Rowland, D. W., 404.
Williams, Samuel, D. W., 410.
Williams, Thomas, Aug. Rec., 2, 50; D. W., 410; H. S., 7, 224; Va. Mag. 1, 385; Wash. Mss., 112, 82.
Williams, Walter, Va. Mag., 1, 379; Wash. Mss., 112, 88.

Williams, William, H. S., 7, 203; Va. Mag., 2, 47.
Williamson, David, D. W., 421; J., 155.
Williamson, James, Wash. Mss., 112, 86.
Williamson, Samuel, J., 111.
Williamson, Smith, F. I. B. W., 2, 349; V. C. M., 38.
Williamson, William, Wash. Mss., 1460.
Willimore, James, Va. Mag., 1, 385.
Willis, Henry, D. W., 403.
Willis, Joseph, F. I. B. W., 2, 414; V. C. M., 43.
Willis, Richard, Va. Mag., 1, 386; Wash. Mss., 112, 83.
Willis, Robert, H. B., 1761-65. 57; H. B., 1766-69, 46, 50.
Willmore, James, Wash. Mss., 112, 82, 83.1; Wash. Mss., 1467.
Willock, James, H. S., 7, 222.
Willoughby, John (maj.), Wash. Mss., 1478.
Willow, Joseph, Va. Mag., 1, 381.
Willow, Joshua, Wash. Mss., 112, 95.
Wills, Joseph, L. to Wash., 1, 300; Va. Mag., 2, 41; Wash. Mss., 112, 86.
Wills, Joshua, Wash. Mss., 112, 85.1.
Wills, Josiah, Va. Mag., 1, 390.
Wills, Justinian, F. I. B. W., 2, 508; V. C. M., 51.
Willson, George (capt.), Aug. Rec., 1, 75.
Willson, Richard, D. W., 407.
Willson, William, V. C. M., 97; Va. Mag., 7, 306.
Wilmoth, William, D. W., 402.
Wilmouth, Thomas, H. S., 7, 186.
Wilson, Aquilla, Va. Mag., 2, 46.
Wilson, Benjamin, D. W., 421; Va. Mag., 1, 390; Wash. Mss., 112, 85.1, 96.
Wilson, Charles (lt.), H. S., 7, 191.
Wilson, Edward, D. W., 408.
Wilson, George (maj.), H. B., 1766-69, 71.
Wilson, George (capt.), Aug. Rec., 1, 317; H. B., 1761-65, 248, 253.
Wilson, George, Aug. Rec., 1, 72; H. S., 7, 191.
Wilson, Henry, J., 97.
Wilson, Hugh, H. S., 7, 186.
Wilson, James, D. W., 411; H. B., 1761-65, 214, 220; H. S., 7, 195, 196.
Wilson, John (capt.), D. W., 425.
Wilson, John, H. B., 1742-49, 94, 175; H. S., 7, 192, 197, 201; Va. Mag., 1, 283.

Wright, Thomas, H. S., 7, 202; L. to
  Wash., 1, 300; Va. Mag., 1, 381;
  Va. Mag., 2, 47; Wash. Mss., 112,
  86, 95.
Wright, William (lt.), V. H. C., 4,
  92.
Wright, William, Aug., Rec., 1, 478;
  Va. Mag., 1, 379; Wash. Mss.,
  112, 88.
Wyche, James (capt.), H. S., 7, 230.
Wyley, Alexander, Va. Mag., 2, 48.

Y.

Yacome, Filey, H. S., 7, 196.
Yancey, John, H. S., 7, 213; Wash.
  Mss., 1555.
Yancy, Charles, H. S., 7, 214.
Yarborough, Jeremiah (en.), H. S.,
  7, 207.
Yates, John, H. S., 7, 207.
Yates, Thomas, Wash. Mss., 1555.
Yates, William, H. S., 7, 205.

Yeates, Thomas, Jr., H. S., 7, 214.
Yeats, Robert, Wash. Mss., 112, 114.
Yedley, Richard, H. S., 7, 179.
Young, Daniel, H. S., 8, 129.
Young, Edmund, H. S., 8, 129.
Young, Ezekiel, Va. Mag., 1, 387;
  Wash. Mss., 112, 82.2.
Young, George, H. S., 7, 220.
Young. Israel, H. S., 7, 209.
Young, James, H. S., 7, 179, 187, 188,
  195; Wash. Mss., 112, 114; Wash.
  Mss., 1485.
Young, John, Aug. Rec., 1, 331, 349;
  F. I. B. W., 2, 431, 521; H. S.,
  7, 180, 184, 185, 187, 191, 216.
Young, Peter, H. S., 7, 224.
Young, Robert, H. S., 7, 191.

Z.

Zane, Ebenezer, D. W., 421.
Ziglar, Christopher, H. S., 7, 214.